Bureaucracy and Self-Government

Bureaucracy and Self-Government

Reconsidering the Role of Public Administration in American Politics

SECOND EDITION

Brian J. Cook

Johns Hopkins University Press
Baltimore

© 2014 Johns Hopkins University Press
All rights reserved. Published 2014
Printed in the United States of America on acid-free paper
9 8 7 6 5 4 3 2 1

Johns Hopkins University Press
2715 North Charles Street
Baltimore, Maryland 21218-4363
www.press.jhu.edu

Cataloging-in-Publication Data is available from the Library of Congress.

A catalog record for this book is available from the British Library.

ISBN-13: 978-1-4214-1552-9 (pbk. : alk. paper)
ISBN-10: 1-4214-1552-6 (pbk. : alk. paper)
ISBN-13: 978-1-4214-1553-6 (electronic)
ISBN-10: 1-4214-1553-4 (electronic)

Special discounts are available for bulk purchases of this book.
For more information, please contact Special Sales at 410-516-6936
or specialsales@press.jhu.edu.

Johns Hopkins University Press uses environmentally friendly book
materials, including recycled text paper that is composed of at least
30 percent post-consumer waste, whenever possible.

The essence of obedience consists in the fact that a person comes to view himself as the instrument for carrying out another person's wishes, and he therefore no longer regards himself as responsible for his actions.

STANLEY MILGRAM

Administration is more than the tool, the unquestioning servant of whatever party happens to be in power. Administration plans. Administration is not merely a lifeless form. It is an active, originating, inventing, contriving element in the body politic.

MARSHALL DIMOCK

Democracy is for friends and citizens, not masters and slaves.

WILSON CAREY MCWILLIAMS

Contents

Preface to the Second Edition

Before he announced his retirement in 2014, Senator Tom Coburn (R-OK) was one of the most persistent critics of the federal bureaucracy. He scrutinized all proposed legislation for its potential to contribute to wasteful spending, particularly if waste will occur through growth in administrative positions. In December 2009, he hit upon a clever if symbolic ploy to constrain the size and scope of the federal executive. He introduced an amendment titled "Bureaucrat Limitation" to modify the proposed Service Members Home Ownership Tax Act of 2009, a relatively innocuous legislative proposal to make the first-time homebuyers tax credit more easily accessible to members of the armed services. Coburn worded the amendment generically so that it could apply to many proposed laws. The amendment stated, "For each new bureaucrat added to any department or agency of the Federal Government for the purpose of implementing the provisions of this Act (or any amendment made by this Act), the head of such department or agency shall ensure that the addition of such new bureaucrat is offset by a reduction of 1 existing bureaucrat at such department or agency" (*Congressional Record* 2009, S12167). Of course, Senator Coburn did not think his amendment would be debated, let alone adopted. The message he conveyed, whether or not he fully intended it, was clear and unmistakable, however. The men and women who administer the nation's vast edifice of public programs, whether portrayed respectfully as public servants or dismissively as bureaucrats, are essentially interchangeable parts, mere cogs in the machinery of a federal government that has grown vast and imposing.

The dominant concern regarding government in the United States for the past generation, indeed for most of the nation's history, has fixated on its size and scope. This is particularly true with respect to the federal government, but the attention to size and scope has been a prominent obsession with political leaders and citizens at all levels of the American federal system. Size and scope, of course, are really proxies for the real concern, namely, government's intrusiveness into the private lives of citizens, especially its encroachment on property, including the burden of taxation. The question of the proper boundaries between public and private is a complex matter, however. It is easier to deal with the question simplistically by considering numbers of bureaucrats and the sizes of administrative agencies. More important, this obsession with size and scope is a manifestation of a more general and prominent way of thinking about governance in general, which sees government administration as merely the means to achieve collective ends. Governments, especially administrative agencies, are instruments to serve public needs and public aims. Machines are instruments. If machines have interchangeable parts, then public bureaucracies must have them too. Thus, one bureaucrat is as good (or as bad) as another, and if additional productivity can be squeezed out of each one, there is no need to add more. This thinking governs the private sector, so why should it differ in government?

In this book, I aim to introduce and grapple with ways of thinking about government and public administration that move beyond debates about size, numbers, and scope to address the function and role of public administration in a system predicated on self-government. By revisiting and refreshing my historical exploration of the treatment of competing conceptions of politics, government, and public administration with a new edition, I offer students and colleagues engaged in the study of politics and public affairs ways of *thinking constitutionally* about public administration that go beyond the instrumentalist orientation that dominates discourse in American politics regarding bureaucracy and the work of public servants. After all, public servants engage in the day-to-day activities that constitute governance while their fellow citizens are busy doing other things. There is much more that they do than the admittedly complex task of putting means into effect to satisfy collectively chosen ends.

My method is to combine historical analysis with normative theory. I draw on carefully selected primary and secondary sources and scholarly interpretations to develop my own interpretations of the nature and impacts of public debates about public administration that have occurred at critical junctures in American political development, from the founding to the present day. I then draw on this historical analysis to offer a summary account of the instrumentally oriented normative theory of public administration under the Constitution that has emerged and solidified over the course of American political development, the consequences it has wrought, how a more complete theory might be fashioned from ideas about the nature of political institutions, and how political leaders might be engaged in considering this more comprehensive view.

I focus my historical analysis on a single critical thread—how political leaders have, in political action and in public debate, grappled with the complex character of public administration as both instrumental to and constitutive of public purposes. I follow this thread across the course of American political development, observing the shifting context in which political leaders have attempted to deal with public administration's dual character and how that context has impinged on their struggles. Because my historical contextualizing is relatively general so that I can concentrate on the critical thread, which is my main concern, my analysis may invite criticism as historically superficial. I prefer to consider it selective and purposely so. If criticizing my method for constructing my argument draws attention to the normative argument that grows out of it, then the scholarly discourse that might follow will have demonstrated the value of this undertaking.

The revisions I have incorporated into this work, updated from nearly two decades ago, center on enriching the historical analysis with new, or newly found, scholarship, extending the historical analysis to the present by considering developments since the mid-1990s, and sharpening the focus of the final two chapters on how to incorporate a constitutive dimension into normative theorizing about public administration under the Constitution. Thus, for example, I have added material on the Jeffersonian impacts on administrative theory and practice, on the Jacksonian developments in national administrative structures and functions, on administrative theorizing and practice that presaged progressive reforms, and on the curious and confounding complexities that characterize public thinking about administration in the post–New Deal political order. I have drawn on a remarkably rich and varied lode of scholarship and public commentary to anchor the modest expansion and updates I have incorporated into my analysis. To accommodate the changes and additions, I have reorganized material to create a separate chapter for the post–New Deal analysis (chapter 6), with chapters 7 and 8 still centered on the normative argument. However, this revised edition adheres to the structure and flow of the original work.

With these revisions and refinements, I expect the book to hold its grip even more firmly on a special niche in public administration scholarship and teaching as the only single-volume treatment of the close intertwining of American political development and the evolution of ideas about the proper role and function of public administration in the American regime. A part of that niche is its invitation to scholarly and political discourse on how the stunting of that evolution of ideas and arguments might be transcended so that public administration may be considered a legitimate political institution in its own right, not an enemy but a friend of American self-government. To my surprise and dismay, such discourse is needed now more than ever.

Revising a single-authored book is a solitary endeavor even more so than the original research and writing. Nevertheless, in addition to those who helped me bring the first edition to publication, several individuals helped me complete this revised edition. Thanks go first to those faculty colleagues in the Center for Public Administration and Policy (CPAP) at Virginia Tech who adopted the first edition of this book for a doctoral seminar in public administration theory and context over the past five years. Their feedback, my own experience using the book in that seminar, and the comments and observations of the students enrolled, spurred my thinking on the need for a revision. A special thank-you goes to David Rosenbloom for writing a positive review of my proposal for the revised edition, in which he advocated for more pages to give me space to expand my analysis and argument. David also lent his time to discuss suggestions for how I might improve and enrich the analysis. He is not, of course, responsible for my failure to follow all of his guidance. My thanks also to Rick Green for the further guidance he provided on understanding the ideas and actions of Alexander Hamilton and Thomas Jefferson. Suzanne Flinchbaugh, associate editor for acquisitions at Johns Hopkins University Press, responded positively from the very beginning to my idea for a revised edition. I thank her for her skill, attentiveness, and enthusiasm in shepherding both the proposal and the final manuscript through the editorial review and approval process. My thanks also to Andre Barnett, senior production editor, whose manuscript editing caught many errors large and small, and spruced up the prose in ways that only a fresh pair of eyes can.

I received superb research support from Nicky Rishel Elias, who, while finishing her dissertation in CPAP, found time to track down a wealth of sources I might use to enhance or to correct my analysis. Nicky also offered commentary on passages in the first edition that needed my attention. Her dissertation successfully defended, she is now an assistant professor in the Department of Public Management at John Jay College in New York. I also received additional research assistance from Jake Paysour, my graduate assistant in CPAP during the 2013–14 academic year. Although I asked him to help primarily with work on an entirely different research project, Jake found additional references as well as critical primary source data for me, both of which helped round out the revisions and analysis. Finally, at the last critical juncture, when I needed help getting my references updated and properly organized and my manuscript files in good order, my daughter Lauren came to my aid. She carefully combed through the manuscript pages and helped me organize the references from the scattered mess of materials I had amassed. With her assistance I managed for the first time to deliver a book manuscript by the contractual deadline.

I dedicated the first edition of this book to Lauren and her older sister, Meredith. Their love and support as well as that from my dear wife and partner in life, Ruth, made the labors necessary to produce this volume a joy rather than a burden. Dedicating the new edition to them seems a rather trivial gesture in comparison to what they have given me.

It is not a trivial act, however, to dedicate this revised edition to Charles T. Goodsell, a scholar and teacher, colleague, mentor, and friend, whose remarkable intellectual drive, unquenchable curiosity, analytical creativity, and dedication to the public good is the equal of any in our profession. Thank you, Charles, for your support and encouragement, and frequent opportunities to share ideas.

Series Editor's Foreword

In the view of most Americans, the proper role of public administration in a democracy is that of a tool—"a hammer or a saw," in Herbert Kaufman's famous formulation—to be used by elected officials for the sole purpose of carrying out popularly ordained public policies. But such a narrow, *instrumental* view of administration is naïve, according to Brian J. Cook. Even simple tools are more than instruments; they have *constitutive*, or formative, effects on those who use them. "With a hammer in one's hand," the maxim goes, "the world looks surprisingly like a nail." Or, in Montesquieu's more ominous observation, "At the birth of societies, the rulers establish institutions; and afterwards, the institutions mold the rulers."

Americans' narrowly and naïvely instrumental view of public administration has deep roots in both theory and history, Cook argues. Theoretically, to confront the constitutive influence of unelected bureaucrats would render the deep cultural commitment to popular sovereignty problematic. It also is difficult to reconcile the power of administration with a constitution that devotes separate articles to Congress, the presidency, and the judiciary but scarcely mentions, much less empowers, the bureaucracy.

Historically, Americans have spent more than two centuries establishing and trying to breathe life into their instrumental conception of bureaucracy. The framers of the Constitution were, of necessity, inexperienced at administration—during colonial times, the legislature was their domain and administrators were appointees of the British crown. At the convention, the framers naturally inclined to a view of administration as purely instrumental, rejecting the idea, for example, that department heads, like judges, should serve "during good behavior."

As Cook shows, the instrumental approach to administration has been strengthened by every subsequent wave of bureaucratic reform: Andrew Jackson's spoils system and administrative reorganization, the sharp distinction Woodrow Wilson drew between politics and administration, Franklin D. Roosevelt's alphabet agencies to combat the Depression, and so on. The efforts of President Bill Clinton and Vice President Al Gore to "reinvent government" have been grounded in an image of administration scarcely less naïve than hammers and saws: on the ship of state, suggest David Osborne and Ted Gaebler, the leading theorists of the Clinton-Gore reforms, political officers "steer" and administrators "row."

The history of bureaucratic reform has not been the history of bureaucracy, however. Indeed, administrative power had grown in the face of every effort to domesticate it. The primary reason it has done so is that the tasks of government have grown dramatically more extensive and complex, forcing elected officials both to rely on administrators for advice in policy making and to allow them considerable discretion in policy implementation.

As the gap has grown between instrumental theory and constitutive reality, Cook notes despairingly, the American people have grown increasingly angry at and disenchanted with bureaucracy. Just as, in Richard Fenno's classic statement, modern candidates run *for* Congress by running *against* Congress, so do presidential candidates run for chief executive by running against the executive branch.

Cook has little doubt about what the political system needs to do to resolve its bureaucracy problem: acknowledge that public administration has powerful constitutive effects, and work to make those effects beneficial. He is equally emphatic in his advice to those who teach public administration, namely, strive to develop Aristotle's *phronesis*, or practical wisdom, in their students. "To conjoin knowledge of principles of right with considerations of what is suitable" is no small aspiration for the public administration profession.

Michael Nelson

Preface to the First Edition

Specialists in Soviet politics had a devil of a time in the early 1990s coming to grips with their slide toward irrelevance. The political, economic, social, and cultural system at the core of their scholarly careers had disintegrated in the historical equivalent of a blink of an eye. Their search for new and securely relevant research and teaching specialties looked much like the academic version of a mad scramble. A departmental colleague of mine, of Ukrainian heritage, successfully maneuvered through these dangerous straits by transforming herself into a specialist in Ukrainian politics. What she observed in the midst of that difficult scholarly transition, during a journey to a conference in the western Ukrainian city of Lviv, was quite illuminating.

As striking as what had changed since the crumbling of the Soviet system was what had stayed the same. And what had remained the same most emphatically was the essential character of the old Soviet bureaucracy. Upon arriving in Lviv on a plane from Warsaw, the passengers disembarked to face one-and-a-half hours of tortuous passport control. Two officials were available for processing 150 people. No information was offered regarding where the proper forms could be found or how they should be filled out. Nor did it seem absurd to these two officials that all these people, with all their luggage, were to get through a set of double doors, one side of which was closed and locked, to reach them. The bus trip from the airport to the hotel was just as bad, turning into a three-hour nightmare of official processing, bargaining about routes and stops, and unplanned side trips.

Confirmed were my colleague's long-held suspicions that the most notable features of the old Soviet bureaucratic system, often perceived as the result of incompetence and bureaucratic pathology, were intentional. They served to subjugate and demean citizens and visitors, forcing them into submission and dependence. The bureaucrats were the masters, and all others who entered their sphere of officialdom were subjects to be controlled.

For the better part of the twentieth century, Western democracies, and the United States in particular, have expended tremendous effort to avoid the totalitarian bureaucratic nightmare. My neighbors in Worcester may insist, only half-jokingly, that a visit to the Massachusetts Registry of Motor Vehicles for new license plates is not much different from a trip to Lviv. In truth, however, Americans have been wildly successful at keeping public or "state" bureaucracy under control. Formal and informal restraints abound, and American political culture is suffused with messages reminding public administrators of their proper place: the people are the masters, and bureaucrats are, quite literally, the servants.

Despite this triumph, the American people are at best ambivalent and apprehensive about public bureaucracy, reflecting a tradition that reaches to the very taproot of American political culture. At worst, evidence from recent public opinion polls and popular culture outlets suggests that segments of the public have become truly antigovernment. They are angered by the behavior of the federal government in particular, including federal administrative officials. For these citizens, the threats that officialdom poses to the American way of life are evident on a daily basis.

Michael Sandel has observed that all this anger and apprehension directed toward government signals "the fear that we are losing control of the forces that govern our lives" (McWilliams 1995, 197). This sense of loss of control, I would argue, reflects in part the loss of genuine aspirations to self-government. Public bureaucracy is implicated in this loss to the extent that, in the eyes of many Americans, it is not subject to citizen control. Many citizens may sense that, quite the opposite, they are subject to the control of bureaucrats, who answer only to politically powerful groups or to other bureaucrats. To them, public bureaucracy is deeply and permanently involved in structuring relations between groups of citizens and in shaping public purposes. Thus, public bureaucracy, when seen as master rather than servant, represents the central impediment to the full realization of popular self-rule.

Moreover, this range of citizen reaction to government bureaucracy, from ambivalence to angry rejection, indicates that the idea of public administration and its status as a political institution are in extreme flux. The time is ripe, then, for a thorough reconsideration of the role of public administration in American government and politics. In my attempt at such a reconsideration, I tapped into several intellectual movements in the study of government and politics in the United States.

The first of these movements has emerged from the conclusion reached by a considerable number of political scientists that their discipline has become nearly ahistorical. To counteract this, they have sought to stress in their work the importance of historical context in explaining currently prominent features of the American political landscape. In doing so, they have closely investigated the possibility that the basis for many current problems and controversies can be found in the major ideas and forces that have shaped American political development.

Scholars leading the second movement have raised serious questions about the capacity of liberal democratic regimes to sustain themselves in their current form. They have tackled anew the core question of what constitutes a good society. In the process, they have returned to the early intellectual foundations of a political science oriented toward finding the combination of elements that could produce more capable, more resilient democratic polities.

Finally, a third movement has engaged in a searching reappraisal of the status of public administration in the American constitutional system. Spurred by increasingly strident assaults on public bureaucracy, specialists in public administration have been in the vanguard of this endeavor. They have produced scholarship of considerable intellectual richness and originality, the conclusions of which have, however, not been embraced by all.

Drawing upon all three of these intellectual currents, I argue that public bureaucracy is deeply and permanently involved in structuring relations between groups of citizens and in shaping public purposes. This is an inevitable fact of life in a modern liberal democratic regime. It will always have both positive and negative consequences, but which predominates will be a function of how well citizens and political leaders understand and deal with the basic fact.

Conceptions of public administration and its place in the American constitutional system, it turns out, have been an important motif in the public discourse and political action that have propelled American political development. Unfortunately, the rhetoric and ideology that have emerged, and the public expectations about popular control of bureaucracy that have accumulated across time as a result, have increasingly deviated from the basic fact of public administration's formative role in the regime. The consequence has actually been less popular influence on bureaucracy. Worse, it has produced untoward limitations on the capacity of public administration to contribute, within its proper sphere, to the maintenance and enhancement of American self-government.

I present my argument in the form of an extended essay, or perhaps more accurately, in the form of a proposition or a hypothesis. My principal concerns are the development of ideas about public administration across the course of American political development, the discontent with government and public bureaucracy that has arisen, and how past ideas and current theory can contribute to an appropriate response. The conceptual core of my argument is the distinction between the instrumental and constitutive qualities of political institutions, including public administration.

I begin by establishing the contemporary context of the problem and proceed then to explore the differences between instrumental and constitutive reasoning. All of this unfolds in chapter 1. I try to show in particular how the two kinds of reason can, considered separately and together, contribute to our understanding of politics and political institutions, including public administration.

I apply this conceptual frame in an analysis of the ideas about public administration that were given voice in public debates that epitomized the political struggles of major eras in the development of the United States. In chapter 2, for example, I examine in detail the original debates sparked by Congress's creation of the first executive departments and the question of the president's power to remove from office department heads and other executive officers. I conclude that the character of this debate—the depth of the insights and the crystallization of distinctive conceptions of administration's place under the Constitution—as well as the outcome, set the principal boundaries for most of the subsequent confrontations over the status of administrative power in the constitutional system. The seeds of the divergence between public belief and administrative reality were planted there.

In chapters 3, 4, and 5, I follow the progression of that divergence, manifested as an increasingly narrow and intense commitment to a strictly instrumental conception of public administration in American public affairs. I examine, in particular, the confrontation between Andrew Jackson and Senate Whigs over the president's removal power, the debates spawned by civil service reform and regulation of interstate commerce, the efforts of the progressives to redefine executive power, and the New Deal struggle over executive reorganization.

In the final two chapters, I consider the prospects for rejuvenating the idea of public administration in American politics. I begin by considering the implications of a predominantly instrumental conception of public administration in American politics. This is prelude to an appraisal of the benefits of resuscitating and invigorating the constitutive dimension of public administration and to a delineation of what needs to be considered, and accomplished, to realize those benefits. I conclude by renewing the call for a constitutional theory of public administration. I discuss the basic principles, centered on fostering responsible administrative discretion, on which such a theory might be established.

No one should expect, of course, that a precise delineation of the scope and meaning of public administration in American government will ever be realized. It will remain forever subject to political contention and debate. Understanding systemic and institutional fundamentals and their implications can, however, inform the debate. Hence, the theory building I advocate is crucial intellectual work if we are ever again to see a time when thoughtful citizens, and men and women in public life, regard public administration as a vital part of a distinctively American capacity for self-government.

Acknowledgments to the First Edition

I have many people to thank, and much to be thankful for, as I reach a new milestone with the publication of this book. Sid Milkis of Brandeis University regarded my ideas, and the scholarly endeavor I envisioned, with respect and seriousness from the very beginning. He provided superb guidance on early chapter drafts, and his own work stood as a model of scholarly craftsmanship while providing the foundation for key portions of my analysis. Steve Elkin of the University of Maryland remains the central source of intellectual substance for much of my work. He read parts of the manuscript at various stages of development, offering strategic direction and helping me polish various dimensions of the argument.

Larry Terry, Rick Green, Martha Derthick, Theodore Lowi, Drew McCoy, and the anonymous reader for Johns Hopkins University Press read all or part of the manuscript and provided helpful criticism that improved the final product. They also offered words of support that increased my confidence that I indeed have said something worth saying. Series editor Michael Nelson provided reasoned advice and oversight and enthusiastic support for the project from the very beginning. I hope in the end that I met his expectations. Henry Tom, executive editor for Johns Hopkins University Press, proved to be a pillar of patience and flexibility when I missed several deadlines. He also made easy the path through final review, approval, and production. Anne Whitmore edited the manuscript. She rescued me from many of the worst idiosyncrasies in my writing style. I thank her for her skill, her hard work, and her generous encouragement.

Clark University Librarian Sue Baughman and reference librarians Mary Hartman and Ed McDermott furnished me with a spare yet cozy and quiet space to work, friendly greetings on oh so many 8:00 a.m. arrivals in the library, and expert, efficient service in finding vital material.

My thanks also to the many other public administration scholars and political scientists from whom I have learned so much. They just keep generating new and exciting ideas, leaving me busy and content to follow in their wake.

My warmest and most affectionate thanks I reserve for my wife, Ruth, and my daughters, Meredith and Lauren. Their unqualified love, support, concern, and curiosity granted me the power and inspiration to keep going and provided me refuge from the pressures of trying to complete a book manuscript and chair a political science department at the same time. They know there will be other projects to follow, but we will also take time to relax, reflect, and have some fun.

Bureaucracy and Self-Government

Chapter One

Public Administration as Instrument and Institution

Washington, D.C.'s summers of 2010, 2011, and 2012 were the three hottest on record going back over 140 years (Rogers 2012). That warmth, however, was nothing like the political heat directed toward government administration in the nation's capital in 2013. First, observers and analysts raised serious questions about the capabilities and dedication of the U.S. State Department toward keeping its diplomats safe in the wake of the September 2012 terrorist attack on the U.S. facilities in Benghazi, Libya. The assault killed four U.S. government personnel, including the U.S. Ambassador to Libya, John Christopher Stevens (Hirsh 2013; U.S. Department of State 2013). Second, U.S. Internal Revenue Service (IRS) officials revealed that IRS staff in the Tax Exempt and Government Entities Division had scrutinized applications for tax-exempt status by the many new, politically active citizens groups organized in response to the election of President Barack Obama using criteria that appeared, at least initially, to target ideologically conservative groups (U.S. Department of Treasury 2013; but see Weisman 2013). Third, an employee of the private consulting firm Booz Allen Hamilton, working under contract to the U.S. National Security Agency (NSA), surreptitiously revealed the agency's domestic surveillance program involving the compilation of massive phone and Internet records databases (Savage and Wyatt 2013; Savage, Wyatt, and Baker 2013). The furor raised in response to this convergence of events generated questions both serious and silly about the competence of federal bureaucrats and their insidious intrusion into the public and private lives of American citizens. Rep. Paul Gosar (R-AZ) and three of his colleagues in the Arizona delegation to the U.S. House of Representatives seized the opportunity created by this furor to organize a congressional field hearing entitled, "The I.R.S. and the E.P.A.—Bureaucrats Out-of-Control" and invited "victims" of "I.R.S. abuse or E.P.A. overreach" to testify (Gosar 2013).

In contrast to the fallout from these events, conservatives in the U.S. Congress proposed a near doubling of the U.S. Border Patrol as part of their price for supporting immigration policy reform (Parker 2013). One newspaper columnist observed, if "you think that the government . . . is incompetent . . . you certainly wouldn't think it able to manage a task as difficult as locking down the Southwest border" (Klein 2013). Similarly, toward the end of the federal government shutdown in October 2013, the second longest of three such closures in less than 20 years (Brass 2013), congressional Republicans expressed outrage that the National Park Service had swiftly closed and barricaded most national parks and monuments, an action that seemingly indicated effective administration in a dire fiscal crisis but which critics saw as denying citizens access to cherished public assets and services administered directly by federal bureaucrats.

The juxtaposition of attacks on government bureaucracy with calls for expanding it in response to a threat or for keeping it operating to protect a right, even without the funds to pay the bills, reflects just the most current manifestation of the congenital confusion American political leaders and citizens alike exhibit about public administration and its place in a regime predicated on the belief that the people are sovereign and fully capable of governing themselves. A periodic inquiry into the sources and evolution of this confusion is critical because the continuance of the confusion poses a danger to those beliefs and aspirations for self-government.

How the Republic can best administer its affairs has been at the center of nearly every political conflict that has marked a new stage in the nation's development—from the replacement of the Articles of Confederation with the Constitution, to the emergence of an "administrative state" in the Progressive Era, to a twenty-first-century American state that looks like "an insurance company with an army" (Krugman 2011). In the past two decades, all levels of American government have been through a process of crisis, reform, and reinvention of their administrative organizations and management processes. Yet the stream of new schools of thought, techniques imported from business management reforms, and proposals for administrative change or dissolution has left the American people as conflicted as ever about the meaning of self-government when public administration seems to occupy so much of the politics of the nation.

American citizens have long recognized that their governments, in particular government agencies and the officials who manage them, exert considerable influence on their lives. With this recognition may come an "implicit bargain" that such influence and the dependence on "state institutions" it reflects would remain "invisible, and that for all intents and purposes each citizen could continue to believe that she was sovereign over her life" (J. M. Bernstein 2010). Indeed, the notion that the state, especially the national government, exerts a formidable governing influence while remaining "hidden in plain sight" is a prominent theme in recent scholarship on American political development (Balogh 2009). Whatever one may make of claims about implicit bargains or a government out of sight—and they are not easily dismissed—it is even harder to refute that, in growing numbers over the past 40 years, albeit with notable fluctuations, members of the American public have come to see government officials as poorly controlled and unresponsive (see, for example, ANES 2008, tables 5A.1–5A.4, 5B.2–5B.3). To some, possibly now even a majority, the actions of the federal government may even pose an imminent threat to their personal freedom (Pew Research Center 2013a). This abstract animosity toward, and even fear of, government and government officers, seems to dissipate considerably, however, when it comes to specifics.

Since the mid-1990s, strong majorities of people surveyed have favorably viewed state and local government (Pew Research Center 2013b). Although the proportion holding a favorable view of the federal government declined sharply after 2001, public views about specific federal agencies are much more sanguine, although these views have eroded in recent years. For instance, in the late 1980s and again in the 1990s, majorities favorably viewed all but one of a baker's dozen of federal agencies, with more than 70 percent viewing some agencies favorably. The IRS was the exception. Even with the more recent plunge in favorable public views of government—the federal government in particular—in 2010, a majority of the public still viewed favorably 10 out of 13 of the same agencies, although the sizes of the majorities had declined in most instances. The least favorably viewed agency, the U.S. Department of Education, at 40 percent, still easily exceeded the sorry public regard for the U.S. Congress, at 26 percent. The favorability of the IRS had actually increased, although it remained below a majority (Pew Research Center 2010, 55).

Similar patterns can be found in the data from the American Customer Satisfaction Index (ACSI), which claims a more robust and valid methodology for measuring industry and government performance than the standard public opinion survey (ACSI 2014). In its most recent commentary on government performance, ACSI found that "although government services [overall] continue to score significantly below private sector services, some federal agencies show levels of user satisfaction similar to high performing private sector companies." In comparing agency-level trust with general trust in the federal government, the organization found that "while citizens have very low trust in the federal government in the abstract, they tend to report much higher trust in the particular agencies with which they actually interact" (ACSI 2013).

Two prominent public administration scholars have offered interpretations of the discrepancies between general and specific public satisfaction with government performance and trust in government and its administration. First, George Frederickson, with David Frederickson, explained the deviation between general opinion survey results and specific performance assessments as the result of the "paradox of distance" and the "lack of role differentiation." In the paradox of distance, "people trust and even revere those government officials who are near at hand," while they "believe that government officials who are far away are lazy, incompetent, and probably dishonest" (H. Frederickson and Frederickson 1995, 167). Lack of role differentiation refers to the public's tendency "not to distinguish between persons elected to legislative bodies, persons elected as executives, persons politically appointed, and permanent civil servants" (165). Because of this lack of differentiation, inept and corrupt behavior by elected and appointed officials taints the public's perceptions of the competence and integrity of all officials. Second, Charles Goodsell concluded from his own review of the evidence that "citizens' views of government as an abstraction are influenced by the cultural myth that government fails. Citizens' views of their individual bureaucratic experiences are, by contrast, controlled by direct experience—which tells them that government usually works" (Goodsell 2004, 33).

These two interpretations are not mutually exclusive, of course, since physical and experiential distance are likely correlated. These notions of distance and experience and their associations with citizens' satisfaction with and trust in government, and with their capacity to hold government to account have deep historical roots in governing philosophies associated with the American founding and the early years of the Republic. Prominent among these philosophies were the arguments of the Antifederalists and Thomas Jefferson's embrace of localism

(Balogh 2009, 36), which he articulated most extensively in his now largely forgotten ward system scheme (e.g., Matthews 1984, 81–89). At its core, however, the incongruity between the general and the specific in public perceptions of government and public administration reflects the refusal of the America people and their political leaders, from the founding to the present day, to accept the contributions of more formalized and centralized administration to American self-government. The paradox of distance and the myth that government fails imply that public perceptions of government administration, generated by a distant, broad, and general perspective, are more abstract and less real, while perceptions created through close, focused contact or specific interactions are more concrete and authentic. This dichotomy does not withstand scrutiny, however. Both perspectives—the general and the specific and the perceptions they generate—are equally valid and real. Both are derived from concrete government action filtered through numerous lenses. It is only the experience derived from the specific perspective, however, that matches public expectations about the role of public administration in American public life established at the founding and further shaped and reinforced over two centuries of further national development.

When government bureaucrats function as the instrument of individual welfare, serving people's wants and needs, which is usually the case with local government or in close, specific, client-oriented encounters with state or federal agencies, public bureaucracies and public administrators are judged positively. However, when administrative agencies from a broad, general, and distant perspective are considered, or when agencies are observed performing less direct service-oriented functions, people more readily see the impact of public administration on the shape and substance of public policy, especially on the general patterns of interactions among citizens that comprise social life, and thus the very complex character of modern public governance. The reality of that impact violates basic expectations of the servile role public agencies ought only to fulfill, so public reactions are then almost wholly negative, sometimes manifested as anger, denunciation, vandalism, and even threats of violence toward public servants (ADL 2009; Knickerbocker 2010; Yoder 2013). Some citizens, organized by several of the most antigovernment leaders in Congress, stormed the barricades at several national parks and monuments during the 2013 shutdown in such a display (NBC Washington 2013)

These expectations for a wholly instrumental, service-oriented public administration have been built up over the long American struggle with one of the most enduring dilemmas in liberal democratic politics and government: How can a broad-based, long-range, stable, even permanent exercise of governmental authority be reconciled with a regime of popular sovereignty? The answer that has dominated public thinking and political rhetoric in the United States is that public agencies are best understood, and treated, as subordinate instruments or servants of the public will. As the broad, distant perspective on government administration reveals to many citizens, however, the picture is much more subtle and complex. Administrative agencies, in their multiple and varied forms, are engaged in more than achieving goals already designated for them. They shape public purposes and order the relations among citizens in American society, as individuals and in groups, in intricate and far-reaching ways.

In the public experience, if not in the expectations of many American citizens, then, public administrators and their organizations not only help to serve the goals, wants, and needs of the people but also help to determine those goals, wants, and needs, in complex and sometimes worrisome ways. This is the fundamental reality that scholars, political leaders, and attentive citizens must examine, understand, and ultimately accept if they wish to dispel the contradictions and conflicts, disruptions, and diminished self-governing power that ensue from misplaced notions about the place of public bureaucracy in the nation's political and social life. The examination can best begin with a consideration of distinctive kinds of reasoning, and such a consideration can in turn serve as an effective device for developing in more detail a multidimensional understanding of political institutions and of public administration in particular.

Instrumental and Constitutive Reasoning

Consider a common household tool—the claw hammer. It may be used to drive a nail, to prop open a window, or to smash open a piggy bank. In each case, the hammer is merely the means to an end designated by the user. In other words, the hammer has no *intrinsic* significance. It has no "essential nature" because its use determines its identity. All tools or instruments—the power drill, the automobile, the smartphone—are similarly means, simple or complex, for achieving some externally defined purpose by some human user. They do not define ends and are not ends themselves.

This way of speaking and thinking about the world and its objects is *instrumental*, or *means-end*, rationality. It is also called economic rationality, or *economizing*, because it is the epistemological foundation of economics, and of the social institution called the market economy, in which everything bought and sold is seen as the means to an ultimate end: human want satisfaction (Diesing 1962, ch. 2; Elkin

1985, 253–56). Instrumentalism is a particularly powerful form of reason, and in many ways, it is the defining form of rationality in Western culture, underlying as it does the market economy's advancing reach (Kuttner 1999; Sandel 2012). "The increasing scope of the economy forces people to make an increasing number of allocation decisions, in which means are allocated to alternative ends. Hence people come to think of decisions in terms of means and ends; they come to believe . . . that all practical questions are questions of means and ends" (Diesing 1962, 36).

The reach of instrumentalism, or economizing, has extended, quite easily, to policy making and political institutions. Before appraising that, however, it is important to see that instrumentalism is not the only form of reason. "The efficient achievement of predetermined goals is a special kind of effectiveness. If there are other kinds of value besides goal values then there are presumably also other kinds of effectiveness or rationality" (Diesing 1962, 3). So, consider again the hammer, and the adage that "with a hammer in one's hand, the world looks surprisingly like a nail." Informally codified as the Law of the Hammer (D. A. Stone 1988, 144; see Kaplan 1964; Maslow 1966), this apothegm expresses the idea that a tool, or more expansively a technology, can have a "profoundly formative influence" (Tribe 1973, 652).

Most people, adults anyway, are able to control the influence that their use of a simple tool has on their psyches and worldviews. This may be less true for more complex technologies. The growing ubiquity of smartphones and other personal communications devices appears to have brought with it notable changes in public behavior and social relations—talking out loud to no one nearby, sitting with one's head down and eyes fixed on one's lap during dinner at a restaurant—that while not yet completely unremarkable have certainly become almost commonplace. The choice and use of even a simple tool, and certainly of more sophisticated technologies, can therefore have at least some perceptible impact on the end toward which one is using it. "For virtually every human action . . . is at once both operational (or 'instrumental') *and* self-forming (or 'constitutive')" (Tribe 1973, 635; emphasis in original). One can take this a step further and note that the hammer or smartphone may not only shape the end but also *become* the end. One's purpose in life becomes to hammer or to communicate via smartphone. What were once simply tools devoid of meaning except through use have become intrinsically significant.

In contrast to instrumental rationality, *constitutive* rationality is reasoning about forms and purposes. Constitutive rationality refers to individuals, or even societies, making sense of the composition of something, reasoning about how to make something into what they wish it to be, or even deciding what it is they desire in the first place. The effects of a public policy and the institutions that undergird it, for instance, can be judged not only on the basis of whether specifically designated objectives are achieved but also against broader standards that members of a society hold for the form or composition of the social fabric. Society's members may consider whether the policy alters the relations between particular classes of citizens in ways that do not accord with the conception of their society that they hold and seek to maintain. Hence, constitutive rationality can inform policy evaluation because it encompasses value other than that of means meeting ends and therefore is about another kind of effectiveness.

Consider the relatively familiar activity of painting a picture. One can speak of it quite readily in instrumental terms by stating that painting a picture makes one feel good. Painting is the means to an end—personal pleasure. To address why an artist has painted a particular canvas in a particular way is difficult for instrumental reasoning, however. The artist may say she has painted the sky in a landscape a particular color or positioned trees in a particular way because that is her preference. It is the means to her preference satisfaction. She may argue that she chose a particular color or placement of trees to achieve an intended effect. But the question of why that intended effect and not another cannot be answered instrumentally. Instrumental rationality, involving as it does the search for and matching of appropriate means to *given* ends, can say little about how the ends are chosen, except that "the specification of goals, values, or ends must ultimately rest on logically arbitrary . . . expressions of will and desire as opposed to acts of reason and understanding" (Tribe 1973, 636; see also MacIntyre 1981, 84–102; J. D. White 1990, 134–37).

However, if one can cite reasons for choosing the end, such as affinity with a moral system, code of ethics, or, in the case of the artist, a particular school or period in landscape art, one is being rational rather than arbitrary. By choosing ends and by articulating reasons for that choice, beyond arbitrary will or preference, one shapes one's character or identity. Through a painting, an artist expresses the kind of landscape artist she is, and with a particular painting further shapes, or *constitutes*, herself as a landscape artist. Painting is thus an end in itself—it has intrinsic significance—and it is formative.

These several facets of constitutive rationality apply with equal if not greater force to whole societies. Take war for example. At the height of the Persian Gulf War in 1991, much of the public discussion centered on the nature of the ultimate goals of the U.S.-led allied forces. Many observers noted that the conduct of the war had a determinative effect on American objectives. Columnist George Will, for example, contended that "American policy is to inflict from the air sufficient attrition on Iraq's defenses to achieve American war aims—*whatever they eventually will be*—without crossing the crucial threshold to intolerable casualties" (Will 1991; emphasis added). Observers made similar arguments about the shifting rationales for the invasion and occupation of Iraq that began in 2003 (Sandalow 2004).

In the aftermath of the first Gulf War, agreement was widespread, if not unanimous, that the war had exerted a transformative influence on the nation, a consequence that President George H. W. Bush emphasized (Bush 1991). The same has been said about nearly every other war, including the Afghanistan and Iraq wars, but little attention has been paid to the significance of such a notion. If one accepts war as the ultimate instrumentality employed by a nation-state to achieve its goals and protect its interests, one must nevertheless also accept that war cannot be judged solely on whether national goals were successfully achieved and national interests successfully protected. Studs Terkel (1984) explored precisely this noninstrumental dimension of war in his oral history of World War II, and it is reflected in the book's title: *The Good War.* The darker side of this phenomenon is the devastating human, environmental, societal, and fiscal costs and transformative cultural impact of war. For the generations coming of age after World War II, the dark effects from the wars in Vietnam, Iraq, and Afghanistan, have been just as real and traumatic.

Tools and technologies have "the effect of significantly altering the ends—and indeed the basic character—of the individuals [or] societies that choose them" (Tribe 1973, 642). The import of this phenomenon is that "social choices serve not merely to implement 'given' systems of values, but also to define and sometimes to reshape the values—indeed the very identity—of the choosing . . . community" (634; see also Leiss 1990). A society may even seek to define its identity in terms of particular artifacts or technologies. One can think of the cargo cults of Melanesia, or even the United States during the several decades of this century when it appeared that the nation's chief if not sole purpose was to be a nuclear superpower. And it is certainly not unreasonable to speak of war as becoming, for some individuals, groups, or whole societies, an end in itself and a way of life.

If tools and technologies can at least in part be understood as constitutive of individuals and societies, as at least in part making individuals or societies what they are, then that effect must apply *a fortiori* to the institutions of society. This is so for the institutions of politics and government, because they are the building blocks, the basic organizing units, of polities. It is important to recognize that heavily relying on instrumental reasoning and an instrumental understanding of public affairs can leave a nation blind to formative consequences. The added cost of failing to embrace a constitutive understanding of public action, it turns out, is a negated politics, a degenerative political science, and an impaired day-to-day management of public life.

Neutralizing Politics and Administration

The predominance of instrumental reason in the American public philosophy makes the conception and use of social structures—the market or market-like arrangements, or public agencies—as problem-solving tools seem altogether sensible. To employ them for relatively narrowly specified objectives is "programmatic" economizing, and it is ubiquitous, as in the "tools of government" perspective characterized as the "new governance" (Salamon 2000).

A grander version of economizing is also prevalent in public affairs and in modern theories of democratic politics and constitutional government. In this grander version, political institutions, and politics in general, are the instruments for achieving some ultimate social goal or the vehicles for reaching some ideal social end-state. In Harold Lasswell's well-known formulation (1958), for example, politics involves principally "who gets what, when, where, and why." That is, politics distributes social goods (and bads). In a somewhat different formulation, David Truman (1971) concluded his exhaustive study of group organization and political involvement by arguing that "the total pattern of government over a period of time . . . presents a protean complex of crisscrossing relationships that change in strength and direction with alterations in the power and standing of interests, organized and unorganized." In E. E. Schattschneider's influential description (1960), a governmental institution, or government as a whole, is an "arena of conflict," in which relatively advantaged or disadvantaged interests seek, respectively, to limit or expand the scope of conflict, in an effort to advance their chosen ends. The central notion in all these conceptions of politics was perhaps most succinctly put by Arthur Bentley: "We are forcibly reminded that the governing body has no value in itself, except as one aspect of the process, and cannot even be adequately described except in terms of the deep-lying interests which function through it" (Bentley 1908, 300; quoted in Easton 1971, 149).

Whether in the micro or the macro sense, politics and political institutions are without meaning if they are not used by segments of society. They are either instruments to which society gives meaning only when they are employed to achieve some externally defined end or they are mere stages or backdrops on which a complex calculus, like preference aggregation, is practiced, or great political dramas, like interest-group conflict, are played out.

Public administration is particularly susceptible to being conceived of as an instrument. Policy makers and the public generally understand regulation and regulatory agencies, for example, as the primary mechanisms for informing, guiding, manipulating, or even coercing citizens to behave in ways that will allow the community to achieve its objectives. "The boundaries of the 'public administration' problem have leapt far beyond the question of how to effectively organize and run a public institution and now encompass the far more vexing question of how to change some aspect of the behavior of a whole society" (Schultze 1977, 12). The reason for attempting such behavioral change is to reach some grand social goal, whether it is "prosperity and price stability" or "equitable income distribution" (1).

Most public organizations are not even privileged enough to be seen as engaging in such a grand social endeavor. Instead, they are stuck in a programmatic economizing world, understandable, for example, as a "system of administration viewed as industry structures . . . composed of diverse, independent agencies, collaborating in supplying and arranging for the availability of different bundles of collective goods and services. . . . Once one begins to think in this way, one can imagine the possibility of an education industry, a police industry, a fire-protection industry, a trash and garbage disposal industry, a welfare industry, a health-services industry, and many other public-service industries that would appropriately characterize . . . public administration" (Ostrom 1987, 204). Indeed, this is precisely what has happened, as exemplified by the inclusion of government services in the American Customer Satisfaction Index, and the widespread blurring of boundaries between public and private entities delivering such services in this age of "the new governance" (Salamon 2000).

This way of thinking, not only about government agencies but also about all large social and political institutions, prompted Theodore Lowi to proclaim the existence of a Republic of Service Delivery (1985, 96). "Thus, firmly embedded in the public mind is the relatively new idea that institutions, including government, are to be trusted and accorded legitimacy not in terms of the effort they make or in terms of the amount and character of the representation they provide but in terms of service delivery" (94). It is important not to construe Lowi's Republic of Service Delivery as simply a consequence of economists invading the public realm, although the increasing influence of economic thinking and economic advice in public affairs after World War II is one strand in the story. An instrumental conception of politics and public institutions has a number of deeper roots.

First, the cornerstone of this conception is liberalism because "liberals . . . regard political community as an instrumental rather than intrinsic good" (Barber 2003, 7). In his extensive dissection of liberal democracy in *Strong Democracy*, Barber repeatedly stresses that it is liberalism that treats political institutions, indeed all of politics, as an instrument for the achievement of largely private wants, and he especially notes the instrumentalism inherent in the "peculiar logic" of social-contract theory (67).

Furthermore, liberalism is the philosophical anchor for economic thought. Hence, instrumentalism, or the "means-ends schema," is a central element in "the value system developed by economic progress" (Diesing 1962, 36). And the effects of economic progress, and thus of liberalism, have been substantial. "One cultural element after another has been absorbed into the ever-widening economy, subjected to the test of economic rationality, rationalized, and turned into a commodity or factor of production. So pervasive has this process been that it now seems that anything can be thought of as a commodity and its value measured by a price, and that all values can be thought of as utilities" (24).

The increasing influence of economists in public affairs may be regarded as a particular effect of the general trend of economic progress. Although the effect of economic progress has not yet been to transform or "rationalize" political institutions into commodities with prices attached, it has had the effect of "neutralizing" them (Diesing 1962, 25); that is, they have increasingly come to be regarded as neutral, interchangeable devices for attaining whatever society deems most important. As Barber states it, "politics is prudence in the service of *homo economicus*—the solitary seeker of material happiness and bodily security" (Barber 2003, 20).

This is especially so for public administration. In particular, the privatization thrust and its successor, the new governance or networked governance, that have arisen in the past 30 years are extensions of the logic of economizing, wherein public agencies become interchangeable with private entities in the pursuit of some program objective or, much less often, some grand social goal (see Goodsell 2004, 145–56; Kettl 1988, 1993; Salamon 1989; Savas 1987).

Second, quite distinct but not wholly separate from economic progress is the influence of *democratic* progress. Democracy—as a theory of government and a way of life, at least in the form Barber labels "unitary" (2003, 149)—has the effect of subjugating and instrumentalizing public institutions. Alexis de Tocqueville observed the several dimensions of this characteristic of democracy and considered its consequences throughout *Democracy in America* (1988). Democratic progress can be linked with economic progress in that economic progress may provide for greater equality in economic conditions. Democracy, however, is concerned with the equality of *all* social conditions. As a society moves closer to the equality of social conditions, popular pressures increase and the mass of the people press the institutions of government, and the officials who staff them, into service to satisfy society's wants. "Democratization opened up the possibility that citizens might now use government for their own benefit, rather than simply watching government being used for the benefit of others. . . . Once citizens perceived that government could operate in response to their demands, [they] became increasingly willing to support the expansion of government" (Lowi and Ginsberg 1990, 23; see also J. Q. Wilson 1975).

Third, political science has played a small but significant role in promoting an instrumental conception of politics and public institutions by assuming a neutral orientation toward them. Whereas American political science in its original conception scrutinized the practice of government with an eye toward the "maintenance and improvement of the liberal democratic experiment" (Anderson 1990, 195), since the 1950s and the so-called behavioralist revolution (Dahl 1961), the discipline has for the most part approached politics and political institutions as phenomena, to be examined with the value-neutral tools of scientific method. The effect was to cut loose political institutions from the context of the regime that gives them meaning. They became simply arenas in which individual actors do battle in a civilized form of combat called politics. Conceived thus, the institutions are valueless, as Bentley asserted, until they are occupied and used for particular purposes.

The consequence of the "revolution" in political science was particularly pronounced with respect to the discipline's treatment of public administration. For a time, political scientists seemed to regard public bureaucracies as nonentities, that is, as having no intrinsic political value worthy of study (see Hill 1992, 33–36). The more general point, however, is that the education of several generations of American public officials in American universities reinforced the more widespread effect from economic progress: conceptualizing political institutions as instruments, amenable to (instrumentally) rational, objective, or value-neutral analysis of their effectiveness in achieving ends defined externally to them. Within the academy, there eventually arose fairly vigorous counterattacks on the behavioralist, instrumentalist orientation to politics and political institutions, offering a number of alternative approaches, in both political science and the study of public administration, for "thinking institutionally about politics and public administration (Heclo 2008; see also Spicer 2010). Whether this effort can exert influence on politics and the public philosophy remains to be seen.

Finally, quite apart from and in addition to a grounding in liberalism, the Constitution and the mythology that has grown up around it have had their own impact on public thinking about politics and government. The Constitution has come to be regarded as the profound and singular constitutive act of the American people. In his treatise on the constitutional legitimacy of the administrative state, for instance, John Rohr argues that the Constitution has a special "moral vitality," because it is "the great work of the founding period of the Republic" (1986, 8). In turn, the nation's founding and the Constitution it produced are unique because they represent the decisive acts "of the sovereign" (80). Hence, to paraphrase Woodrow Wilson (and the title of Rohr's book), everything that has come after the founding has been about *running* the Constitution, filling in the details, striving to achieve its purposes.

Indeed, nearly every new goal or purpose the American people have defined for themselves over 230 years has been anchored in the Constitution, or at least in constitutional rhetoric. That has proved vital to the survival and stability of the nation, but it has also made everything else that has come after seem merely instrumental in character. The ideal end-state, presumed to be readable between the lines of the Constitution's text, is a perpetually receding horizon. The American people are ceaseless in their pursuit of that horizon, rarely pausing to reflect on how they may have changed in their relationships with one another as citizens during the pursuit or how their perception of what stands on that horizon may have changed as well.

A wholly instrumental conception of American politics and government, and thus of public administration as well, is thus likely to be not only inadequate but ultimately debilitating. Understanding more fully how constitutive rationality applies to political institutions, and to public bureaucracy specifically, is essential to realizing other possibilities.

Politics: The Shape and Substance of Public Life

The idea that societal institutions, especially political and governmental institutions, can shape the manner in which individuals behave, as well as the ends toward which they strive collectively, is hardly new. The eighteenth-century French philosopher Montesquieu remarked, "At the birth of societies, the leaders of republics create the institutions; thereafter, it is the institutions that form the leaders of republics" (Montesquieu 1734, 25). Woodrow Wilson echoed Montesquieu but went much further. "Institutions are subsequent to character. They do not create character, but are created and sustained by it. After being successfully established, however, they both confirm and modify national character, forming in no small degree both national thought and national purpose—certainly national ideals" (Link et al. 1966–1994, 11:239).

The American founders were quite cognizant of the formative quality of political institutions. For example, in advocating the peculiar arrangement of republican institutions and practices embodied in the Constitution, Alexander Hamilton saw not only a greater general prosperity accruing to the American people but also that this "commercial republic" he sought would form a particular kind of citizenry, with attachments to and preferences for particular institutions (Green 2002).

In *The Federalist* No. 10, James Madison offered an especially powerful example of constitutive reasoning in his comparative analysis of democratic and republican government. In one of the most famous passages in the *Federalist* papers, Madison argued that the effect of representation, a distinguishing feature of republican government, "is, on the one hand, to refine and enlarge the public views by passing them through the medium of a chosen body of citizens, whose wisdom may best discern the true interest of their country and whose patriotism and love of justice will be least likely to sacrifice it to temporary or partial considerations." The second half of Madison's point is less well known, but it adds considerable force by virtue of the negative images it conjures up: "On the other hand, the effect may be inverted. Men of factious tempers, of local prejudices, or of sinister designs, may, by intrigue, by corruption, or by other means, first obtain the suffrages, and then betray the interests of the people." In neither case does it make sense to think about the conditions that Madison described only as ends for which representation is the means. Instead, representation is the end as well as the means. It is the state of political existence created by particular constitutional forms. Moreover, it embodies particular features and imparts certain qualities on, or constitutes, public opinion, depending on whether another condition is present or absent, namely, size, as in the extended republic.

Constitutions and constitution making are, not surprisingly then, rich sources of constitutive thinking about politics and government because constitutions make a people by creating the framework that will condition what they know or do not know. "In designing our political institutions we are sculpting our knowledge. In founding a constitution, we are determining the shape and character of our political epistemology" (Barber 2003, 170). A constitution "regulates a long-term pattern of interactions. It establishes conventions . . . that make it easier for us to cooperate and to coordinate in particular moments" (Hardin 1989, 101). At base, then, constitutions are highly elaborate structures of "constitutive rules" (Wagner 1990). Reflecting these characteristics, although the U.S. Constitution "reflects Lockean values, it also has affected their evolution and extension. This effect is clear with respect to the political liberties which are defined in the Constitution but which have also evolved within the constitutional framework." Hence, the "Constitution's significance . . . is not limited to generating issues that at times dominate American politics. It also shapes how groups define the issues they raise" (Nardulli 1992, 15).

Constitutive reasoning is not restricted to foundings, however, nor are constitutions the only political constructs that exert a formative influence on a polity. The greatest observer of and commentator on the formative effects of social, economic, and political institutions on the American polity, or more precisely on how these institutions have made the American polity what it is, remains Alexis de Tocqueville. *Democracy in America* is a bountiful source of material about how political parties, interest groups, judicial power, and town government go into the mix that is the distinctive regime called the United States. Tocqueville concluded, for example, that "the strength of free peoples resides in the local community. Local institutions are to liberty what primary schools are to science; they put it within the people's reach; they teach the people to appreciate its peaceful enjoyment and accustom them to make use of it. Without local institutions a nation may give itself a free government, but it has not got the spirit of liberty" (1988, 62–63). The Henry Reeve translation is even clearer on the central point: "municipal institutions *constitute* the strength of free nations," that is, they are what we mean by a free nation; they impart the qualities that define a nation as free (Tocqueville [1835] 1945, 63; emphasis added).

It is with his brief but penetrating observations of the comparative effects of slavery, however, that Tocqueville captured all the subtleties of the formative effects of institutions—their constitutiveness—that are at once social, economic, and political.

> On the left bank of the Ohio work is connected with the idea of slavery, but on the right with well-being and progress; on the one side it is degrading, but on the other honorable; on the left bank no white laborers are to be found, for they would be afraid of being like the slaves; for work people must rely on the Negroes; but one will never see a man of leisure on the right bank: the white man's intelligent activity is used for work of every sort. . . .

The American on the left bank scorns not only work itself but also enterprises in which work is necessary to success; living in idle ease, he has the
tastes of idle men; money has lost some of its value in his eyes; he is less interested in wealth than in excitement and pleasure and expends in that direction
the energy which his neighbor puts to other use; he is passionately fond of
hunting and war; he enjoys all the most strenuous forms of bodily exercise;
he is accustomed to the use of weapons and from childhood has been ready to
risk his life in single combat. Slavery therefore not only prevents the white
men from making their fortunes but even diverts them from wishing to do so.
(Tocqueville [1835] 1988, 346–48)

As these commentaries reveal, the constitutiveness of political institutions, like
constitutive reasoning more generally, can be understood along several dimensions. First, political institutions are constitutive in the sense that they are among
the fundamental elements, or constituent parts, of the whole system of government and politics created by a constitution—what is commonly called a regime.
In other words, they are institutions in the core meaning of a "custom, practice,
relationship, or behavioral pattern of importance in the life of a community or
society" (*The American Heritage Dictionary*, 3rd ed., 1992, s.v. "institution").

It is simply too narrow a view, then, to regard the American regime as consist-
ing of the Constitution and the American people, with the institutions of government and the people who populate them merely devices or tools for achieving
the people's ends. Indeed, a distinctive American political regime does not exist
absent a peculiar arrangement of institutions and cadre of public officials. From
this perspective, the republicanism of the Constitution holds that the people,
who are the ultimate sovereigns, and the institutions and officers of government
in their representative and governing capacities, *together* constitute the regime.
That is what the Constitution stands for.

Carrying this line of reasoning one step further, one may even contend that
an identifiable American people could not exist if there were no political institutions to give them a distinctive identity. Political institutions "say who the people
are by defining their way of life, by creating a body of activities which helps to
define their purposes. We may call this political way of life the 'regime,' and political institutions are fundamental to defining it" (Elkin 1985, 264).

This second dimension of the constitutiveness of political institutions is their
"formative bearing" (Elkin 1987, 104). It has two dimensions of its own (107). For
the psychological and educational, or tutelary, component, the effect is principally

on individual attributes and character. The individual citizen comes to define himself, his political identity, and his relationships with others partly through the formative influence of political institutions. Even for highly pluralistic institutional arrangements, in which "structures and consciousness are loosely coupled . . . , social structures and civic consciousness do influence one another. To what extent, then, must democratic pluralism necessarily weaken civic virtue by fostering egoism and political conflict?" (Dahl 1982, 138). Fundamental concepts in political science—personal and political efficacy, for example—have no operative meaning, therefore, without some reference to the manner in which political institutions shape the political identities of citizens.

Robert Dahl's reference to civic virtue further reinforces the tutelary effect of political institutions, because it brings to mind the American Antifederalists, concerned as they were with the promotion of civic virtue, which they saw as achievable through the "educative function" of the "whole organization of the polity" (Storing 1981, 21). This concern reflected the civic republican roots of Antifederalist thought. The focus in civic republicanism is on political deliberation and its "transformational power" (Seidenfeld 1992, 1529), particularly through education. "By informing citizens about others' conceptions of the public interest and by revealing to them how their own conceptions might harm others, the deliberative process can help educate citizens and unmask self-delusions" (1537; see also Barber 2003, chs. 8, 9).

Beyond the individual psychological and educative impacts, however, the formative bearing of political institutions also exerts its influence at a collective level, on the whole polity, providing the citizenry "an organized existence" (Elkin 1985, 262). Political institutions have this effect because they operate like constitutive rules (Elkin 1987, 108). They are far more than just sets of rules, however. They create the entire setting within which relations between members of a polity form and evolve. "Institutions cannot be understood simply as a collection of rules that those who operate them follow. They are, instead, ongoing forms of relation among those who operate and are affected by them—and, as such, they are complex political entities, with all that entails by way of conflict, consensus, strategic behavior, responses to uncertainty, and the like" (Elkin 2006, 77; see also Heclo 2008). Institutions also provide the setting for political-moral reasoning and, thus, create an "environment of choice" (Elkin 2006, 94).

The creation of the basic rules for politics and government in a constitution is simultaneously the creation of the institutional superstructure for the practice of politics and government. The institutions are, first, the expression of the basic rules and thus the central shapers of the actual practice of politics and government. Second, by creating political institutions, a polity defines the meaning of citizenship and of what the collectivity is by creating purposes and the means to achieve them. "Institutions are then simultaneously ends and means" (Elkin 2006, 111). It is only in this context, in fact, that the connection between specific institutional or programmatic means and general societal ends makes any sense. Instrumental reasoning is therefore subordinate to constitutive reasoning when the composition and ongoing activity or life of the society is the object of the reasoning.

The individual psychological and collective components of the formative bearing of political institutions do overlap. The "teaching" function of political institutions is in fact critical to understanding the proper forms of activity and the relations between citizens that take place within those institutions vital to the regime, and to understanding the place of these activities and relations in the way of life of the polity. So, political institutions teach individuals about the nature of the regime of which they are a part and about how that regime may be maintained. "Democratic political institutions must be judged, therefore, at least in part on the extent to which they pose policy questions in civic as opposed to self-interested terms. It is through the deliberative discussions of such questions that citizens develop, discover, and clarify their own understanding of their mutual rights and responsibilities" (Landy, Roberts, and Thomas 1990, 280).

Because political institutions are not merely means to externally defined ends, the whole notion that the goals a community of individuals seeks to achieve could come from outside that community and the structures that order its active public life is deeply misleading. Because political institutions define the types of relations and forms of activity occurring among the individuals who regard themselves as citizens of that political community, they enable representatives to give "concrete meaning" to the public interest (Elkin 2006, 138–39). Thus, they help to create, and not just realize, a nation's public purposes.

Different institutions do define different relationships and forms of activity. What people come to expect of themselves and others in one institutional context may nevertheless carry over to other contexts (Elkin 1987, 109), tying together different forms of political activity and understandings of citizenship in that overall political way of life, the regime. The intrinsic significance of a political institution thus is tied to the particularities of a given regime. "The value of institutions and the politics that defines their operation thus lies in their being part of a certain kind of regime that is itself of value" (Elkin 2006, 111). This emphasizes further the appropriateness of questioning a wholly neutral, subordinate public administration.

Political institutions are therefore central to the ongoing process of constituting a regime. They give operative meaning and formal organization to a political way of life consistent with the aspirations of members of a polity. A political community that aspires to be just, for example, cannot conceive of the value of justice separate from its system of justice—its courts, law enforcement, and legal representation. Moreover, across time, judicial and law enforcement institutions continue to shape the meaning of justice in a regime, that is, how citizens relate to one another in just or unjust ways. An ongoing refinement of purposes, of the character of institutions, and thus of the meaning, purposes, and basic rules of the regime, thus emerges from actual political practice. This is readily evident in the more than 200 years of American political development. The institutions established by the founders in accord with their aspirations to republican government, especially the principle of popular sovereignty, spawned and have subsequently been shaped by increasingly populist aspirations (Morone 1990; see also Adams et al. 1990, 220–27; Herson 1984, chs. 10, 11). Indeed, this interactive quality of political institutions provides citizens their primary opportunity to rethink and reform the purposes of the regime and, by definition, the principal political institutions.

Public Administration as a Political Institution

Although legislatures and courts are often in session, the regime-shaping effects of political practice happen most often in the context of day-to-day governing, that is, administration. Given that administrative agencies are the basic organizational tools modern societies use to educate children; to protect life, limb, and property; and to stabilize currency markets, among many other things that embody the idea of a public or civil *service*, making the case that characteristics of the constitutiveness of political institutions apply to public administration as manifested in public bureaucracies requires considerable effort, especially so as not to lose sight of the instrumental nature of administration. Tocqueville's observations and arguments are a good place to start.

The Political Effects of Administration

Among the institutions to receive his special scrutiny Tocqueville included public administration. Perhaps his most widely known observations in this regard pertain to the extremely decentralized character of public administration in the United States, a degree of decentralization that Tocqueville concluded made for an extremely unstable, underdeveloped, even "stateless" administration (also see Stillman 1991, chs. 1–2). Yet Tocqueville's observations about public administration are also quite revealing about the formative effects administrative arrangements can exert on individuals, their interactions, and the character of the whole society. Tocqueville noted, for example, "A vast number of people make a good thing for themselves out of the [fragmented] power of the community and are interested in administration for selfish reasons" (Tocqueville [1835] 1988, 69). He surmised that "peoples who make use of elections to fill the secondary grades in their government are bound greatly to rely on judicial punishments as a weapon of administration" (75). It is in his comparative analysis of centralized and decentralized administration, however, that Tocqueville offers his most important conclusions about public administration as a shaper of individuals and societies.

He admitted that a certain degree of administrative centralization was desirable, to keep "the spirit of innovation in bounds" (Tocqueville [1835] 1988, 130). Stability was thus maintained, avoiding the abrupt substitution of one set of administrative principles with another. Nevertheless, Tocqueville contended that taken too far, "administrative centralization only serves to enervate the peoples that submit to it, because it constantly tends to diminish their civic spirit" (88). The administrative consequences of extreme decentralization could also be undesirable, including excessive autonomy and discretion. Because of limited tenure, limited control by the courts, filling of offices by election, and the absence of central control or standardization, each administrator became "virtually a law unto himself" (quoted in L. Smith 1942, 231). More broadly, the effect of extremely decentralized administration was the virtual absence of carefully planned and managed collective endeavors. "Useful undertakings requiring continuous care and rigorous exactitude for success are often abandoned in the end, for . . . the people proceed by sudden impulses and momentary exertions" (Tocqueville [1835] 1988, 92). Ultimately, Tocqueville admired principally the "political effects" of administrative decentralization, which were to teach the "multitude" to use liberty well in "small matters," thus preserving it in "great matters" as well (96). The result was that the high potential for despotism in democracy, by the majority, could be broken, or at least diminished.

BUILDING AND TEACHING SOCIETY

Although most later observers of the political nature and effects of administration have not drawn from Tocqueville's remarkable insights, the past 60 years have seen several bursts of intellectual energy and attention directed at public administration and questions about its character and its status in a democratic polity. The cumulative result has been to illuminate aspects of administration's constitutiveness along both the individual and collective dimensions.

Writing as one of the premiere voices for progressivism, Herbert Croly characterized the "democratic administrator" as "more of a probation officer than a policeman," and "more of a counsellor and instructor than a probation officer. He is the agent not of a merely disciplinary policy, but one of social enlightenment and upbuilding" (Croly 1914, 354). Croly's characterization is somewhat ambiguous, reflecting the acute struggle of the Progressives to reconcile competing conceptions of administration (see chapter 4). His statement can, however, be read as capturing both an educative and a reconstitutive role for public administration.

Slightly more than 20 years later, Marshall Dimock offered a clearer statement, calling public administration "more than a lifeless pawn. It plans, it contrives, it philosophizes, it educates, it builds for the community as a whole" (Dimock 1936, 133; see also Herring 1936). Norton Long rejected "the view of bureaucracy as instrument and Caliban" (Long 1952, 810) and promoted public bureaucracy as critical to the "working" constitution precisely because it was not a neutral instrument but a representative institution that also gave added meaning to—helped to constitute—the "division of power in government" (817).

With the work of Arthur Maass and Lawrence Radway (1959) as prelude, scholars of the New Public Administration movement (e.g., Marini 1971) pushed hard for the realization that public agencies could not simply function as helots to the powerful. Instead, agencies and administrators could and should work to alter the structure and distribution of power relations in American society. Similarly, beginning with the Friedrich-Finer debate (see Jackson 2009) and the work of Paul Appleby (1952), the now vast literature on administrative ethics at least implies that the actions of administrative officials have substantial effects— formative and transformative—on society and therefore need to be guided by strong ethical principles. Such an idea was, in a rough sense, first promoted by the Jacksonians, as chapter 3 explores.

The late 1980s and early 1990s brought a broad, rich, and sustained scholarly examination of the nature of public administration and its role in a liberal democracy. In his eloquent defense of the legitimacy of the modern administrative state, for example, John Rohr argued that it "offers millions of employees the opportunity to fulfill the aspirations of citizenship—to rule and be ruled. Of these millions, thousands have the opportunity to instruct millions of nongovernmental employees in the ways of citizenship. Thus the administrative state has the capacity to increase and multiply public spiritedness and thereby infuse the regime with active citizens" (1986, 53). Richard Green, Lawrence Keller, and Gary Wamsley argued that "public administration constantly presents people with political and moral choices that define and redefine good living. It contributes to the formation of habits and character" (Green, Keller, and Wamsley 1993, 519). Robert Denhardt contended that at "the root of every act of every public official, whether in the development or execution of public policy, there is a moral or ethical question" (1993, 263). All these observations echo Stephen Elkin's conclusion that political institutions are constitutive because they "concern the morality of a people—or, perhaps it is best to say, their mores" (1987, 109).

Of much more recent vintage is the growing body of evidence in public policy scholarship on the formative nature of administrative action. This scholarship has revealed that different policy designs in programs as diverse as welfare, early childhood education, and the GI Bill, have differential effects on the tendency of clients to be politically engaged, on the extent of their sense of political efficacy, and on their broad conceptions of the character of the American polity (e.g., Mettler and Soss 2004). To a very limited extent, some of the work has noted that the differential effects may reflect in part variations in discretion granted, intentionally or by default, to program administrators, and especially to frontline operators, for whom Michael Lipsky coined the phrase "street-level bureaucrats." Indeed, it is worth quoting from Lipsky's initial insight, since his work is one of the anchors for at least some of this more recent scholarship. "Street-level bureaucrats . . . 'represent' American government to its citizens. They are the people citizens encounter when they seek help from, or are controlled by, the American political system. . . . Citizens *perceive* these public employees as most influential in shaping their lives" (Lipsky 1971, 392; emphasis in original).

This policy feedback scholarship has tended to focus on policy design and implementation politics, that is, on large-scale external forces generating the constitutive impacts of government action. Beyond Lipsky's long-ago observation, there is some work in this line of scholarship that does at least consider how managerial patterns and systems, personnel training and acculturation, and uses of even very limited discretion may formatively affect, in both negative and positive ways, not only the recipients of government benefits, but those who only come into indirect contact with the agencies that distribute the benefits. Much richer treatment of the formative effects of agency structure and operations, and the values of administrative personnel, must, however, be found elsewhere. One very effective account is Maynard-Moody and Musheno (2003), who show that "street-level workers . . . are producers of values and character" (94). They "imbue citizen-clients with complex identities" (84). This power to define citizen-client identities "affects the interactions between worker and client and, by extension, defines the relationship between state and citizen" (155).

Constitutional Design, Societal Values, and Public Goals

What one can read out of this wide spectrum of scholarship, particularly that of the past two decades, is a fairly consistent message: like legislatures, courts, political parties, and other political institutions that are created by constitutions or emerge within constitutional frameworks, public administration exhibits constitutive qualities. For at least three reasons, administration must therefore be considered a fundamental political institution of the regime in its own right, with some of the formative and tutelary characteristics such institutions exhibit.

Public administration is, first of all, a unique, constitutionally recognized component of the regime. It singularly fulfills critical elements of constitutional design (Cook 1992; Long 1952; Rohr 1986; but see Lowi 1993b). Most apparent, it is responsible for organizing or facilitating, if not always directly undertaking and completing, public tasks, particularly the collective endeavors, whether modest or great in scope, without which no liberal democracy could long survive and prosper. As a result, some public bureaucracies perform fundamental social functions, and they work to conserve the basic values associated with those functions (Terry 2003). Second, public administration as a whole gives concrete, institutional embodiment to values critical to defining and sustaining the regime. These values include stability and continuity in public policy, a reliance at least in part on special knowledge and expertise in public decision making, and perhaps most important, the need to balance reasoning about means and ends, that is, practical reason or *phronesis* (see, for example, Ruderman 1997). Third, even when tightly controlled in their decisions and actions, public agencies independently influence the ideas and interactions of citizens by, among other actions, shaping the public goals the agencies will be instructed to pursue. They thereby give form to public life in efficacious, but also possibly deleterious, ways.

It is relatively easy—too easy—to personify these multidimensional political qualities of administration. Gifford Pinchot, Robert Moses, David Lilienthal, and Hyman Rickover, for example, in their capacities as administrators and by virtue of their personal talents and energies, unquestionably shaped the character and direction of the nation for both good and ill. It is much more difficult to demonstrate the independent effect of public administration on regimes from an institutional perspective, because the work of officials and their agencies is so tightly intertwined with the actions of legislatures, elected executives, and organized interests. This is in part what gives credence to the concept of the old iron triangle or, more recently, the policy network. More important, it is precisely the point about public administration's political nature, and thus its constitutiveness. Consider two brief examples, each of which captures in its own distinctive way something of the integral and formative impact of public bureaucracies on the regime.

The U.S. Customs Service is one of the oldest federal agencies. Its establishment in July 1789 predated the founding of its current organizational superior, the Treasury Department. In the early years of the Republic, the Customs Service was "perhaps the most important body of federal agents dealing directly with citizens" (L. D. White 1951, 148), and its impact on the formative development of the constitutional regime was substantial.

Collectors of customs operated "under instructions that were designed to reduce discretion to a minimum, but still with a large degree of autonomy" (L. D. White 1951, 157). Under these conditions, customs officers shaped commercial relations and business–government interactions in the early republic by striking "a delicate balance between convenience to . . . importers and protection of the revenue" (148). Customs collectors thus gave concrete meaning to the Madisonian–Hamiltonian idea of a commercial republic. The operation of the Customs Service under both the Federalists and the Jeffersonians also substantially shaped early public images of civil service and the trustworthiness of executive power in a republic (White 1948, 515; 1951, 157, 413–14). In their interactions with administrative and political superiors, customs officers contributed mightily to the conceptions of administrative discretion and control that developed in the early republic (L. D. White 1948, 204–5). Finally, the Customs Service influenced the lives of many Americans, not the least of whom were the people employed in the customs houses. Nathaniel Hawthorne wrote personally and vividly about this influence, both positive and negative, in the "Introductory" to *The Scarlet Letter*.

A second example is the National Park Service. In 1916, when it was established, Americans made approximately 168,000 visits to the magnificent western jewels of the national park system: Glacier, Mount Rainier, Rocky Mountain, Sequoia, Yellowstone, and Yosemite. In 2012, these same six parks hosted nearly 15 million visits (U.S. Department of Interior 2013). The National Park Service has had a profound effect on how visitors to any of its many sites think of recreation and the nation's natural and historic heritage, how they see their relationship to the natural world, and how they conceive of the meaning of collective responsibility to future generations, all of which come bundled with a distinctive image of the park ranger that is "part naturalist, part policeman, part resource manager, and even part educator" (Foresta 1984, 1).

Through fire management policy, for example, the National Park Service has shaped, more than once, the very physical experience of natural, scenic areas. During the California gold rush, before the establishment of the first western parks, those who had crossed the Sierra Nevada reported seeing "wide-spaced columns of mature trees that grew on the lower western slope in gigantic magnificence. The ground was a grass parkland, in springtime carpeted with wildflowers." By virtue of an absolute fire suppression policy that lasted into the late 1960s, however, the areas under park service supervision had become impenetrable thickets where "wildflowers [were] sparse, and to some at least the vegetative tangle [was] depressing, not uplifting" (Leopold et al. 1963, and quoted in van Wagtendonk 1991, 12). After implementation of a prescribed natural fire management policy, visitors could again see such areas as Yosemite and Sequoia in their more "natural" states. Moreover, the devastating fires in the greater Yellowstone area in 1988 and the scrutiny of park service fire policy that followed influenced how Americans thought and talked about nature and human attempts to manage wilderness and wild forces. This dialogue and changing conceptions of wilderness continue as the National Park Service and its companion resource management agencies, the Bureau of Land Management and the U.S. Forest Service, grapple with the increasing encroachment of human settlements on the boundaries of national parks, national forests, and other public lands.

Certainly, both the U.S. Customs Service and the National Park Service have been buffeted by powerful social, economic, and political forces. The American people have, after all, intended them to be instruments for achieving some public objectives in the vital areas of international commerce and natural resource preservation, so they are purposely vulnerable to influence and control. These agencies have also been critical to developing and refining our understanding of commerce and natural resource preservation, however, and what we want to achieve as a polity in these areas. In subtle yet deep and lasting ways, these two administrative agencies and the multitude of others at the national, state, and local levels have exerted marked influences on citizen experience with the day-to-day essentials of self-government, and thus on the character of the regime.

Conclusion and Overview of the Analysis

Comprehending public organizations such as the Customs Service and the National Park Service, and public administration more generally, from a constitutive perspective opens up a much broader vista on the implications of large, formal state entities for American aspirations for self-government than the narrow perspective of an instrumental conception of public action allows. These possibilities include the improvement of the conduct of the public's business, as well as, paradoxically, the resuscitation of the American people's understanding of and energetic engagement in self-government.

What remains largely absent from both public dialogue and the substantial scholarly treatment of public administration, however, is an explicit recognition and systematic assessment of public administration's constitutiveness *in combination* with its obvious instrumental qualities. It is an appreciation for the combination of the instrumental and the constitutive that lies at the heart of a political understanding of public administration and an appreciation for its role in self-government.

This most essential characteristic of public administration as a political institution—its simultaneously instrument and constitutive nature and the tensions that ensue—must be the starting point for a refreshed and reengaged debate about public bureaucracy's role in the American system of self-government. That dual character and its implications for the regime, moreover, can only be fully appraised in historical context, for the way our effort to comprehend and address public administration has unfolded has had a profound effect on the authority, competence, and legitimacy administration has come to possess. That effort at comprehension has encompassed how much emphasis to place on an instrumental conception of public administration versus a constitutive conception and how well political leaders have grappled with the tensions between the instrumental and constitutive qualities that administration embodies. The outcome has, to a considerable extent, determined whether public administration now essentially undermines or gives sustenance to American aspirations to self-government.

THE PROCESSION OF DEMOCRACY

At the beginning of *Democracy in America*, Tocqueville explained that what he found most remarkable during his visit to the United States was "the equality of conditions" ([1835] 1988, 9). He argued that the force behind this was not found only in the United States. He proclaimed a "great democratic revolution . . . taking place in our midst. . . . Everywhere the diverse happenings in the lives of people have turned to democracy's profit" (11). Among the principal features of the "gradual progress of equality" (12) were its universality and its permanency.

American public philosophy has generally incorporated the notion that democratic governance and equality of social conditions are best for society, indeed, that the former should encompass the latter. Tocqueville generally agreed, although most of *Democracy in America* is intended as a warning about the dire endings to which democracy and egalitarianism could lead and the need for particular sentiments, mores, and institutional arrangements to shape and direct the unstoppable democratic tide. This, according to Ann Stuart Diamond, is exactly what the Constitution's framers, Madison especially, were up to. In explaining the whole context of the constitutional convention debate on the composition of the House of Representatives, for example, Diamond stressed that the "very intensity of the concern about the dangers of the democratic form demonstrates that the framers were determined both to be democratic and to avoid the classic problems of democracies." Something happened, however, to lead the American experiment in properly chastened democracy to deviate from the "decent, even though democratic" regime the framers intended (1980, 25). In other words, "it is the break upon public opinion [in the Constitution] rather than the provision for its influence that causes skepticism today" (Tulis 1987, 35–36).

Numerous answers to the question of what happened have been forthcoming. The "modern success of utopianism interposes between us and the American founding a radical theory of democracy" (A. S. Diamond 1980, 18) and that, absent an aristocratic heritage, Americans make the "error of mistaking for an aristocratic manifestation whatever slows the expression of the majority will" (19). The "answer may lie in the nineteenth century's growing push for an expanded suffrage that ties, in turn, to the egalitarian lifestyle and political demands of the western frontier. Or, the answer may lie in the . . . lengthening stability of our political system [that] gradually removed public apprehensions over democracy" (Herson 1984, 61).

Quite provocatively, Gordon Wood argued that the Federalists were themselves to blame. He contended that what the Constitution wrought was closely akin to an "aristocratic system" (1980, 17). To win approval in the campaign for ratification, the Federalists had to usurp "the popular revolutionary language that rightfully belonged to their opponents and, in the process, helped to further the extraordinary changes taking place in the American conception of politics and democracy" (15). No wonder, then, that one finds Alexander Hamilton, the quintessential Federalist, denounced as a monarchist by his enemies, arguing in *The Federalist* (No. 22) in favor of "the necessity of laying the foundations of our national government deeper than in the mere sanction of delegated authority. The fabric of American empire ought to rest on the solid basis of THE CONSENT OF THE PEOPLE. The streams of national power ought to flow immediately from that pure, original fountain of all legitimate authority" (emphasis in original).

Finally, Tocqueville's answer captures elements of the arguments of Diamond, Herson, and Wood, firmly anchored as it is in the idea of the inevitability of democracy and the steady progress of equality. He contended that after the Revolutionary War, the nation was divided by two philosophies with deep and venerable roots in human society. He associated the Federalists with the desire to restrict popular power and the Republicans with the desire to extend popular power indefinitely. Tocqueville concluded that it was inevitable in the United States, as the land of democracy, that doctrines favoring popular power would become dominant. Yet the moral authority of the minority view of the Federalists, enshrined in the Constitution, allowed the "new republic time to settle down and afterwards to face without ill consequences the rapid development" of democracy ([1835] 1988, 177). By the time Tocqueville visited America, the effect of democratic politics and government on public administration was clear and consequential. "The majority, being in absolute command both of lawmaking and of the execution of the laws, and equally controlling both rulers and ruled, regards public functionaries as its passive agents. . . . It treats them as a master might treat his servants if, always seeing them act under his eyes, he could direct or correct them at any moment" (Tocqueville [1835] 1988, 253–54).

The arguments about the role of public administration as an institution in American politics and government advanced by statesmen and commentators, at least with respect to the establishment of federal administrative units and a federal civil service, nevertheless experienced substantial elaboration and development before, during, and after the founding. To assess the characteristics of those and subsequent instances of such elaboration and development, a brief review of the structure of American political development is helpful.

A DEVELOPMENTAL SEQUENCE

Historians and political scientists have developed a variety of conceptual frames for imposing order on and providing explanations for American political and governmental development. Most of these schemes identify eras defined by a distinctive set of characteristics embracing both the ideology and practice of politics and government. The termination of one era and the inception of another are typically marked by a major crisis that is followed by a response that captures widespread support. Such is the framework of Stephen Skowronek's analysis of presidents and political time (1997). Some of the resulting transformations have been so substantial, in the estimation of some scholars, as to mark the initiation of new regimes, because of the extensive constitutional expansion or reinterpretation they produced (see, for example, Lowi 1979; Tulis 1987).

In particular, the organization, conduct, and character of the people involved in public administration have been vehicles for and targets of the reform movements that have shaped American political development. Scholars have applied a variety of very similar developmental sequences to capture the effect of such reform movements and chart the evolution of American public administration within the developmental arc driven by reform movements. For example, Leonard White's series of studies in administrative history encompassed what he called the "Federalist," "Jeffersonian," and "Jacksonian" periods and the "Republican Era." Frederick Mosher's treatment of the evolution of civil service concepts identifies six periods: government by gentlemen, by the common man, by the good, by the efficient, by administrators, and by the professional (1968, ch. 3). Michael Nelson (1982) charted four sometimes overlapping periods of public administration development characterized by the distinctive ironies of revolution, Jacksonian democracy, reform, and representation. Herbert Kaufman (1965) identified three more encompassing periods: "the stable years" (1789–1829), "the rhythm of the spoils system" (1829–83), and "neutralizing the civil service" (1883–1964).

Closer to the structure, subject matter, and central conceptual components of the argument I develop, however, is the approach taken by James Morone (1990, esp. xii, 15–30). Morone examined the impact of populist aspirations on American political development associated with the founding and Jacksonian, progressive, and New Deal politics. His central objective was to explain how the "democratic impulse" shaped the construction of the American administrative state. I tell a similar story but focus on the development of the *idea* of public administration and its manifestation within the broad ideas about and evolving practices of American government. Specifically, I am concerned with the "distinction between ideological commitments and institutional outcomes" (R. R. John and Young 2002, 101), or the contrasts between rhetorical claims and actual practices that have exacerbated the already existing tensions between administration and democracy in the American regime.

The disjunction between the real and the ideal across the course of American political development is not surprising, of course. As Albert Shaw observed with respect to the persistence of the ideology of laissez-faire, "The average American has an unequaled capacity for the entertainment of legal fictions and kindred delusions. He lives in one world of theory and another world of practice. . . . Never for a moment relinquishing their theory, the people of the United States have assiduously pursued and cherished a practical policy utterly inconsistent with that theory, and have not perceived the discrepancy" (Shaw 1887; see more generally Novak 2008). A less exasperated perspective on the matter recognizes that human actions rarely conform perfectly to human ideals because human cognition cannot anticipate all the complexities that social reality has in store. Yet the disjunction between ideology and reality with respect to administration reflects more than the imperfections of human nature. Governing practice deviates from governing ideals because of the pursuit of political power. A good example is the emergence during the Jacksonian era of a bureau system within the federal government's administrative structure. These bureaus "tended to become autonomous principalities, pursuing their own policy with support drawn from beyond the boundaries of the department to which they belonged" (L. D. White 1954, 538). This is a tale extensively told by Daniel Carpenter (2001). The rise of autonomous bureaucratic power is intertwined in fundamental ways with the problem of administration's constitutiveness, and this poses serious questions about American self-government, questions that have been posed before but require further consideration when cast in a new light.

The standard demarcation of epochs in administrative and political development provides firm and familiar foundations for investigating the origins and progression of distinctive conceptions of public administration in American politics and government. The outcomes of the struggles, in political thought and in the practice of government, to accommodate such conceptions still reverberate strongly today. What follows is an attempt to describe and examine those struggles through a distinctive lens and discern the implications of their outcomes for the present and future health of American self-government.

Chapter Two

Preserving the Chain of Dependence

The Ideas of the Founding and Early Republic

O n May 19, 1789, Representative Elias Boudinot of New Jersey introduced a resolution on the floor of the U.S. House of Representatives to establish a department of finance. "If we take up the present Constitution," he declared, "we shall find it contemplates departments of an Executive nature in aid of the President; it then remains for us to carry this intention into effect, which I take it will be best done by settling principles for organizing them in this place" (*Annals of the Congress of the United States* 1834, 368; hereafter cited as *Annals*).

In the style of the early Congress, in which much of the legislative drafting occurred first on the floor of the House and Senate, several representatives offered amendments to improve and expand on Boudinot's resolution. Egbert Benson of New York called for the creation of the three most necessary departments: Foreign Affairs (later State), Treasury, and War. James Madison, representing Virginia, then "took charge of the question" (Elkins and McKitrick 1993, 51) and proposed just such an all-encompassing substitute. He moved to begin work first on the Department of Foreign Affairs, to be headed by a secretary, to be "appointed by the President, by and with the advice and consent of the Senate, and to be removable by the President" (*Annals*, 370–71).

When the House, in Committee of the Whole, began debate on the mode of appointment for the secretary of foreign affairs, William Smith of South Carolina objected to Madison's language, particularly the provision that the president alone would have the power of removal. On the heels of Smith's objection, Richard

Bland Lee of Virginia argued that the secretary should be considered an inferior officer. The president was the "great and responsible officer of the Government" (*Annals* 372) and the secretary was only to aid him in performing his executive duties. Smith replied, "This officer is at the head of a department, and one of those who are to advise the President; the inferior officers mentioned in the Constitution are clerks and other subordinates" (372). Smith contended that as the head of a department, a position mentioned explicitly in the Constitution, the secretary could only be removed by constitutionally prescribed means, namely, impeachment and conviction.

This brief exchange held the seeds of two competing perspectives on the status of administration under the Constitution. The influence of each view waxed and waned during the six days of debate on the removal power. The first perspective conceived of public administrators, both heads of departments and "inferior officers," as pure agents or instruments of the "political" branches. The function of public administrators in this view was to aid the president and Congress in the performance of their constitutional duties and to undertake any other tasks assigned to them. The second view conceived of administrative officials, or department heads at the very least, as constitutional officers in their own right and not just as legal or political subordinates. This competing perspective at least implied that public administration was a distinctive, semiautonomous institution in the constitutional scheme.

The two understandings of administration articulated during the debate on the president's removal power, which led up to what has come to be called the Decision of 1789, reflect to a remarkable extent the instrumental and constitutive conceptions of administration. Through the efforts of a small band of representatives in the First Congress, the two conceptions were contemplated together in a single time and place and under real decision conditions requiring tests of constitutional principles in the crucible of politics and the necessities of governing. The new nation's political leaders thus could seize the opportunity to sort out the two perspectives and consider situating and building a public administration within the Constitution's framework in a manner that embraced both qualities.

Notwithstanding its somewhat ambiguous expression in the debate, the instrumental conception decisively prevailed. The Decision of 1789 did not forever foreclose public discussion and contemplation of the constitutive qualities of public administration. Furthermore, the initial development of national governing (i.e., *administrative*) capacity under the Constitution, in the hands of the Federalists, embodied both the instrumental and constitutive dimensions and the inherent tensions between them. Nevertheless, the main thrust of the 1789 decision, the Jeffersonian response to Federalist nation-building, and the long-run impact of both on subsequent generations of political leaders, diminished the possibility that a public administration embodying both constitutive and instrumental characteristics would be fully recognized and consciously embraced as an important component of the peculiarly American form of republican government.

This chapter commences an exploration of the conceptual and practical origins of, and the development of political responses to, the dilemma public administration poses for American constitutional democracy. The focus is on how political leaders have thought and spoken about public administration in the practice of politics, through their own words or the interpretations of scholars and commentators. Following the framework presented at the conclusion of chapter 1, this exploration uses as guideposts the most familiar and widely studied stages of American political development, training attention especially on the struggles of political leaders to respond to the instrumental and constitutive qualities embodied in public administration, and on the consequences of their responses for administration's public standing and its capacity to contribute to sustaining self-government. Although ideas are at the center of this attention, the struggles for power that often accompany the promotion of particular governing ideas also comes under scrutiny.

It is clear from the evidence and scholarly assessments that public administration has had a prominent role, as both a means and an object, in every major effort at political and governmental reform associated with the political development of the United States. This is not surprising, since the Constitution itself was intended, in part, as a solution to the abundant problems of national administration encountered under the Articles of Confederation. Despite the conscious efforts of founding statesmen, particularly Alexander Hamilton, the design of the Constitution and the governing philosophies advanced before, during, and after its ratification have left public administration insufficiently reconciled in the public mind with the principle of self-government. Indeed, for one prominent strain of American political philosophy, formal administration in whatever form is the very antithesis of self-government.

Reform movements arising after the founding generation departed the scene, including the Jacksonians, the Progressives, the New Dealers, the activists of the 1960s and 1970s, managerialists of the 1990s, and conservative reactionaries in the early twenty-first century, all animated by populists pressures, ideology, and political strategy, have had to grapple further with this central dilemma: how to recognize and legitimate the constitutive qualities of public administration in a regime that privileges the instrumental. Shaped by the founding and the consequent struggles over the creation of national governing capacity, the responses of these reform movements have distinctively and cumulatively made the instrumental conception of administration even more prominent in mainstream political thought and political practice. This has had marked consequences for the status, organization, function, and competence of public administration in the United States, and thus for its capacity to contribute to the maintenance and refinement of American self-government.

The Founding: Temporary and Dependent Administration

The likes of George Washington, Alexander Hamilton, Robert Morris, Gouverneur Morris, and even Thomas Jefferson gained administrative experience in war or in American colonial and then state government (Beach et al. 1997, 524–26). Yet administration was not the preferred mode of public service for most of America's revolutionary statesmen. The most active and engaged political leaders of the American founding gained their political training and experience in legislative assemblies, while administration was reserved for royal governors and their underlings. A simple reading of the Declaration of Independence, moreover, shows that the dissension and anger of the colonists and their leaders toward the Crown and acts of Parliament was directed primarily at the abuse of administrative power. The consequence was that administration as a public activity, and thus as a political and governmental institution, was seriously suspect. It was to be kept subordinate, dependent, and minimized. Four interdependent concerns of the leaders of the Revolution and of the Republic under the Articles of Confederation worked together to produce this characterization of administration in American government.

First, the orientation to governing of America's founding statesmen was strongly anchored in English Whig philosophy, which conditioned them to react strongly to "even the smallest perceived threats to liberty" (Lowery 1993, 187). Whiggish thought viewed administrative agents as the greatest threat to the liberties of Englishmen because of their potential capacity to interfere in the individual lives of citizens and to upset the proper constitutional balance between executive and legislative powers that protected those liberties. Hence, many of America's revolutionary leaders worried about administration's threats to liberty even when administration existed in only a most rudimentary form (Lowery 1993, 187–88).

Second, for many political leaders of the founding generation, true republican government meant legislative supremacy. This was the proper constitutional balance of powers. In the extreme thinking of Samuel Adams and the "liberative, expulsive, or destructive school" (Sanders 1935, 3; also Short 1923, 51–53, following Wharton 1889), no permanent and distinct executive institution at the national level should have been contemplated. Others, less extreme in their thinking, saw "as eminently proper and in keeping with republican notions of government" (Sanders 1935, 4) that administration be merely "adjunct" (i.e., "attached to another in a dependent or subordinate position," *The American Heritage Dictionary*, 3rd ed., 1992, s.v. "adjunct," def. 1). This was the case whether administration was to be by committees composed of legislators, by independent boards or commissions, or by departments led by single executives, which was the developmental progression for American administration before the Constitutional Convention. The heads of the relatively mature executive departments, for instance, were elected by and answerable exclusively to Congress, although they were not members of Congress. As the idea of separate but coordinated powers among three distinct branches took firmer hold in American constitutional thinking, acceptance of legislative supremacy still prevailed, certainly in constitution making at the state level (Williams 1988). It is no accident, of course, that Congress is the first branch in the new American Constitution fashioned in 1787.

Third, in light of the dominant republican notions of the time, formed in part by the rabid fear of monarchical tyranny through its administrative agents, many political leaders regarded administration as a *temporary tool*, born of the necessity of meeting the single and relatively clearly defined objective of winning a war and gaining independence. In fact, the Continental Congress was itself "regarded as a temporary body, assembled for a temporary purpose; and consequently no need for a permanent executive was at first experienced" (Short 1923, 37, quoting Bullock 1895). Even after the necessity of a more permanent governing body became evident during prosecution of the War for Independence and contemplation of what might follow victory, the "most outstanding feature of administrative organization" remained "the total absence of any element of permanency" (Short 1923, 50).

Fourth, the need for more permanent executive units—again, eventually departments headed by single executives—was driven by the need for "compatibility" with a military campaign (to paraphrase George Washington, as quoted in M. Nelson 1982, 751). Consequently, the extant conception of administration as temporary, subordinate to legislating, and simply a tool was reinforced and ex-

tended to its taking a form to suit the hierarchical and thus demonstrably instrumental design of military command. No less than the likes of Alexander Hamilton and Andrew Jackson, hardly soul mates in political philosophy, would base
their notions of administrative organization and function at least in part on military command structure (Green 2002, 551–52; Somit 1948, 188–89).

Thus was an instrumental conception of administration firmly embedded in
the very wellsprings of the Republic, and directly connected to the republican,
that is to say, *democratic,* ideology of the Revolution. Nevertheless, hints of a less
stringent instrumentalism, if not of a distinctly constitutive conception, emerged
in response. Opposed to Sam Adams's "town-meeting ideas" (Sanders 1935, 4)
was a "constructive or remedial" school (Short 1923, 51), espousing ideas of "ex-
ecutivism" (Sanders 1935, 5). Alexander Hamilton was its "most outspoken advocate" (Short 1923, 53). Hamilton and the other constructivists were the force behind the move away from administration by committees and boards and toward
single-headed executive departments. They conceived of administration as a distinctly important component of sound government, deserving of its own structure, even if the units in that structure remained wholly subordinate to the
legislature.

During the decade of governance under the Articles of Confederation, in the
Constitutional Convention debates, and in the campaign for ratification of the
Constitution, conceptions of public administration and its place in an American
system of government and politics were subjected to further development—one
might even say further experimentation. A remarkable dimension of this development was the idea that administrators might even be part of the formative
(e.g., deliberative) activities of government. In 1785, for example, James Madison
remarked, "I have always conceived the several ministerial departments of Congress, to be provisions for *aiding their councils* as well as executing their resolu-
tions, and that consequently whilst they retain the right of rejecting the advice
which may come from either of them, they ought not to renounce the opportunity of making use of it" (Short 1923, 60; emphasis added; see Madison 1785).

More significant were the numerous proposals proffered during the Philadelphia Convention for some form of an executive council as the proper executive
structure. Such bodies were prevalent in the states during and immediately after
the Revolutionary War (Blunt 1990). In many of the proposals in Philadelphia,
the heads of the principal executive departments would form the council; and in
some versions of this arrangement, the executive council would even *govern with*
the president (see, for example, Thach 1922, 121–23). James Madison, the "first to

advocate such a council, . . . before the opening of the convention, suggested . . . the idea of associating the heads of departments with the executive in a 'Council of Revision,' with authority to examine and pass upon all legislative acts" (Short 1923, 82). John Randolph and Charles Pinckney offered similar plans. Suggesting a representative function for the council, Elbridge Gerry asserted "that a Council ought to be the medium through which the feelings of the people ought to be communicated to the Executive" (Short 1923, 83).

On the whole, however, the conception of administration as a tool of the people and the people's representatives remained prominent. By June 1787, Madison supported a single executive, "aided by a Council, who should have the right to advise and record their proceedings, but not to control his authority" (Short 1923, 83). James Wilson rejected the idea of a multiple executive as threatening to "interrupt the public administration" (L. D. White 1948, 14). Making the status of appointed officials quite clear, Gouvernor Morris stated, "there must be certain great officers of State; a minister of finance, of war, of foreign affairs, etc. These . . . will exercise their functions in subordination to the Executive" (Short 1923, 81). It would take Alexander Hamilton's distinctive intellectual qualities to devise an arrangement his fellow founders might accept, combining a unitary executive with an administrative structure having the governing importance of the executive council without the constitutional standing or clout.

The Hamiltonian Solution

The executive council failed to win support for inclusion in the Constitution, except in the clause of Article II, Section 2, stating that the president "may require the Opinion, in writing, of the principal Officer in each of the executive Departments, upon any Subject relating to the Duties of their respective Offices." This indicates that the founders not only rejected the idea of heads of executive departments giving collective advice to the president but that the chief administrative officers should be subordinate assistants to the president (Rohr 1986, 142–43). In *The Federalist* No. 72, Hamilton articulated the idea more expansively, arguing that the principal administrative officers "ought to be considered as the assistants or deputies of the Chief Magistrate, and on this account they ought to derive their offices from his appointment, at least his nomination, and ought to be subject to his superintendence."

Hamilton's conception of administrators as subordinate to, and dependent on, the president should not be read too narrowly, however. It was Hamilton, after all, more than any other member of the founding generation, who engaged in a genuine struggle to think through the effective design and legitimation of a national system of public administration for a liberal democratic regime. And in articulating his ideas, Hamilton recognized and sought to validate peculiarly constitutive qualities in administration within a system that already accepted administration as primarily, if not exclusively, instrumental (see Caldwell 1988, Part 1; Green 1990, 2002).

Evidence for Hamilton's more expansive thinking about administration appears in the often quoted opening passage of *The Federalist* No. 72, in which he offers a definition of public administration that, by its very sweep, would appear to encompass not only the identification and development of means but the formation of ends as well. "The administration of government, in its largest sense, comprehends all the operations of the body politic, whether legislative, executive, or judiciary." This passage signaled Hamilton's conception of public administration "as the governing dimension of public life . . . , and contrasts sharply with the prevailing view of public administration today as that apparatus that is subordinate to policy makers" (Green 2002, 544). Hamilton was particularly revealing about his conception of the systemic political reach, impact, and status of administration in a rarely quoted but extraordinary passage in *The Federalist* No. 27. It appeared in the midst of his argument that obedience to federal law would not require any more extraordinary coercion than the laws of the individual states had required.

> I will, in this place, hazard an observation which will not be the less just because to some it may appear new; which is, that the more the operations of the national authority are intermingled in the ordinary exercise of government, the more the citizens are accustomed to meet with it in common occurrences of their political life, the more it is familiarized to their sight and to their feelings, the further it enters into those objects which touch the most sensible chords and put in motion the most active springs of the human heart, the greater will be the probability that it will conciliate the respect and attachment of the community.

The effect Hamilton describes in this passage, that of public administration's permeating the very foundations of the public life of the citizenry and winning its allegiance to the regime, is extraordinary, given the founders' intentions to create a limited government and thus a large, protected sphere of private activity. This "administrative" republic (Flaumenhaft 1981, 103) would not come about, however, unless it rested firmly on the foundation of an "efficacious" administration, an argument that Hamilton took great pains to make clear by advancing it in *The Federalist* No. 17 and again in No. 69, and with Madison's help in No. 46. The consequence of good administration would be a stable, long-lasting regime, the affinity of the people for the regime, and more—their attachment "to civic virtue itself." Thus, government "that can actually accomplish its resolves, that can keep the peace, protect property, and promote the prosperity of the country, will be a government respected and obeyed by its citizens. It will, moreover, promote private and public morality by providing them with effective protection" (Storing 1981, 43).

Although the Constitution defines certain general goals for the regime, it also sets the framework for the elaboration and extension of those purposes, the creation of new ends, and the promotion of a particular kind of citizenry defined by its public and private morality. It also aims for a regime that is "truly popular" because it is founded on a citizenry that will come to prefer "the long-run and long-lasting outcomes of government" rather than "what is immediately popular" (Flaumenhaft 1981, 75). Public administration is integral to all of this, Hamilton argued, but he also warned that a "principle like this was hard to make immediately clear to the people," a warning that would be borne out by subsequent events.

Despite his emphatic acknowledgment of public administration's essential constitutiveness as an integral part of a liberal democracy, helping to shape the character of the citizenry, refine the regime's purposes, and thus guide its development, Hamilton accepted that administration had to fit properly within the well-accepted tripartite structure of the Constitution. Being of strong "executivist" proclivities, Hamilton's principle supporting a solution was relatively simple. The opening passage of *The Federalist* No. 72 continues, "but in its most usual and perhaps in its most precise signification, [administration] falls peculiarly within the province of the executive department." It also followed logically that administrative officers would be subject to presidential superintendence. With a strong and energetic executive, moreover, this structural arrangement would produce the efficacious administration, with its salutary constitutive effects, that Hamilton envisioned.

Hamilton's statement of the solution obscured, however, a complex and subtle conception of the executive energy and unity he championed in *The Federalist*. "Although the principle of executive unity was symbolized by the person of the chief executive, Hamilton conceived 'the executive' as more than a single personality. The executive was a composite individual, and . . . functioned through diverse ministers acting in its name and under its authority" (Caldwell 1988, 44). Hence, "the administrative structure of the federal Union, as Hamilton would have it, embraced even more than the presidency and the great executive departments" (45). Similarly, the complex treatment of administration in *The Federalist* indicates that although it was conceived as "instrumental for achieving higher political ends, such as winning support for the new government" (Rohr 1989b, 8), it would be erroneous to interpret the founders' vision of administration as a "corporate structure, with a president as the chief executive officer of a tightly organized firm whose subordinates are merely the instruments of the president's will" (10). The "model of administration was more political than managerial." The function of the heads of departments "was to assist the president in exercising his constitutional duty to take care that the laws be faithfully executed; they were not simply to do the president's bidding" (10; also see Caldwell 1988, 98). Thus, "Hamilton expected the elements of energy to percolate through many areas and levels of the subordinate public administration. . . . [He] advocated much the same degree of independence among at least the president's principal officers and varying degrees of independent judgment to even the lowest-level officials" (Green 2002, 550). Furthermore, Hamilton envisioned the heads of departments as a stabilizing force to counterbalance his energetic yet republican executive, expecting them "to remain in office well past that of the appointing president" (Green 2002, 549; also Bailey 2008). As Hamilton forcefully learned during his service in Washington's first cabinet, however, other founders with more pronounced Whiggish proclivities were not so receptive to his ideas for a subordinate administration with such sweeping influences.

At the founding, an instrumental linkage between administration and the will of the people in a hierarchical arrangement was at the center of public thinking about politics and government. Indeed, it was, according to Herbert Storing, what governance under the Constitution was all about. "Government was no longer seen as directing and shaping human existence, but as having the much narrower (though indispensable) function of facilitating the peaceful enjoyment of the private life. In this view, government and the whole public sphere are decisively instrumental; government is reduced to administration" (1980, 97). Hamilton's response to this narrow view was brilliant, because he was able to situate, and legitimate, a constitutive understanding of administration within the predominantly instrumental conception. His model of administration, resting on "four interconnected pillars" of "politics, organization design, ethics, and law" (Green 2002, 542), and structured so that the heads of the "great" departments would be supervised by but not subjugated to the president, was nevertheless problematic, revealing underlying tensions generated by the philosophy and design of the Constitution that would not be resolved effortlessly, and raising important questions that could not be easily answered.

For example, how much leeway should subordinate administrators be allowed in providing assistance in faithful execution of the laws? This is the longstanding problem of administrative discretion, and Hamilton came down on the side of broad leeway. He was "emphatic about the need to recognize that the business of administration cannot be fully subordinated to rule as some would wish; the machinery cannot work without latitude in interpreting the rules" (Flaumenhaft 1981, 82). Much, if not most, of the discretion should flow through the president as the only constitutionally designated executive officer and should be restricted to the highest ranks of administrative officials, unless differentially specified in law (L. D. White 1948, 449–51; Caldwell 1988, 90). Yet federal administrative officials would inevitably exercise authority without the direct supervision of either the president or department heads. If citizens found such discretionary actions benign, or even positively helpful, would they come to accept the efficacious effects of discretionary administration, as Hamilton anticipated? Or would they reject those effects on principle rooted in Whiggish fears of a slippery slope toward tyranny? If the actions of some administrators proved derelict, did presidential superintendence mean that the president had exclusive, constitutionally sanctioned power to remove administrators from office? Beyond exclusive focus on the president, what hand could Congress have in influencing the assistance administrators rendered in executing the laws? Perhaps most important, did the constitutive effect of administration and its inevitable role in shaping the character of the regime require that the authority under which administrators operated be anchored directly and independently in the Constitution rather than indirectly as a derivative of the constitutional authority of the president or of Congress?

These were questions of theory and principle, to be sure, but they were also questions of practical politics and governance. In the first years under the new Constitution, Congress addressed such questions, and its decisions and actions, and the reactions to them, shaped fundamentally how subsequent generations of American political leaders thought about and responded to public administration's intertwined instrumental and constitutive qualities.

The Decision of 1789: Dependency and Responsibility Affirmed

The debates surrounding the establishment of the first executive departments have received considerable acclaim as momentous. They appear, for example, in a compilation of material from the *Annals* of the First Congress entitled *A Second Federalist* (Hyneman and Carey 1967). More significantly, Leonard White described the Decision of 1789 as the "first major constitutional debate" to take place in Congress (1948, 20). Charles Thach went so far as to argue that it was "a constitutional convention, so far as subject matter is a criterion," with its work "simply a continuation of that done in Philadelphia two years before" (1922, 141). The extension of that work, with its focus on administrative structure, was necessary because the "American Constitution creates a political system for governance, but it does not establish a government. Governments are not run by legislators, judges, or even Presidents. They are run by administrators" (Mashaw 2006, 1276). Students of the debate have also generally concluded that an instrumental, subordinate status for public administrators was already widely accepted before commencement of the debate. For administrators, the 1789 debate on establishing executive departments and on the president's power of removal was exclusively about deciding "the fundamental question of whether the legislature or the chief executive was their master" (Thach 1922, 141).

Nevertheless, the 1789 debate on the removal power is worthy of further scrutiny, because some of the most articulate representatives who participated in the debate were not entirely convinced by the proposition that administrators were simply subordinate to one or both political branches. Such thinking was not completely unprecedented, as several states toyed with nonhierarchical forms of administration in the "critical period" before the Constitutional Convention (Beach et al. 1997). Although only a small minority, these legislators resolutely sought an alternative conception of the constitutional status of public administrators by attempting to define a constitutionally independent role for the heads of departments mentioned in the Constitution. Thus, the competing conceptions of the place of public administration in the constitutional system debated in 1789 had a direct bearing on developing ideas and practices related to public administration's status, structure, legitimacy, and contributions to the regime.

THE PRESIDENT'S ARM AND EYE

It is important to keep in mind, in assessing the debate, that the subject was the president's power to remove specifically the secretary of foreign affairs (soon thereafter secretary of state). Although the Constitution's conception of the presidency and executive power is ambiguous (see Rohr 1989a), in this case, the Constitution gives express power over much of foreign diplomacy to the president, capturing to a considerable extent the concept of the "federative power" (see Scigliano 1989). Hence, a secretary of foreign affairs most closely fits the idea of a presidential instrument. This makes all the more remarkable the alternative conception of administration that was presented during the debate.

The foundation of the instrumental conception championed in the debate was responsibility, and James Madison proved to be its most lucid and persistent advocate (see Bailey 2008, 461–463). Here is how Madison rendered that conception at two points in the debate:

> Now, if the heads of the Executive departments are subjected to removal by the President alone, we have in him security for the good behavior of the officer. If he does not conform to the judgment of the President in doing the executive duties of his office, he can be displaced. This makes him responsible for the great Executive power, and makes the President responsible to the public for the conduct of the person he has nominated and appointed to aid him in the administration of his department. . . . (*Annals*, 379)
>
> . . . If the President should possess alone the power of removal from office, those who are employed in the execution of the law will be in their proper situation, and the chain of dependence be preserved; the lowest officers, the middle grade, and the highest, will depend, as they ought, on the President, and the President on the community. The chain of dependence therefore terminates in the supreme body, namely, in the people, who will possess, besides, in aid of their original power, the decisive engine of impeachment. (499)

Distinctions within this instrumental conception are evident in the debate. Some members argued that executive officers were agents purely of the president, as originally insisted by Richard Bland Lee. For example, John Vining of Delaware likened the secretary of foreign affairs to an arm and eye of the president, who "sees and writes his secret dispatches, [and] is an instrument over which the President ought to have complete command" (*Annals*, 511). Similarly, Theodore Sedgwick of Massachusetts perceived the secretary "as much an instrument in the hands of the president, as the pen is the instrument in the hands of the Secretary in corresponding with foreign courts. . . . This officer should be dependent upon him" (522). Most forcefully, Michael Stone of Maryland and

Elias Boudinot argued that whatever authority department heads could exercise was derived from the president.

> The power of appointing an officer arises from the power over the subject on which an officer is to act. It arises from the principal who appoints having an interest in and right to conduct business, which he does by means of an agent. Therefore, this officer appears to be nothing more than an agent, appointed for the convenient dispatch of business . . . and the principle will operate from the Minister of State down to the tide-waiter. (*Annals* [Stone], 492)

> The President nominates and appoints; he is further expressly authorized to commission all officers. . . . Who vests the officer with authority? Who commissions him? The President does these acts by his sole power, but they are exercised in consequence of the advice of another branch of government. If, therefore, the officer receives his authority and commission from the President, surely the removal follows as coincident. ([Boudinot], 527)

Echoing in some ways the legislative supremacy thinking of the revolutionary period, other members contended that administrators were largely agents of the law and thus of the legislature, under the Constitution's "necessary and proper" clause. Roger Sherman of Connecticut argued, "As the officer is the mere creature of the Legislature, we may form it under such regulations as we please, with such powers and duration as we think good policy requires" (*Annals*, 492). Anticipating arguments advanced by Senate Whigs in their battle with Andrew Jackson 45 years hence, Elbridge Gerry of Massachusetts warned that if the president had unlimited control over treasury officers, we might "expect to see institutions arising under the control of the revenue, and not of the law" (502).

Out of these two lines of argument from the 1789 debate emerged the view of public administrators as agents of both the president and Congress. As Madison stated it late in the debate, "the powers relative to offices are partly Legislative and partly Executive" (*Annals*, 581). Congress would adopt this doctrine most clearly in its creation of the Treasury Department (see Mashaw 2006, 1284–88; L. D. White 1948, 118–19). Madison also later anticipated officials with a mix of legislative and judicial duties (*Annals*, 611–14). Congress and the president, and at times the courts, have struggled over control of administration ever since, a struggle that intensified as the conception of administration that prevailed in the 1789 debate expanded its reach (see, for example, Aberbach and Rockman 1988; Corwin 1984, ch. 3; Fisher 1985, 66–98).

Independence and Firmness in Administration

An appreciation for the importance of the 1789 debate cannot end here, however, for a number of representatives were clearly uneasy about making an executive officer "the mere State-dependent, the abject slave" of the president (*Annals* [Alexander White], 458), as suggested by the instrumental conception of administration given voice in the debate. Mr. White, of Virginia, later asked,

> Who are the heads of departments? We are to have a Secretary of Foreign Affairs, another for War, and another for Treasury; now are not these the principal officers in these departments? . . . But who are their inferior officers? The chief clerks and all others who may depend on them. These, then, are the inferior officers, whose appointments may be vested in the respective heads of departments. . . . The gentlemen who formed the Constitution seem not inclined, at all events, to give to the President the power of appointing even these inferior officers, to which is attached the power of removal. (518)

John Page of Virginia observed, "To the argument [supporting the President's removal power], which is drawn from the necessity of having energy in Government, despatch, secrecy, and decision; I think all these advantages may be had without putting the respectable heads of departments in a situation so humiliating, that I can scarcely suppose a man of true independent spirit, and fit to be in such an office, could submit to" (*Annals*, 549).

It was left to William Smith of South Carolina and James Jackson of Georgia, however, to articulate fully an alternative to the strict subordination of Madison's instrumental conception. Smith opened the June deliberations with some potent ammunition: the opening paragraph from *The Federalist* No. 77, wherein Alexander Hamilton argued that the "consent of that body [the Senate] would be necessary to displace as well as to appoint," a requirement that would contribute to stability in administration. Theodorick Bland of Virginia had made the same argument in May without reference to Hamilton. Some have called this passage mere "musings" on Hamilton's part, and "merely speculative" (Rohr 1986, 141), or have suggested (Flaumenhaft 1981, 102) that Hamilton may have taken this position strategically, to advance ratification and make a larger point about stability. Hamilton apparently later repudiated or at least clarified his position in advice to Washington during the controversy over the Neutrality Proclamation of 1793 (Fisher 1985, 66; Goldsmith 1974, 181–82). It is equally possible that indeed Hamilton meant exactly what he wrote in *The Federalist*, relying in particular on the stabilizing force of the Senate (Bailey 2008). In the 1789 debate, William Smith sought to expand on the stability argument by linking stability not with the Senate so much as with executive officers holding office "on a better tenure" (*Annals*, 472).

Smith argued that if the Constitution stated that Congress could vest appointment of inferior officers in heads of departments, that vestiture made department heads "principal" officers, removable only by impeachment. Smith said his opponents on the question considered the head of a department "an inferior officer in aid of the President. This, I think, is going too far; because the Constitution, in the words authorizing the President to call on the heads of departments for their opinions in writing, contemplates several departments. It says, 'the principal officer in each of the Executive departments'" (*Annals*, 459). Smith went on to contend that as advisors to the president, as designated in the Constitution, heads of departments were more than merely the president's subordinates, reflecting some of the thinking from the Constitutional Convention on the role of heads of departments in an executive council.

Initially, in May, Smith based his position on impeachment as the sole method of removal on the argument that offices were a form of property. Incumbents of executive offices thus could not be deprived of their property without something approximating a judicial proceeding, a requirement that impeachment satisfied. Many of his colleagues derided this aspect of Smith's argument, along with his more general proposition that impeachment was the only constitutionally prescribed method for removing principal executive officers. In response, Smith let his property argument fade into the background while remaining steadfast in his defense of impeachment as the sole means of removal. A statement Smith made in the middle of the June proceedings compared the tenure of judges, elected officials, and heads of departments and is a better representation of his overall position. It shows that his arguments were not isolated or extreme. Although scholarly consensus has relegated Smith to a marginal role in the debate, his ideas were important in shaping the course of the debate and spoke to the question of the proper role for administration within the constitutional system.

> It has been inferred from the clause in the constitution, declaring judges to hold their offices during good behavior, that there are no other officers who hold their offices by this tenure. Now, I apprehend, that this clause was inserted to distinguish them from other officers who hold their offices for a limited period. . . . It was seen to be proper to have them independent; and that

could only be secured by such a declaration in the constitution. . . . With respect to the other offices to be established by law, there is nothing to prevent
us from limiting their appointment. . . . Let us then limit the duration of the
Secretary of Foreign Affairs for as short a period as is thought to be salutary.
Here we are not restricted. But I conceive, as the constitution now stands,
they cannot be removed in any other way but by impeachment. (*Annals*,
507–8)

James Jackson's principal arguments reinforced Smith's position, and provided perhaps the clearest expression of the view that department heads de-
served special constitutional status.

> I appeal to the good sense of the committee to determine whether these offi-
> cers are not established by the Constitution as heads of departments. How
> then can they be merely instruments of the President, to conform implicitly to
> his will? for I deny the principle that they are mere creatures of the law. They
> have Constitutional rights that they may exercise. If the president alone is
> the head of the whole Executive Department, and these the mere creatures of
> the law, where is the necessity of calling them heads of departments in the
> Constitution? . . . (*Annals*, 530)
>   . . . I call upon gentlemen to show me, why heads of departments are nec-
> essarily dependent upon the President, when the Constitution specifically
> points them out. I cannot, for my part, admit that any part of the Constitution
> authorizes the President to exercise an uncontrolled power over them, be-
> cause I perceive, as a fundamental principle in the Constitution, that the exer-
> cise of all power should be properly checked and guarded. (532)

Jackson's arguments quoted here are particularly interesting. He insisted that
the highest ranking administrative officials have a constitutionally recognized
independent status. As John Rohr has observed, "surely a constitutional provision for a principal officer in each of several executive departments implies that
these high officials hold some sort of executive power in their own right" (1989a,
110). Beyond even that, however, Jackson contended that the highest-ranking administrators play a special role that would be fully consistent with a basic constitutional principle—checking the power of the president. Administrators exercising some sort of check on the president is much the same idea as that on which
the advocates of an executive council had based their arguments, and it would
reappear in later legal and political battles involving administration as an object

of governmental and political reform. One might even count it as being among the elements that made for an efficacious administration. Combining the Smith and Jackson arguments, the thrust of their contention seems to be that, although administrators are subject to substantial control by statute and presidential command, they nevertheless retain a constitutionally recognized status and function that cannot be altered.

The proponents of the strictly instrumental conception never fully neutralized Jackson's and Smith's constitutional arguments, because they could never provide an explanation for why the framers, a number of whom were participants in the House debate, specifically included department heads in the Constitution if they did not intend them to have special status. Faced with a stalemate on the constitutional arguments, the two sides turned the issue into a question of practical (i.e., instrumental) politics and governance. What purposes would administration best serve?

The utility of granting special constitutional status to department heads and protecting them from arbitrary removal is that executive officers could provide stability in government and in the regime and could act as an additional check on the president. These may be counted among the "higher political ends" toward which the constitutional status of public administrators may be aimed (Rohr 1989c, 84). With few exceptions, the parties to the 1789 debate agreed that stability was a critical contribution that administration could make to the new regime created by the Constitution, with Alexander Hamilton, in absentia, being the most vigorous proponent. The disagreement was over how stability through administration would best be achieved and whether administration could serve as an effective constitutional check on the president. Madison argued that the inability to weed out incompetent or corrupt officials because of the lack of a presidential removal power would most likely corrode responsibility and, by extension, undermine the stability of administration and thus of the regime. Smith, Jackson, White, and a few others argued that a public administration completely at the mercy of the president would destroy stability because, as Bland contended, every new president would be tempted to turn out "the great officers, . . . and throw the affairs of the Union into disorder" (*Annals*, 381), the very argument advanced by Hamilton in *The Federalist* No. 72.

Madison and others argued against allowing department heads to serve during good behavior (that is, indefinitely unless impeached) precisely because such tenure would provide them with the power to resist presidential commands. Such power would weaken unity and energy in the executive, creating a multiheaded monster that would smash the "great principle" of responsibility. In fact, during the debate, members of the House spouted a cascade of references regarding how many heads and how monstrous the new government would become. Such references became increasingly derisive in mocking the arguments of Smith and Jackson (see, for example, the remarks of Reps. Vining [*Annals*, 511] and Sylvester [560]).

By pointing out that "the Constitution also has confidence in the heads of departments" (*Annals*, 519), by warning of the risks in depriving department heads "of their independency and firmness" (488), and in asserting the benefits of a department head "invulnerable in his integrity," who could serve as "a barrier to your Executive officer" (472), however, a small band of holdouts in the 1789 debate provided the political leaders of the young nation the opportunity to appraise an independent constitutional foundation for administration that might more securely legitimate the constitutive qualities Alexander Hamilton envisioned. Their arguments favoring independence and a distinctive constitutional status for department heads captured a way of thinking about administration that showed its significance to democratic governance beyond even its service in the achievement of higher political ends.

William Smith, James Jackson, John Page, and perhaps one or two others argued that administration was a unique institutional component of government under the Constitution and that it had to be recognized as such, because it would, from the very beginning, help to shape the character of the government and the nature of political life in the regime. However, like the more hierarchical, subordinate scheme articulated so well by Madison in the debate, this alternative conception was problematic as well, because it raised the red flag of accountability and control that has remained the central focus of American thinking about public administration to the present day. This demonstrates just how difficult a challenge equilibrating the instrumental and constitutive qualities of administration within a liberal democracy really is, and why sustained attention to it in theory and in practice is critical.

The Meaning of the Hamiltonian Solution and the Decision of 1789

Two of its features made the Decision of 1789 as distinctive and important as any action affecting administration taken during the Philadelphia Convention or the ratification debates. First, in an open public forum, in the context of making decisions about the actual structure and function of the constitutional scheme, political leaders grappled with the instrumental and constitutive in public administration and the evaluative perspectives associated with each. A considerable majority of representatives embraced the instrumental conception and argued that administrators ought to be evaluated on how well they served the ends of the Constitution, as those ends might be further shaped and refined exclusively by the people and their elected representatives. The minority contended that administrative officials ought to be understood as a vital influence on the purpose-creating and refining activities of elected representatives, that they would, further, have a hand directly in shaping and refining the aims and purposes of the regime, and thus that they ought to be evaluated on these grounds. This set the pattern for subsequent struggles with the administrative dilemma, although the circumspection of 1789 would never be attained again, and, with only rare exceptions, the public expression by practicing politicians of the idea of constitutive administration would become weaker or at least more diffuse.

Assessing the impact of Federalist ratification strategy, Gordon Wood contended that "the Federalists helped to foreclose the development of an American intellectual tradition in which differing ideas of politics would be intimately and genuinely related to differing social interests." Using "the most popular and democratic rhetoric, the Federalists of 1787 furthered the American disavowal of any sort of aristocratic conception of politics and encouraged the American belief that the ills of democracy can be cured by more democracy" (G. S. Wood 1980, 17). There is great irony in this, of course, as Thomas Jefferson and his followers would in short order accuse the Federalists of promoting not just aristocratic but monarchist government. The Decision of 1789, with its confirmation of executive unity, responsibility, and administrative dependence and subordination, may have been vital to ensuring the governing capacity of the constitutional system, as Leonard White (1948, 25) concluded. As a second distinctive feature of its importance, however, and again because the forum was public and required decisions about putting the Constitution into operation, the Decision of 1789 had consequences much like those Wood attributed to the Federalist ratification effort. It was a decisive reinforcement of the idea of administration as principally if not exclusively an instrument of popular rule. In its immediate aftermath, the dominant rhetoric of the debate, if not the legal effect of the decision, forged this link most closely to the presidency through the emphasis on executive unity. The ambiguities in the decision with respect to who held the controlling end of Madison's chain of dependence—the president or Congress—would, however, become the source of continuing and sometimes bitter dispute.

In significant ways, the conception of administration advanced by Alexander Hamilton—administration of the central government subject to a superintending but not directly controlling president—nicely resolved the dilemma posed for liberal democracy by the need for a vigorous, permanent public administration. Hamilton's solution was nevertheless problematic, because it conceived of administration's constitutiveness as subject to political control, which was clearly necessary to reassure American citizens that they ultimately controlled how the government would operate day to day. This invited political struggles over the control of administration and thus the need by those claiming control to demonstrate they were *in control*. Yet Hamilton "favored the establishment of a close, direct working relationship between the administration and the Congress, the administration to furnish the expert opinion and information necessary to the intelligent deliberation of the legislative body" (Caldwell 1988, 35). Just who is in control under such an arrangement? Whiggish sensitivities would certainly be aroused. Further, because public administration is fundamentally a political institution, it is by definition constitutive. This was bound to become evident in practice, at least occasionally in ways that would seem to belie claims of adequate political control, thus reinforcing in the public mind the fundamental suspicions from American revolutionary ideology about administration as a threat to liberty and self-rule. Making the linkage of public administration's authority to the Constitution indirect, through the control of the political branches, in turn could greatly diminish the chance for popular understanding and acceptance of administration's essential contributions to the regime.

The losers in the 1789 debate strove to establish a direct constitutional linkage and insisted that public administration be evaluated not just for how well it filled in the details and achieved policy objectives but also for its overall contribution to the definition, maintenance, and active expression of constitutional principles. This they found difficult to do, because administration is "missing" (Mashaw 2006, 1316) from the Constitution, appearing only in bits and pieces, mostly within Article II. Thus, the most basic feature of the Constitution's design—the tripartite distribution of powers—is at the heart of the problem of recognizing administration's dual character. American political leaders had to work with what they had, nevertheless, which should have meant, ideally, locating, designing, and practicing a public administration that would balance its instrumental and constitutive qualities, and so help maintain and enhance its best qualities in service to the regime.

As national growth and other changes in American society occurred and problems surfaced in the practice of politics and government under the Constitution, however, the response of political reformers at successive stages of American political development was not only the addition of more democracy in some form, as Tocqueville had indicated would be inevitable, but also more sweeping claims about the political subjugation and instrumental character of public administration. The result has been to aggravate the inherent tensions public administration poses for democracy, thus keeping popular regard for public administration's constitutive character from developing in the manner Hamilton had envisioned. This has left attentive citizens with little reason to accept that public administration might be involved in something as fundamental as shaping the public ends toward which public resources are employed.

With an irony beyond that uncovered by Michael Nelson (1982), in which successive reform efforts aimed at bringing administration under tighter political control have actually increased its political independence, American public administration has suffered an erosion of its public support, a weakening of its ties to the governing order, and thus its potential for contributing to the healthy development of the regime. This has occurred even though each reform effort has been, in many respects, an attempt through further subordination and control to tie administration more closely to the regime in ways that would preserve increasingly popular aspirations to self-government. This developmental pattern emerged in dramatic fashion during the decade after the Decision of 1789.

Federalist Administration in Practice and the Jeffersonian Response

During their relatively brief period of control of the new national government, the Federalists filled in many of the Constitution's gaps, creating through varying approaches a national administrative structure and presence in the lives of their fellow citizens. The extent to which citizens recognized that presence as a function of central government administration is a matter of scholarly debate, but even proponents of the thesis that state builders in the early republic fashioned a central government largely "out of sight" admit that the most prominent federal institution of the time, Hamilton's Treasury Department, "touched the lives of many Americans through customs and excise officers and through land agents" (Balogh 2009, 101). The handiwork of Hamilton and the Federalist majorities in Congress encompassed stabilizing government finances by establishing a functional revenue collection system and a system for the disposition of public lands, resurrecting a domestic economy by creating a stable, well-regulated national financial system along with a basic patent approval system, and creating a nationwide system of communication and internal movement through a postal system and a network of post offices and post roads.

Along with this initial state building, the Federalists appeared to have also integrated successfully the wide-ranging albeit still embryonic administrative system within the confines of the Constitution and the theory of presidential superintendence and overhead political control articulated in the Decision of 1789. In the first months of his presidency, for example, Washington declared that the officers of the "great departments" were to "assist the supreme magistrate in discharging the duties of his trust" (Short 1923, 106). More to the point, Washington's ministers, "even the transcendently able Secretaries of State and Treasury, were never actually denied authority, but at the same time they were given no final authority that they could count upon" (Flexner 1969, 403). A decade after he left the presidency, Jefferson remarked that the president could seek the advice of the heads of departments "either separately or all together, and remedy their decisions by adopting or controlling their opinions at his discretion" (Short 1923, 110). Taking a broader sounding, Herbert Kaufman noted that "not one of the first five Presidents ever expressed any concern about the dangers of sabotage of their policies by a hostile public service—an anxiety not all of their successors escaped" (1965, 19).

The residual ambiguity of the 1789 decision, as well as a political environment in flux with respect to ruling doctrines, nevertheless gave the Federalists plenty of leeway to experiment in ways that deviated from the general notions of presidential superintendence and more general political control the decision conveyed. In most instances, enabling statutes were very broad and general, requiring development of rules and regulations by administrators. Even in key instances where the central government would have a direct presence and the enabling statutes were much more detailed, considerable administrative discretion in further development and exercise of federal authority was still necessary, one might say even inevitable. Hence, because there was no well-developed doctrine of strict construction to follow, the first Congresses "delegated broad policymaking powers to the President and to others, combined policymaking, enforcement, and adjudication in the same administrative hands, created administrative bodies outside of executive departments, provided for the direct responsibility of some administrators to Congress itself, and assigned 'nonjudicial' business to the

courts" (Mashaw 2006, 1268), much as the states had done in the years immediately preceding the Constitutional Convention (Beach et al. 1997).

Governing experience also revealed that the role administration would play
in the new nation could not be so easily confined within the constitutional constraints initially defined by the Decision of 1789. For example, Washington's use
of "fitness of character" (Schroeder 1855, 79) as the primary basis for determining the suitability of men for high office in the new government was grounded in
part on local public standing among peers (R. N. Roberts and Doss 1997, 5),
which often meant previous electoral success. This brought politicians into administration, there being no conception or practice of neutral expertise. This
guaranteed in turn that at least high-level administrators would be regarded as
politicians and thus administration as a political undertaking. Indeed, at least
until the presidency of Andrew Jackson, cabinet secretaries operated as politicians and statesmen (see Fowler 1943).

The premier examples, of course, are Hamilton and Jefferson, the intellectual
leaders of the opposing political parties taking form at the time. Although Hamilton's actions as treasury secretary largely personified his notion that quite
broad discretion and independent action should be granted to heads of departments, many of his deeds as secretary pushed the limits of his authority and
further exposed the ambiguities of the Decision of 1789 with respect to administrative dependence and overhead political control. If Hamilton's actions were
nevertheless fundamentally honorable, anchored as they were in his overarching
aims for securing the future security and stability of the republic through efficacious administration, the independent political behavior of some department
heads turned out to be merely crass politicking by ambitious politicians seeking
the presidency within the congressional caucus nominating system (M. Nelson
1982, 753). If administration was a mere instrument, after all, then political men
could put it to many uses, not all of them necessarily in service of broad public
ends.

If the new government was on the whole well administered at the start,
Washington, Hamilton, and the Federalists had to contend, nevertheless, with
the Whiggish proclivities of many of their countrymen. With respect to the most
important needs of the new national government—generating a stable stream of
revenue that could help service the debt and establish good credit domestically
and internationally—they had to tread very carefully around the already well-
rooted animosity of Americans toward direct taxation. The challenge was all the
greater because the Federalists had chosen to anchor the theory of their new

Constitution in a popular sovereignty that served to constrain the sovereignty of the states of the union. If Hamilton's administrative republic was to succeed, Americans had to see themselves as first citizens of the nation, and they would have to experience firsthand a direct and very visible administration that proved firm, yet far less a threat and far more an aid to the conceptions of self-government rooted in self-interest that had also won the day with the ratification of the Constitution. Although the Federalists did impose some internal direct taxes, they shied away from the most sweeping implications of the Hamilton administrative republic as too politically risky (Balogh 2009, 72–110). If the administrative republic could not be fully realized under the firm and able hand of Alexander Hamilton, the chances that Americans might come to appreciate administration as a political institution, whose power could enable rather than undermine self-government, were slim indeed.

Finally, congressional participation in controlling the administrative instrument, inherent in the Constitution's design and forcefully defended by many senators and representatives during the 1789 debates, became increasingly assertive after Washington retired to Mount Vernon. Congress pursued increasingly bold efforts to place limits on presidential power, exerting control over administration by granting administrative officers ministerial discretion that was direct rather than derivative from the president, specifying and thus limiting the grounds for removal of officials from office, and building a patronage system involving the federal workforce that was initially enshrined in law by the Tenure of Office Act of 1820 (L. D. White 1951, 387–90).

With respect to the problem of dual presidential and congressional control of administration, Michael Nelson argued that "agencies, forced to live with the ambiguities of control from both elected branches, set about developing power resources of their own. . . . [They] began to play one branch off against another; if neither president nor Congress was supreme, then law was, and the agencies interpreted and implemented the law" (1982, 755). Nelson sees in this the irony of a system of dual control becoming one of limited control that ultimately enhances the power of bureaucracy. Yet dual control also illuminates the difficulty inherent in attempting to ignore or suppress the essential governing role administration plays even in a popular regime, and it clarifies the necessity of grounding that role in the ultimate legitimating source, namely, the Constitution. From the perspective of the American democratic ideology, however, which sees administration, indeed most of politics, as instrumental, such a necessity is difficult to understand and accept, and the Hamiltonian solution did not adequately address it. In the "revolution" of 1800, Jefferson and Madison aimed to put to an end decisively what Madison called Hamilton's "wishing . . . to administer the Government into what he thought it ought to be" (Farrand 1911, 3:534).

Mr. Jefferson's Revolution and the Formative Consequences of Administration

Despite James Madison's status as premiere theorist of the new constitutional system, Hamilton and Jefferson must be regarded as the foremost visionaries for how that system would be further shaped and practiced over the long term. With Madison, Washington, and many other founders, Hamilton and Jefferson shared a "developmental" vision for the American republic (Balogh 2009, 65–72). They thus also shared an understanding that government is constitutive in the most fundamental political sense: formative of citizen norms and ties, and thus of the critical relations with public authority that define a regime. Hamilton and Jefferson dramatically parted company, however, on the fundamental question of the proper conceptual foundations for securing the constitutive effects of their developmental vision and sustaining the republic over the long run. Hamilton's commentary in *The Federalist* No. 27 encapsulated well his thinking about efficacious administration as the path to securing citizen allegiance to a well-ordered republican regime. Jefferson was convinced, in stark contrast to Hamilton's vision, that a citizenry of independent farmers with land aplenty engaged in "friendly intercourse would do far more than government to ensure the loyalty of Americans" (Balogh 2009, 71). In Jefferson's calculation, then, "it was precisely because national government could rely on the bonds of citizens' affections" built up from independent interactions among equals without government involvement, that "no elaborate administrative machinery" was required (76).

Thus, a division over the constitutive effects of administration lay at the core of the Hamilton–Jefferson rift. A bridge across the divide might have been found, but men of high intelligence, vision, and ambition do not easily submit to compromise. In the clash between the Federalists and Jefferson's Republicans, Jefferson and Madison chose the risky path of forming an opposing political party, with all its implications for the dangers of factional government. Through that avenue they attacked the Federalists, and Hamilton in particular, with vehemence and even vitriol. In later retrospect, Madison placed the ultimate responsibility for the fate of the Federalists on Hamilton's doorstep, stating in the same reminiscence in which he accused Hamilton of departing from the Constitution in his effort to form his desired republic administratively, that "I deserted Colonel Hamilton, or rather Colonel H. deserted me" (Farrand 1911, 3:534). Jefferson for his part was clearly driven in part by ideological conviction and more than a bit of romanticism about agrarian idylls, revolutions, and self-rule, all tied to his recognized need to secure political power in order to actuate those convictions. Although the words seem mild to twenty-first-century eyes, Jefferson's critique was of the harshest kind. He "discerned nothing less than a settled Federalist design to anglicize American society and create a monarchical form of government along British lines" (quoted in Bassani 2010, 147).

In his inaugural address, Jefferson sought to soften the harsh divisions between his Republicans and the Federalists, divisions he had so artfully stoked. He famously declared that "every difference of opinion is not a difference of principle. We have called by different names brethren of the same principle. We are all Republicans, we are all Federalists." And he urged his fellow citizens, "with courage and confidence," to "pursue our own Federal and Republican principles, our attachment to union and representative government." Yet Jefferson also made clear that his election, which he would later declare "as real a revolution in the principles of our government as that of 1776 was in its form" (Jefferson 1819), was aimed squarely at weakening national administrative capacity. He called for "a wise and frugal Government, which shall restrain men from injuring one another, shall leave them otherwise free to regulate their own pursuits of industry and improvement, and shall not take from the mouth of labor the bread it has earned," calling this the "sum of Good Government." Although Jefferson also called for "the preservation of the General Government in its whole constitutional vigor," he insisted on "economy in the public expense, that labor may be lightly burthened," a milder version of an earlier declaration that it was best if "our public oeconomy also is such as to offer drudgery and subsistence only to those entrusted with it's administration, a wise and necessary precaution against the degeneracy of the public servants" (Jefferson 1795). He had also insisted that "our general government may be reduced to a very simple organization, and a very inexpensive one; a few plain duties to be performed by a few servants" (Jefferson 1800). The decentralization of administration that went along with a simple and cheap federal government also "implied frequent rotation of office" to avoid the rise of an administrative class (Caldwell 1988, 116), which, despite Jefferson's claims of effort to the contrary, reinforced patronage-driven appointments to office (194). Closing his declaration of principles in the inaugural address, Jefferson tied his enumeration to "an age of revolution and reformation" in which the "wisdom of our sages and blood of our heroes have been devoted to their attainment."

The tensions in Jefferson's address are significant. His call for bridging divisions reflects the largely bloodless revolution by ballot that he led, adding the key bookend to Washington's decision to retire after two terms. This further signaled to Americans that their democratic republic could peacefully transfer power, boding well for the regime's long-term stability. Yet at the same time, with his claim on a most faithful adherence to the "pure principles of the Revolutionary era" (Caldwell 1988, 109), Jefferson dramatically reinforced the lack of any serious commitment in that revolutionary ideology to a competent, politically adept, and respected public administration that could prove its value to the stability of the still risky venture in a continent-sized democratic republic. This internal tension in Jefferson's portrayal of the implications his election held for American self-government encapsulated well the effects the Jeffersonians wrought on the development of the American state, for they perfected in American political philosophy and political practice, and thus injected into debates about the role of administration in the regime, a conception of self-rule that was fundamentally anti-statist, that regarded well-organized, well-resourced, and energetic government as bordering on tyranny. Writing to Madison from Paris in late 1787, Jefferson offered a lengthy assessment of the newly minted constitution in which he declared, "I am not a friend to a very energetic government. It is always oppressive" (Jefferson 1787).

Once in office, Jefferson did act on his principles in significant ways, primarily with the aim of reducing the hated national debt that Hamilton had used to restore the nation's fiscal health and financial trustworthiness. With Treasury Secretary Albert Gallatin as his primary administrative counselor, Jefferson and the Republican majority in Congress executed his plan to eliminate internal taxes and most of the administrative agents needed to collect them, close most of the nation's foreign missions and reduce the size of those that remained, and most sweepingly, limit appropriations to the army and navy, reducing them to a shadow force (Newbold 2010a, 26–30). Yet Jefferson eventually discovered the imperatives of an energetic government he had disparaged as "always oppressive" and particularly unnecessary in as peaceable a domestic political culture of free and equal farmers, artisan, and merchants as that in the United States.

The Louisiana Purchase has over time achieved status as the prime example of Jefferson's departing from strict adherence to his principles because he went against his own worries about whether the treaty was strictly constitutional.

More important than the general constitutional question, the treaty itself is an "extraordinary example" (Newbold 2010a, 33) of the exercise of administrative discretion that, although not entirely in opposition to Jefferson's thinking allowing exceptions to "literal conformity to the law" for "the conduct of high officers of state in times of crisis" (Caldwell 1988, 138), nevertheless had a profound impact on the nation far beyond anything Jefferson would ever have admitted about the salutary formative effect of government administration. The decision of Robert Livingston and James Monroe, to exceed their instructions and legal authority and accept Napoleon's sweeping offer to sell the Louisiana territory and the port of New Orleans, raised far more than "a mere technical question" about constitutional authority (Mayer 1994, 244–45), for it led to a permanent reconception of the nature of the United States, doubling its physical expanse, and multiplying its developmental possibilities, in the minds of citizens and political leaders alike, beyond anything that could comport with Jefferson's plain and simple government in a yeoman republic.

Still, the imperatives that forced Jefferson to embrace energetic government and employ very visible administration, with formative consequences, are best seen in his infamous embargo. Jefferson's all-out effort to avoid being drawn into a disastrous war during England's long conflict with Napoleonic France—he had no army or navy worth the names to fight it—led Congress to grant him the authority to impose a complete embargo on American international trade, restricting American shipping almost exclusively to interstate coastal trade and eventually restricting overland trade as well.

Leonard White characterized the embargo as an "experiment in peaceable coercion" (1951, 423). That Jefferson felt compelled to employ such coercion via administrative agents of the federal government is itself extraordinary. The reach and control of that deployment of administrative power was truly remarkable, however. The combination of statutes authorizing the embargo "provided remarkably broad grants of enforcement discretion both to the President and to enforcement personnel" (Mashaw 2007, 1657). Moreover, Jefferson delegated most of his discretion to Treasury Secretary Albert Gallatin. Gallatin created an extensive structure of circular letters and other communiqués to guide enforcement personnel in their use of their discretion. Yet that discretionary authority remained far-reaching. "Collectors of revenue, naval personnel, and the masters of revenue cutters could stop sea and land transports on mere suspicion, or on forming the 'opinion,' that violation or evasion of the embargo was intended. No ship could be loaded without a permit, and then only under the watchful eye of a federal official" (Mashaw 2007, 1654). At its full extent, the embargo "marshaled force of every available sort . . . against citizens reluctant to forego what they considered their right to sail the high seas" (L. D. White 1951, 423).

Against fierce opposition, especially in New England, and with the inadequate resources of Jefferson's "frugal" government providing "drudgery and subsistence only to those entrusted with its administration," Gallatin and his enforcement personnel, including revenue officers, naval officers, and U.S. attorneys, administered the embargo surprisingly well. "The record of the normal enforcement agencies was on the whole highly creditable" (L. D. White 1951, 453). The great sweep of the embargo, the severe limits of necessary administrative resources, and citizen reaction to the stunning contradiction between Jefferson's professed governing philosophy and the vigor, even ferocity, with which he pursued enforcement of the embargo (Newbold 2010a, 48–49), ensured the eventual collapse of his "fair experiment" (quoted in L. D. White 1951, 473).

What must most be stressed for present purposes, however, is that despite the likelihood Jefferson would never had admitted it, the actions of the administrators who enforced the embargo taught the American public that the despised administrators of the national government could act with great, albeit imperfect, competence and integrity under extreme duress, that they could use extraordinary discretion in accord with the law and not abuse it, and that when called on to meet a high national purpose they would serve the nation and not just themselves. Of course, what the American public also learned from the embargo was that the contrast between the ideological rhetoric of their leaders envisioning a small, insignificant, and wholly subordinate public administration and the reality of the impact of administration from even the far distant federal government, was just as sharp in dangerous times. If the complete subordination of administration to the people's will was a core principle of American government, should it not apply with as much force in crisis as in peace?

In the wake of the Decision of 1789, the Federalists, particularly Hamilton, sought to develop a balance between the empowerment of administration necessary to build a new nation while simultaneously governing it (and the formative effects of administrative theory, structure, and practice that empowerment implied), with the political accountability necessary to conform to the aspirations toward self-government and protection of individual rights embodied in the new Constitution. In many ways, Hamilton attempted to capture some of the sentiment about a distinct governing role for public administration under the Constitution and the far-reaching political effects this implied that was expressed by the minority position in the 1789 debates. He only partially succeeded, his vision proving stronger than his practices, hemmed in as the latter were by the already deep-seated skepticism about administration in the public mind, the promotion of popular sovereignty by the Federalists in the ratification debates, and the consequent political calculations about constraining the use of visible administrative power that Federalists felt compelled to make.

Jefferson and his followers introduced a much harsher ideological vision, rhetoric, and corresponding set of actions, all aimed at reducing the public administration to a lowest common denominator of mechanistic, routine functions. The Jeffersonian ideology itself, but also subsequent actions by Jefferson and his immediate successors, sharply aggravated the underlying tensions between the instrumental and constitutive in administration, and set in motion a wider and more intense friction in American politics over administration's political role that has persisted across the arc of American political development. It has also vastly diminished what lessons about the political contributions of administration the Federalists managed to offer, has distracted political leaders constantly from the substantive tasks of governance, and has sowed confusion and division among the citizenry about the self-governance of a continental-sized nation where everyday governance means administration. The Jeffersonian rhetoric and animus toward administration would harden further even as more forms of visible administration and its formative effects emerged once the Republicans succumbed to internal divisions and Andrew Jackson's "Democracy" moved to the fore. The vehicle Jefferson and Madison employed to achieve their triumph over the Federalists—the political party—they regarded with unease and hoped that it might be temporary, being representative of the threat that factions still posed to the regime. Under the Jacksonians, however, the party would, working through the president, become a more potent symbol and device for controlling and subordinating administration to the popular will. It would also, with great irony and troubling effect, make administration the vehicle for invasive national political influence on local communities across the growing nation.

Chapter Three

Restoring Republican Virtue

The Impact of Jacksonian Ideals

Daniel Webster made this melodramatically defiant declaration near the conclusion of a speech delivered on May 7, 1834, on the floor of the U.S. Senate:

> A collision has taken place which I could have most anxiously wished to avoid; but it was not to be shunned. We have not sought this controversy; it has met us, and been forced upon us. In my judgment, the law has been disregarded, and the Constitution transgressed; the fortress of liberty has been assaulted, and circumstances have placed the Senate in the breach; and although we may perish in it, I know we shall not fly from it. . . . We shall hold on, Sir, and hold out, till the people themselves come to its defence. (Wiltse and Berolzheimer 1988, 34–71)

Webster's speech climaxed three weeks of Senate debate. A Senate resolution had charged that President Andrew Jackson, in his removal of Secretary of the Treasury William J. Duane, had assumed "upon himself authority and power not conferred by the constitution and laws, but in derogation of both" (Richardson 1911, 3:69). On April 15, 1834, Jackson had sent to the Senate a message of protest, requesting that it be entered in the Senate's journal. All of this was, in turn, part of the larger battle between Jackson and Senate Whigs over the Second Bank of the United States, national economic policy, presidential power, and executive patronage. This placed the growing federal bureaucracy at the focal point of a contest of competing conceptions of the Republic and its foundations. Public administration and questions about its political status and structure within the regime were subjected to sustained public debate.

The federal service was a critical component in the efforts of Andrew Jackson and his supporters to restore republican virtues they believed had been lost after the end of the Jefferson administration. The Jacksonians' conception of the administrative structure that would be needed to realize their restoration project changed over time from personal to impersonal organization. More important, their most forceful public rhetoric about what they believed the status of public administration should be departed from, if not openly contradicted, their own expectations for the role administrative service would fulfill in their restoration project. Views of the structure and status of public administration under the Constitution emerged from other quarters as well, generating dynamic tensions and a vigorous interplay of ideas with Jacksonian ideology. An examination of Whig ideology stressing a conception of administration based on responsible discretion and fidelity to law is thus also critical to understanding Jacksonian era contributions to the further development of ideas about the role of public administration in the American regime.

The ideas and arguments about public administration that surfaced during the Jacksonian era served primarily to amplify the effects of the Decision of 1789. The ideas and actions of the Jacksonians and their opponents heightened the tensions between the ideology of subordinate and instrumental administration and the reality, even in a regime of limited government under a written constitution, that appointed officials would be deeply and continuously involved in shaping the aims of the polity and defining the character of the citizenry. The vigorous new assertion of popular control that marked this era thus heightened more than it clarified the ambiguities and conflicts regarding how the instrumental and constitutive qualities of administration might be reasonably balanced under the Constitution.

Jacksonian Restoration: Personal and Unitary Administration

By most accounts, great changes were occurring in American society at the time of Andrew Jackson's election (see, for example, Mashaw 2008, 1570–74; Pessen 1978; L. D. White 1954, 8–10). Many of them had a distinctly democratic cast: more concretely structured and active political parties, presidential nominating conventions, expansion of the franchise, expansion of markets for American goods, and the emergence of both an urban laboring class and a middle class of craftsmen, shopkeepers, tradesmen, and successful farmers. Many of these democratizing changes seemed to emanate from Jackson himself. Lecturing on the Jacksonian "democratization of the Constitution," William Bennett Munro described Old Hickory as "the product of his military experience and his bucolic surroundings, a democrat with a small 'd.' He was of the common people and understood them" (Munro 1930, 96). Jackson's election, in turn, culminated "a great surge of equalitarian sentiment; the greatest, perhaps, that the country has ever known" (97).

A redoubled commitment to the Jeffersonian idea of rotation in office, deeply tied to the democratic sentiment of the time and carrying significant meaning for the form and character of public administration nationally, is the most widely recognized legacy of the Jackson presidency. Yet the "democraticness" of the Jacksonian reform efforts was of a peculiar sort. Making sense of it is central to any appreciation of the Jacksonian contribution to public thinking about, and understanding of, public administration's place in the regime.

As Matthew Crenson explained, the democratic-reform thrust of the Jacksonians was not class based but idea based and emotion based. What they sought was a "return to the old republican virtues" or the "restoration of republican virtue" (Crenson 1975, 24, 27). Furthermore, the Jacksonians confronted and were deeply affected by the fundamental changes in social institutions occurring at the time (Kohl 1989, 9–10). These changes represented for the Jacksonians and their sympathizers the loss of traditional values and ways of life and thus the loss of the anchors of orderliness in society that traditional values provided (15–16). Facing this loss, the Jacksonians also sought in their reform efforts to stem the tide of, or at least to come to grips with, the moral decay emanating from nascent industrialization and the upheaval in major social institutions and the resultant loss of authority these institutions suffered. "Government had a high purpose: to make men good. But republicanism for the Jacksonians was not the classical republican ideal of the pursuit of virtue through civic engagement. It featured instead a commitment to governmental action that would tend to assure that virtue, understood as honesty and hard work, would be rewarded" (Mashaw 2008, 1578–79). Yet the Jacksonians struggled to weave these concerns and efforts into a coherent governing ideology that could guide administrative practice (Crenson 1975, 27–29). The emblematic concerns and governing struggles of the Jacksonians nevertheless had substantial implications for ideas and actions respecting public administration. The first place to look for such effects is in their use of the spoils.

Party Dominance and the Character of the Spoils

As Carl Friedrich (1937) argued, appointing to public office one's supporters, friends, and fellow travelers was well ensconced in Anglo-American political and governmental practice long before 1776. Further, "the spoils system in its modern form as a mainstay of political parties was initiated in the period of, if not by, Washington" (12). The main source of controversy and interparty recrimination surrounding patronage appointments was the "question of removal." Jackson's innovation, in Friedrich's assessment, was to convince his fellow citizens that partisan removals were a democratic virtue because "long tenure spelled bureaucracy and corruption" (14). Such hyperpartisanship thus carried a broader purpose. The aim of the Jacksonians was to keep tight constraints on government, and thus on administrative power, which reflected their commitment to the Jeffersonian ideological aims of small and frugal government and decentralized power, and their beliefs that commitment to such aims had seriously deteriorated under the Federalist-Jeffersonian "fitness of character" standard for selection of officeholders. To the Jacksonians, that standard had produced something akin to an "aristocracy of office" (Mashaw 2008, 1614). The party would, therefore, be the vehicle for imposing the people's control over government and maintaining the proper constraints on the wielding of administrative power to keep it in line with majority will. Thus, in the view of Martin Van Buren, principal architect of the Democratic Party and Jackson's successor as president, the idea was to "constrain excessive personal ambition" by presidents through party control of administrators (Milkis and Nelson 2003, 129), in coincidence with the expansion of popular participation in government (Mashaw 2008, 1616).

The effect in one sense was to subordinate public administration's role in service to the general good to that of party service by making it function as the primary resource, through assessments of officeholders, for the sustenance of party rule. "By the 1850s the partisan political obligations of office holders were so routinized that political contributions were collected on a schedule that looked like progressive taxation" (Mashaw 2008, 1615; also see L. D. White 1954, 335). As Herbert Croly summarized it at the height of the Progressive attack on the spoils, the "adoption of the principle of rotation in elective offices and the application of the spoils system to appointive offices did much to injure the independence of the Federal system and to impair its integrity. The local partisan organization named the Federal officials and took care that they served their real rather than their ostensible master" (1914, 70–71).

If partisan democracy subjugated public administration to majority will through the spoils system, however, that system hardly effected a clean sweep of appointive offices; it appears to have reached only about 10 percent of federal government personnel put in office under Jackson's predecessors (Crenson 1975, 51). Furthermore, "even the highest estimates put removals during [Jackson's] two terms at no more than 20 percent." This "does not tell the whole story," however. It was easy to turn out senior officeholders, given the four-year limit imposed by the Tenure of Office Act of 1820 (Zavodnyik 2007, 154). Still, Jackson's replacements did not differ much in socioeconomic and demographic characteristics from the people they succeeded. Therefore, in Crenson's estimation, "where there are differences between the Jacksonian civil service and its predecessors, they are small, and they appear as continuations of a long-standing and very gradual trend toward democratization of the administrative elite" (16).

It is far more accurate, therefore, to think of the spoils system and the ascent of party dominance as themselves vehicles to effect the changes in the federal government, including personnel administration, that the Jacksonians sought in order to meet their concerns about restoring republican virtue and stemming the loss of moral authority and the institutional anchors for fundamental values. The impact was to alter "relationships between the federal establishment and other political institutions" (Crenson 1975, 166). This change in institutional relationships was significant, for it represented a marked departure along several dimensions from the conception of administration's proper place in the regime as articulated by the Federalists, and even the Jeffersonians.

One of these dimensions was in the extent of the presence of federal officials in the life of states and local communities. To an extent that might have put even Alexander Hamilton in awe, the multiplication of federal offices, primarily post offices and land offices, brought to "thousands of towns . . . a hub of patronage and in turn a center of political power" controlled from Washington (Zavodnyik 2007, 154). As federal administrative positions increased under Jackson's successors, the "influence of federal officials in local politics grew along with the civil list" (255). By the 1850s, the combination of regular appointees, postal contractors, customs house laborers, and census workers, not to mention federal contracts for local newspapers, brought federal political influence to the state and local levels through administration and control of the patronage to such an extent that federal officials not only controlled state party conventions and local political committees but also influenced the congressional votes on major legislation, as in the case of the Kansas-Nebraska Act (Zavodnyik 2007, 257–59, 269–72). What could be a more profound constitutive effect than to influence, through administration, the nature of local politics, the law of the land, and even the makeup of the national legislature? One could argue that all this was evidence of the people's will, controlling the administrative instrument through the vehicle of the party. It is just as possible to imagine, however, that from the point of view of the average citizen it was not so easy to discern who was the controller and who was the controlled.

A second dimension of the Jacksonian departure concerned the conception of office and position and the ordering of offices. The new Jacksonian administrative order was initially a return to simplicity in administrative arrangements, especially to the ideas of personal organization and unity of command (Crenson 1975, 51). That simplicity harkened back to, if it was not consciously grounded in, the allegedly simple and virtuous governance of George Washington's presidency (66–67). Yet Jackson carried the banner of personal organization further and centralized unity of command far more, relative to the size of the federal establishment of his time, which had grown nearly threefold since the Monroe presidency (Zavodnyik 2007, 121). Thus, not only were the operations of each department, bureau, and office to depend on personal organization and unity of command, but the entire executive branch must do so as well, with Jackson at the helm in a nearly single-handed effort "to supervise all of federal administration" (Somit 1948, 191).

The Jacksonian reform and control endeavor evolved, however, in ways that reflected increasing sophistication in thinking about the challenges of administering a growing nation. Far beyond the invasive effect of federal executive patronage on local political life, two prominent features of the Jacksonian efforts further exacerbated the tension between the instrumentalism of public administration portrayed in ideological rhetoric and the constitutiveness of administration in practice. The first was the move from personal organization to depersonalized office and nascent bureaucratization, including the creation of a bureau system in federal administration. The second was Jackson's vigorous reinforcement of the main thrust of the Decision of 1789, given its most powerful formal expression in his protest to the Senate. A harsher instrumental conception of administration and an even greater estrangement of public administration from its constitutional roots was the result.

ADMINISTRATION DEPERSONALIZED

Several of Jackson's closest advisors, some holding important posts in his administration, had realized that the concepts of personal organization and unity of command were inadequate for addressing their concerns about republican virtue and moral decay. Indeed, Jackson stalwarts were concluding that, in many respects, personal organization was *contributing* to the corruption and moral decay within the federal service.

In the institutions from which Jackson, as well as his predecessors, drew most of his appointees—especially law, but also commerce and manufacturing—personal organization predominated. Because the changes under way in American society had affected these institutions greatly (Crenson 1975, ch. 2), they had lost much of their moral authority. Their practitioners could no longer impress upon men the old republican virtues that had made them trustworthy for federal employ. No longer could Jackson or his principal appointees "assume that their subordinates were fundamentally decent and that field administrators practiced the same standards of conduct which had prevailed for generations in the American legal profession and business community" (103). Whether the "great surge of equalitarian sentiment" and the pursuit of economic gain that Tocqueville linked to it (see, for example, Tocqueville 1988, 551–54) were at the root of the problem is not altogether clear. But it was undeniable that the trust in and expectations for personal integrity associated with the administrative orientation of the first five presidents was now naïve, if not debilitating.

The principal response of the Jacksonians, not necessarily in any coordinated fashion, was to begin to separate office from officeholder, to depersonalize the functions of the administrative offices of the federal government. In this effort, the spoils system proved useful as well, for it bore the seeds of bureaucratic structure and of the interchangeability and commensurability associated with economic reasoning. "In this system, individuals could be placed or replaced without upsetting the integrity of the whole. Men were fitted to this system, not it to men. It was the administrative counterpart of the interchangeability of machine parts" (Marshall 1967, 455–56).

Thus, the spoils system could be regarded as "an instrument of bureaucratic depersonalization" (Crenson 1975, 56), and Jackson might "look forward to a time when the personal characteristics of the officeholder would not define the office, when one administrator could be exchanged for another without any disruption of public service" (57). Of course, the purpose for introducing bureaucratic elements into federal administration was not principally the more familiar ones of achieving greater efficiency through division of labor and harnessing specialization and expertise. The object was, instead, to democratize the public administration and then to constrain the administrative iniquity that resulted from the elimination of fitness of character and personal integrity as the primary checks on the behavior of officeholders. "Where the federal government had once relied on good character to assure the successful conduct of public business, it now depended on mechanical checking and balancing devices, arrangements which would make possible an almost automatic supervision of civil servants. Impersonal organization would reduce the government's reliance on 'good character'—so that it could also be freed from the depredations of bad character" (133). It also fit well the party ideal of constraining personal and programmatic ambition in favor of party principle.

In pursuing such internal changes in administrative structure as depersonalization, however, the Jacksonians revealed tensions and discrepancies between their rhetoric of subordination and democratic control, and the reality, which even they recognized, of the influence of public administrators on the character of the polity. Jacksonian rhetoric about public administration, and about politics more generally, was suffused with references to subordinate and dependent agents and instrumentalities. This was most evident in their adherence to the principle of instruction. "Instruction was the right of the people to dictate their views to the elected representatives, and the duty of their representatives to abide by that dictation" (Kohl 1989, 124–25). One logical consequence of the principle was that, "with the people constantly instructing the representative of their will, there was no need for knowledge, wisdom, or discerning judgment" (125). In commenting on attacks in the South against post offices, because of abolitionist pamphlets carried in the mail, Jackson claimed, "we are the instruments of, and executors of the law, we have no power to prohibit anything from being transported in the mail that is authorized by law" (Crenson 1975, 151).

Given the influence of federal officials on local politics through the patronage that the Jacksonians accelerated, the influence of the instructions the people might send by the very officials meant to be instructed is more than a bit incongruent with the Jacksonian celebration of the subordination of administration to the common man. Yet it is an even more jarring inconsistency to discover that Jackson and his supporters had intended for government generally and public administration particularly a more constitutive role, in the formative or tutelary sense, beyond simple politicking. As Crenson concluded, "the moral character of the citizens . . . seems to have caused them considerable worry, and administrative agencies had a role to play in restoring republican virtue to American society. The Jacksonians seem to have held the belief that the character of the nation's civil servants might help to shape the character of its people" (1975, 173).

As Robert Lane pointed out, democratic peoples generally find "the thought of governmental shaping of behavior . . . unattractive" (1981, 12). In its most nightmarish form, such behavior conjures up visions of government controlling citizens' actions as well as their thoughts and feelings. It was the Constitution's framers who sought to place relatively strong constraints on the tendencies of democratic government, in the hands of a passionate majority, to be preoccupied with people's tastes or the purity of their souls (Elkin 1987, 115–16). Surely the irony of the Jacksonian scheme for keeping administrative power in check through adjustments in administrative structure and operations, which were also expected to have some salutary effect on the wider society and individual citizens toward whom government's actions were to be kept in check, would not be lost on reflective citizens even of Jackson's time. They might therefore have asked, "How can public administration be a pure agent and instrument of the people's will if it is to have a hand in shaping that will?"

The problem that the Jacksonians created for themselves, and, in a more long-lasting way, for the effectiveness of American public administration today, was simply that the people's trust in and support for public administrators and administration as an institution could not be built on such an incongruity. Acknowledging the goal-determining and character-shaping qualities as well as the goal-achieving attributes of administration would seem to be essential if citizens were expected to accept as legitimate and thus obey the autonomous decisions and instructions of administrators only generally supervised by elected executives or their immediate subordinates—the heads of departments.

Jackson's forceful commitment to unity of command was in a very important sense an effort to keep in check the discrepancies between his rhetoric of democratic control and administrative subordination and the character-altering aims of his reforms. Citizens could depend on the moral restoration being carried out through administration as being in their best interests because it was under the president's strict control, and voters had entrusted Jackson to carry out the democratizing reforms of which the return to simple republican virtue was a part. Jackson's prime focus in this control effort was on strict limits to administrative discretion to ensure responsibility, applicable from the president himself down to the lowest levels in the chain of command (Somit 1948, 191–92). The emergence of a bureau system of administration and the creation of one of the earliest federal regulatory structures—a steamboat safety system—illustrate further the struggles of Jackson and his successors to keep within reasonable bounds the tensions and contradictions between their ideology and the practical realities of governing, and greatly democratized governing in particular.

Administrative Expansion: Steamboat Regulation and Bureau Government

National regulation in the early American republic was largely restricted to the economy and specifically to the financial system and international commerce, the latter connected to the revenue-raising needs of the federal government and executed through the Customs Service. As internal migration and interstate commerce expanded significantly in the early 1800s, reliance on steamboats grew dramatically. The reliability of the steamboats themselves, and more importantly the dangers they posed to life and limb from exploding boilers, eventually raised a public outcry. The steamboat inspection system, which a Congress under the comfortable control of Jacksonian Democrats initiated in 1838, "wielded the national commerce power to regulate matters of personal safety that were conventionally addressed through the police power of the states" (Mashaw 2008, 1629). Although the policy innovation of the steamboat inspection system was itself a notable departure from the prevailing public philosophy, the evolution of the administrative structure of the system was even more conspicuous.

The 1838 legislation provided only for local, part-time inspectors hired by steamboat owners and operators. The "statute relied heavily on traditional, non-administrative deterrence strategies—enhanced common law civil liability and penalties for specified misconduct. These strategies failed" (Mashaw 2008, 1634). In response to the failure, Congress ordered a report on the system from the Commissioner of Patents. On the basis of the commissioner's thorough report and compelling critique of the system established in 1838, Congress enacted sweeping reforms in the steamboat inspection system in 1852. The new law created a central Board of Supervising Inspectors with reporting responsibility to the Secretary of the Treasury, and a system of "local inspectors of hulls and boilers." These local inspectors "not only inspected and certified vessels and boilers, acting as a local board for each customs district, but they also jointly licensed engineers and pilots of all steamers carrying passengers and granted special licenses for the carriage of flammable or explosive materials. As a board they were further authorized to hear complaints concerning the negligence or incompetence of engineers or pilots and to withdraw their licenses" (1638). The inspectors thus had "considerable discretion," including the leeway to "waive any of the rules in the statute concerning boiler requirements if their application would be unjust and the inspectors determined that variance from the rules could be accomplished with safety" (1639).

The operation of the Board of Supervising Inspectors shows even more dramatically the growth of an autonomous administrative entity that stood in stark contrast to the unity of command and strict subordination at the core of the Jacksonian administrative depersonalization. The Board of Supervising Inspectors had direct and independent rule-making and adjudicative authority and direct reporting authority to Congress. This autonomy and authority were grounded in technical expertise, and although the supervising inspectors were presidential appointees confirmed by the Senate and thus removable by the president, they exercised their authority and discretion with little interference from either Democratic or Whig presidents or Congresses. Thus, "the Board-dominated regulatory regime constructed by the 1852 Steamboat Safety Act was an autonomous bureaucratic enterprise—one designed to apply expert knowledge to the task of promoting steamboat safety. Indeed, the Steamboat Inspection Service combined the multimember structure, single-industry focus and licensing/adjudication features of Progressive and New Deal regulatory commissions, with the rulemaking capacities of later health and safety regulators" (Mashaw 2008, 1641).

This growing professionalism and accompanying administrative autonomy were not restricted only to narrow technical areas that aroused widespread and vociferous public concern. As the tasks and shear workload of the executive departments continued to expand, the heads of the executive departments sought help from professional managers, first informally through the secretaries' own devices, and eventually through statutory means designating new administrative positions. Thus emerged the bureau system, which was intended to relieve "the head of the agency from immediate responsibility for each and every transaction. Responsibility for operations, under direction, could be delegated" (L. D. White 1954, 537). This "direction" very quickly became far more nominal than actual, however, as White showed, quoting an 1846 report of Secretary of the Navy George Bancroft. "The chiefs of the bureau have powers of direction. Their act is esteemed as the act of the Secretary. They have power to originate,

authorize, and sanction expenditures. On their activity, vigilance, and scrupu-
lous supervision . . . success in administering the department must depend"
(537). No longer mere clerks, administrators subordinate to the heads of the
great departments were becoming powerful political actors themselves, influencing public policy and thus the direction of the republic. Even if this influence
was manifested in ways only vaguely perceived by citizens generally, it was nevertheless a far cry from the claims of the Jacksonians that administrators from
the president on down were mere instruments of the law.

Michael Nelson, among others, argued that the spoils system democratized
the public service, thus helping "to legitimate the national government among the
new classes of Jacksonian America and assimilate those that emerged later" (1982,
765). This reflected the fundamental political role of administration. "The federal
establishment was itself an organ of the political order, as much a part of the political struggle as were the party organizations. . . . It was not simply that the executive branch was staffed with party workers but, more important, that the administrative apparatus provided a link between the nation's political authorities
and its citizens. In this capacity, administrative agencies performed functions
very much like those of the modern political party—they helped to organize support for the republic's political regime" (Crenson 1975, 6). Helping to organize
political support surely entails more than merely following the instructions of
the people. It might even include shaping what the people thought their instructions should be.

Neither rotation in office nor depersonalized administration could bear the
weight of the discrepancy between Jacksonian ideology and rhetoric about constraining administrative power and subjugating it to the people's will and their
intended contributions to the regime—increasing citizen attachment and constraining corruption. Nor, given their evident impacts in practice, could rotation
or depersonalization and unity of command any longer help the Jacksonians
keep the internal contradictions of their ideology and public rhetoric at bay. That
ideology and rhetoric were on particular forceful display in the "bank war."

The Presidential Protest

The Bank of the United States was Alexander Hamilton's idea, integral to his
plans to restore the health of the nation's finances under the Constitution and to
create a robust national economy. Hamilton's push to establish the bank contributed substantially to his rift with Jefferson, who argued that it would eventually
lead to unrestrained federal power. Hamilton prevailed in the dispute when

Washington sided with him in support of a charter for the bank. Because of Jeffersonian abhorrence of the bank and its power to influence the national economy, the charter of the First Bank of the United States expired in 1811. A period of economic instability and monetary chaos followed and initially continued even after the chartering of the Second Bank of the United States in 1816. The bank only began to perform effectively under its third president, Nicholas Biddle, appointed in 1823. The bank's charter was subject to renewal in 1836.

The Whig Party, successors of the nationalist wing of the Jeffersonians Republicans and committed to many of the original Federalist notions about national government, supported the bank. Jackson and the Democrats, keepers of the Jeffersonian small-government creed, opposed it. In particular, from Jackson's viewpoint, the bank and the internal improvements it helped to finance represented an unconstitutional expansion of federal power and intrusion in state affairs that added to the undermining of old republican values—honest toil, thrift, and reward for merit (Crenson 1975, 25)—from the Revolution and the founding. The bank was at the center of the bitter presidential contest of 1832, and after he was reelected, Jackson was more determined than ever to destroy the bank. Amos Kendall, a Treasury official and close friend and advisor to Jackson who would soon become Jackson's postmaster general, prepared a plan for removing the bank's assets and depositing them in selected state banks, an example of a "subordinate" official's substantial influence on the shape and direction of public policy.

The bank's congressional charter, however, gave sole authority for removing deposits to the treasury secretary. This reflected the uniquely closer relationship to Congress that Treasury enjoyed as a result of its 1789 enabling act, as well as recurring efforts by Congress to vest discretionary authority directly in department heads rather than indirectly through the president. Moving around departmental appointments and ambassadorships in early fall 1833, Jackson appointed William J. Duane to the Treasury post. Duane was known to oppose the bank, but as it turned out, he supported allowing the bank's charter to expire rather than removing the deposits as the way to kill the bank. Duane thus resisted Jackson's order to remove the deposits, and he refused to resign. Jackson dismissed Duane and installed Attorney General Roger Taney as treasury secretary, who executed the asset transfer plan.

In addition to the influence Amos Kendall exercised in devising the asset transfer plan, it is important to stress further the extent to which appointed officials like Duane possessed such autonomous legal authority and power. Ostensibly a direct subordinate of the president, Duane was nevertheless confident in his refusal to comply with Jackson's order to remove the bank deposits. Further, Jackson exercised his removal power without hesitation, but he did not try to bypass Duane to execute the asset transfer by himself or through another intermediary (see Mashaw 2008, 1596–98). Thus, Jackson's own actions contradicted his claims about unity of command and strict subordination to the people's will of all administrators.

Whig leaders in the Senate, in furious response to Duane's removal, pushed through in early spring 1834 the resolution that accused Jackson of assuming power and authority not granted to him by constitutional provision or statute. Jackson responded with his formal message protesting the Senate resolution. Despite the president's request, the Senate refused to enter the message into the journal of its proceedings. In his protest, prepared with the help of Roger Taney, Amos Kendall, and Attorney General–Designate Benjamin Butler, Jackson challenged the formality of the Senate resolution on constitutional grounds. More importantly, he revisited the Decision of 1789 and found in it an authoritative interpretation of the Constitution in which "the executive power is invested exclusively in the President" (Richardson 1911, 3:71). Jackson repeated this assertion several times and then connected it with the idea of unity of command and the subordination of executive officials.

Being thus made responsible for the entire action of the executive department, it was but reasonable that the power of appointing, overseeing, and controlling those who execute the laws—a power in its nature executive—should remain in his hands. (79)

The whole executive power being vested in the President, who is responsible for its exercise, it is a necessary consequence that he should have a right to employ agents of his own choice to aid him in the performance of his duties, and to discharge them when he is no longer willing to be responsible for their acts. (79–80)

The Secretary of the Treasury being appointed by the President, and being considered as constitutionally removable by him, it appears never to have occurred to anyone in the Congress of 1789, or since until very recently, that he was other than an executive officer, the mere instrument of the Chief Magistrate in the execution of the laws, subject, like all other heads of Departments, to his supervision and control. (81)

Jackson continued throughout the protest to reiterate his conception of the unity of the executive and toward the conclusion he warned, as Madison did in 1789, of the loss of responsibility without that unity. "The President is the direct representative of the American people, but the Secretaries are not. If the Secretary of the Treasury be independent of the President in the execution of the laws, then is there no direct responsibility to the people in that important branch of this Government to which is committed the care of the national finances" (Richardson 1911, 3:90). The persuasive power in Jackson's protest is precisely the link he makes to responsibility, which reaches to the heart of American worries about controlling officials not chosen through the ballot box: How can a people engage in self-government if some officials can act independently of direct, or even indirect, popular influence?

Jackson's conclusion that "it appears never to have occurred to anyone in the Congress of 1789, or since" that administrators were other than mere instruments of the president is, of course, disingenuous, because the historical record is plain that many others thought administrators were more than just implements of the president. What is distinctively absent from the protest, even accepting an exclusively hierarchical line of authority from presidents to administrators, is any idea of a unique contribution administration would make to the regime, like that discernible from the challengers to the Decision of 1789 or Alexander Hamilton's ideas and practices. Executive officials were reduced to a single, indirect link to the Constitution, with no raison d'être other than what the president bid.

The contrast, again, with the reality of even Jackson's own actions is striking. The contrast would grow more obvious as the Jacksonians' depersonalized administration evolved into a formal bureau system, and the democratizing surge of the Jacksonian era generated new demands for government action to protect public health and safety, most prominently in the case of steamboat regulation. With respect to the former, presidential supervision was attenuated, and direct responsibility, and administrative power, located farther from the center of command. The effect was improved efficiency but also the broadening of administrative discretion and the eventual rise of autonomous political power and the influence on public policy and its effects on citizens that went along with that power (L. D. White 1954, 537–40). The epitome of all this, reinforced by being outside even the bureau system, was the broad discretion and autonomy exercised by the mid-1850s by the Board of Supervising Inspectors of the Steamboat Inspection Service (Mashaw 2008, 1638–58). The tensions were heightened further, moreover, by challenges to Jacksonian principles from other quarters.

THE WHIGS: ADMINISTRATION AS THE EXERCISE
OF RESPONSIBLE DISCRETION

Jacksonian ideas about administration, even with their heavy baggage of tensions and contradictions, were clearly triumphant during this turbulent period in the development of American politics and government and in the decades afterward. The ideas did not go completely unchallenged, however. Whig opponents in particular took advantage of the clashes over the Bank of the United States, the presidential protest, and the spoils system to articulate alternative views, with the floor of the Senate proving to be their most effective forum.

Jeffrey Tulis observed that the dispute over the bank, Jackson's protest, and the Senate's reaction "evolved into a deep and serious discussion of the connection of the structure of the bureaucracy to the problem of executive accountability" (1987, 58). In the Senate debate precipitated by Jackson's request to have his protest message entered in the Senate journal, Whig senators spent a good deal of time railing against Jackson's arrogation of the whole executive power to himself. Nevertheless, senators did also deliberate about the structure and status of public administration in the constitutional system, and the Whig view articulated during the debate displayed very interesting qualities.

Senator George Poindexter, a Whig from Mississippi and the first senator to speak after Jackson's protest was read to the Senate on April 17, 1834, observed that the "Secretary of the Treasury, who refused to bend his neck to the yoke of executive power, and to make himself the instrument of violating the solemn obligations of law at the dictation of the Chief Magistrate, was unceremoniously kicked out of office, and another substituted in his place, with a more compliant conscience" (*Register of Debates in Congress* [hereafter cited as *Register*] 1848a, 1336–37). Senator Peleg Sprague, a Whig from Maine, chastised Jackson for designating the Secretary of the Treasury "as the Secretary of the President, and not the Secretary of the law" (*Register* 1848a, 1341).

On April 21 the debate resumed, and Senator Thomas Ewing, a Whig from Ohio, attacked Jackson for speaking "of the Secretaries generally as his Secretaries . . . and thus appropriating those high offices of the law to himself as his sole and exclusive property" (*Register* 1848a, 1405). Senator Ewing's rebuke seemed intended to turn Jackson's own claims against him, given Jackson's attack in his first annual message to Congress on the idea of public office "as a species of property . . . [rather] than as an instrument created solely for the service of the people" (Richardson 1911, 2:1011). Senator Ewing also sharply denied that the Constitution vested the president "with any such power" of removal at will and asserted that "its assumption is against the whole spirit and genius of our institutions. Its tendency is obvious. It makes the President superior to the law" (1418).

Still later in the debate, on April 30, Henry Clay labeled Jackson's idea that the president possessed the sole executive power and that executive officers were exclusively responsible to him as "altogether a military idea, wholly incompatible with free government." Clay then went on to declare, "There exists no such responsibility to the President. All are responsible to the law, and to the law only, or not responsible at all" (*Register* 1848a, 1575). Finally, in his signature speech in the debate, Daniel Webster proclaimed, "There is, there can be, no substantial responsibility, any further than every individual is answerable, not merely in his reputation, not merely in the opinion of mankind, but to the law, for the faithful discharge of his own appropriate duties" (Wiltse and Berolzheimer 1988, 68).

Responsibility to the law was thus a central theme in the Whig attack on the Jacksonian conception of administration. Clay, Webster, and their Whig allies articulated a second theme, however, which emphasized "the importance of the exercise of experienced, informed, responsible discretion as the heart of administration" (Storing 1980, 110). In staking out an early position against the protest message, Senator Theodore Frelinghuysen, a Whig from New Jersey, argued that "when the act of Congress put the public moneys under the discretion of the Secretary of the Treasury, the President did not possess the power of interfering with the full and free exercise of that discretion; much less to substitute his own will for the opinion and conscience of the Secretary" (*Register* 1848a, 1346). Henry Clay contended that "if [executive officers] are bound to conform to the will of the President, and to obey his commands, they cannot be regarded as moral, independent, and responsible beings" (1575). Daniel Webster voiced much the same idea: "And the Protest assumes to the President this whole responsibility for every other officer, for the very purpose of making the President every body, of annihilating everything like independence, responsibility, or character, in all other public agents" (Wiltse and Berolzheimer 1988, 62).

Senator George Bibb of Kentucky delivered perhaps the most interesting, thought-provoking, and surprising speech in the debate, on April 25. Bibb was a Jacksonian Democrat, but in his lengthy speech, he explored the intricate interconnections among responsibility, discretion, and the law facing public administrators. Senator Bibb moved from commentary on the specifics of William Duane's removal, about which he said, "He refused to surrender a duty and trust committed to him by law," to general observations about the duties of appointed officials. He stressed that "where the law itself assigns to an officer the performance of a duty, and the Legislature vests a discretion in that officer, then he is the officer of the law, answerable to the law, responsible for his own conduct" (*Register* 1848a, 1503). After dissecting Jackson's protest, Bibb reached the climax of his speech by elucidating his understanding of "the theory of our Government. Each officer is answerable for his own acts of commission or omission. . . . Each officer swears for himself, judges for himself, is responsible for himself to the public" (1511).

If many of the ideas articulated by these senators ring familiar, it is no accident. Senators Bibb, Clay, Ewing, and Webster in particular examined the records of the Decision of 1789 as intently as had the men who assisted Andrew Jackson in the composition of his protest message. They found intellectual and political kinship with the likes of William Smith, John Page, and James Jackson, who belonged to what Henry Clay labeled "a large and able minority" in the 1789 debate. In fact, Bibb, Clay, and Webster were so emboldened by their examination of the 1789 debate that they were willing to challenge its authoritativeness. Bibb mocked Madison's contention that impeachment provided a "decisive" check on the president. Impeachment, Bibb insisted, "has long since ceased to be any effective protection to the purity of the constitution" (*Register* 1848a, 1510). Clay called the 1789 debate inconclusive; he had argued in early March, in introducing legislation to control executive patronage, that the First Congress had "improvidently" conceded the removal power to the president as "an implied or constructive power" (834). Webster, in turn, had declared in his 1835 speech on the appointment and removal power that "Congress may . . . , hereafter, if necessity shall require it, reverse the decision of 1789" (Wiltse and Berolzheimer 1988, 90).

Their long-running battle with Andrew Jackson drew Whig leaders in the Senate into a searching discussion of the structure and status of public administration in the American regime. In Herbert Storing's interpretation, the conception the Whigs developed was remarkable. "The Whigs saw public administration not as a closed hierarchy leading to the top but as pools of official discretion, loosely connected but largely independent. . . . Sound discretion, not obedience to higher command, is the essence of good administration, though both, of course, are always involved" (1980, 110). Storing compared the Whig conception of the administrator to that of the judge, who is restrained by the limits of the law, and who employs practical reason within those limits to reach a good judgment. Such a conception of administration largely modeled on lawyerly bearing and professional orientation would emerge again in subsequent decades as Congress grappled with the demands on government spawned by a growing nation (Hoffer 2007).

Like their intellectual soul mates from 1789, then, the Whigs sought to define a more independent status for administrators and to anchor that independent status in a particular understanding of the Constitution. Yet the minority in 1789 made a greater effort to be specific about the constitutional provisions that could support their understanding of and claims for administrative independence. Although George Bibb vested administrators with independence, responsibility, and discretion, for example, he linked it all directly to a vague and general "public" rather than to provisos in the Constitution, which might have provided a surer and more permanent foundation for the qualities he enumerated. Moreover, the Whigs hewed closer than the 1789 minority to an exclusively instrumental function for administration. Thus, although many references to the administrative obligation to fulfill the purposes of the law can be found in the presidential protest debate, it evidences few if any references to the duty of administrators, through their discretion, to shape or refine the law, help to define the purposes the law embodies, or place an independent check on the president's interpretation of the law, as the minority in 1789 proposed.

Indeed, many of the Whig paeans to responsibility and fidelity to the law appear to have meant mostly fidelity and subordination to Congress, which, admittedly, does make the law. Webster proclaimed that "the theory of our institutions is plain; it is that government is an agency created for the good of the people, and that every person in office is the agent and servant of the people" (Wiltse and Berolzheimer 1988, 77). The legislature is the supreme agent under "the theory," so Webster continued, "I do not think the Constitution . . . intended to impose any restraint on the legislature, in regard to its authority of regulating the duties, powers, duration or responsibility of office" (89).

Henry Clay similarly placed control over executive power enacted by law with Congress, and argued in his presidential protest speech that "when an officer, no matter what may be the mode of his appointment, or the tenure of his office, is designated by law to perform duties growing out of powers vested in Congress, that officer represents Congress, and is the agent of Congress" (*Register* 1848a, 1577). In his executive patronage speech of 1835, Clay further argued, "The office coming into existence by the will of Congress, the same will may provide how, and in what manner the office and the officer shall both cease to exist—Congress, in pursuit of the public good, brings the office and officer into being, and assigns their purposes" (Colton 1897, 18).

It was John Calhoun, however, who gave clearest expression to the notion that the controlling end of Madison's chain of dependence should rest in Congress's hands. In an 1835 speech on executive patronage, Calhoun offered his own "construction" of the Constitution that "would put down all discretionary power, and convert the Government into what the framers intended it should be—a Government of laws and not of discretion." Calhoun then proceeded to declare that by his construction "no officer, from the President to the constable, and from the Chief Justice to the lowest judicial officer, could exercise any power but what is expressly granted by the Constitution, or by some act of Congress; and thus that which, in a free state, is most odious and dangerous of all things—the discretionary power of those who are charged with the execution of the laws—will be effectually suppressed, and the dominance of the laws be fully established" (*Register*, 1848b, 555).

Herbert Storing's assessment is, therefore, crucial for characterizing Whig thinking about administration. The practical reason of the judge contains a strong element of instrumental rationality. The "severe limits of the law," after all, force the judge to reach a "good" judgment, that is, a judgment that fulfills the law's purposes. But the leeway, or discretion, permitted the judge within those limits means that the judgment will also contribute, perhaps in only a small way, to refining the law's aims, and thus altering the character of relationships between citizens. The struggle the judge faces in accommodating these two dimensions of judgment can be seen in the Whig effort to articulate a coherent understanding of public administration based on the balancing of fidelity to law (the instrumental) and responsible discretion (the constitutive). It is particularly interesting that Calhoun ultimately rejects the struggle of his Senate compatriots to accommodate the instrumental and the constitutive through a conception of the administrator's job that weds obedience to law with responsible discretion. Instead, Calhoun adopts a constitutional ideology, and within it a conception of public administration, that almost perfectly mirrors the instrumentalism of the Jacksonian view.

As a practical matter of public understanding and political practice, the outcome of the 1834–35 debates was much the same as followed the debates of 45 years before. Some of America's foremost statesmen of the time failed again to take advantage of the opportunity to acknowledge explicitly in their political rhetoric, and to embrace fully in the actual operations of government, a more expansive conception of public administration in the regime, one that would encompass its constitutive as well as its instrumental qualities. In this, Jackson's Whig opponents were as much captives of the predominant interpretation of the Decision of 1789 as he was. In an exchange of letters with James Kent, the foremost authority on American constitutional law at the time, Daniel Webster seems convinced by Kent's insistence that "it is too late to call the Presidents [sic] power in question, after a declaratory act of Congress and an acquiescence of half a century" (Wiltse and Allen 1977, 12).

The 1834–35 debates thus failed to alter very much the political status of public administration in the constitutional system that had emerged from the Decision of 1789. Consistent with Charles Thach's (1922) assessment, it remained a question of who—the president or Congress—was the master. After the outcome of two highly charged political contests, this way of framing the matter was likely the most important determinant of broad public thinking and political practice for many decades to follow. In the decades just before, during, and after the Civil War, Congress proved to be the undisputed master and primary institutional battleground for the next set of confrontations over the role of administration in the American regime.

The Jacksonian Legacy

The Jacksonian era featured some of the most powerful, wide-ranging, and illuminating public debates about the role of administration under the Constitution that can be found in American history. Further developments in public ideas, and accompanying struggles for power, occurred in response to competing claims about the nature of public office, the relationship of public offices and officeholders to the citizenry, and the allegiance of public officers to political superiors, the law, and the Constitution. The continuation of these debates a generation after the Decision of 1789 reflects its residual ambiguities. Some of the men who engaged vigorously in the 1789 debate seemed to recognize public administration as having both instrumental and constitutive attributes. A small number even advocated grounding the structure and practice of public administration in this recognition. The Revolution's ideology of subordinate, instrumental administration ultimately won out over this perspective during the debate. Despite the debate's outcome, the governing practices of the Federalists and Jeffersonians generated tensions and contradictions between what was expressed in the debate as ideal and essential for good government, and what was real about administration's role in politics and governance.

Andrew Jackson's presidency proved to be a direct response to the gap between what was publicly pronounced and accepted and what was increasingly practiced with respect to the role of public administration in an increasingly democratic regime. The Jacksonian attack on the Second Bank of the United States, for example, certainly featured a clash of competing interests seeking possession of the political and economic power that control over the currency and management of the nation's debt engendered. The ferocity of the attack, however, reflected the deep-seated principles and consequent worries of the Jacksonians as heirs to the Jeffersonian ideology so fixated on the regime-altering potential of autonomous, discretionary administration. Yet the Jacksonian response, which centered on strengthening democratic control under the president *and* the party, dispersing administrative power to the states, and sharpening the conception of the subordinate administrative instrument, only exacerbated the tensions and contradictions between the sharpening rhetoric and ideology of democracy and the fundamental reality of administrative influence on politics, and the potential for administration to function as a vital component in the ongoing construction of the regime. The strains created were particularly acute because the Jacksonian rhetorical response did not fully comport with the Jacksonians' own understanding, intentions, and actions regarding administration.

The case of rotation in office offers the most obvious of ironies in that reforms born of fears of aristocratic bureaucracy led inexorably to bureaucratic structures and "the rise of bureaucratic power in America" (M. Nelson 1982, 757). Yet, if not under Jackson then certainly under many of his successors, the effects of the spoils system went further by proceeding to turn on its head Jackson's attack on the prevailing, semiaristocratic conception of office as an unwarranted "species of property." Turning public offices over to parties and candidates certainly assured that no officeholder would see the office he occupied as his to hold for life with good behavior. Yet the change, following Amos Kendall's declaration that "offices are the property of the people and the officeholders their hirelings" (quoted in L. D. White 1954, 344), merely made office the property of the parties, to be exchanged like any commodity as each party won or lost majority support. To the extent that the Whigs offered an alternative (L. D. White 1954, 322–24), the electorate expressed decisively a preference for Jacksonian rotation over a course of time stretching more than a generation. Moreover, all the parties competing for office during that time did strive to bring competent men from their ranks into office and to retain many who demonstrated competence or occupied positions that required continuity and stability (Mashaw 2008, 1616). The consequences were, nevertheless, "a foregone conclusion" (L. D. White 1954, 327), in particular, to "demoralize" the public service in all the ways that term connotes. Although the spoils system brought some blatantly corrupt and immoral individuals into government service, the effect of rotation was more far reaching because of its impact on competent officeholders and thus on the competence of day-to-day governance.

The efforts toward the depersonalization of office by the likes of Amos Kendall succeeded in providing the conceptual and structural components for controlling the behavior of officeholders and likely laid the groundwork for the much more ambitious neutralization of public service that progressive reformers would subsequently pursue. The accompanying motive of giving the people possession of office through the parties meant, however, that the Jacksonian administrative reforms came at a very high price. The politicization of administration that Americans eventually associated with rotation was thus not in the fundamentals of strengthening self-government by increasing attachment to the regime, as the Federalists had hoped, or of shaping or reshaping the moral character of the citizens, as was the aim of the Jacksonians, but in the crass, self-interested politicking of the greedy who scrounged for patronage. If public administration as instrument and servant of the people could be bent to this result, how could it ever be trusted, supported, and legitimated as a fundamental shaper of the character of the citizenry and contributor to the improvement of American self-government that the Jacksonians claimed?

Although some political leaders in this era did articulate conceptions of administration that seemed to recognize its constitutive role and the tension with its instrumental role, their efforts proved woefully inadequate, especially in translating this recognition into the practice of politics and government. In the presence of such confusion and suspicion about public administration's place in the regime, distrust could not help but increase among political leaders themselves and the public at large. And this, ultimately, could only contribute to weakening the capacity of public administration to support and improve American self-government. Hence, the theoretical and practical challenges public administration posed for American politics and government would have to be confronted again and would be complicated further by a host of developmental forces: westward expansion, population growth, and accelerating industrialization, not to mention the slow and painful healing of a grave constitutional wound.

Chapter Four

Perfecting the Neutral Instrument

Transformations of the Second State and
Progressive Reforms

W hat makes the murder of President James A. Garfield such an enduring legend? As part of American political folklore, one can find some rendition of it in nearly every introductory text on American government, particularly in those passages concerning the development of national administration. Remarkably, accounts of the event often give prominence not to the president but to Charles Guiteau, the deranged and swindling partisan who gunned down Garfield with a single shot to the back. This is a bit of a surprise, for in his political career that carried him to the White House, Garfield had shown signs of having the potential to break out of the grip of the tiring status quo of post–Civil War political and governmental structures and practices (see Hoffer 2007, 92–97; Peskin 1999). For political reformers of the time, however, as well as for their many ideological descendants, Guiteau and his deadly deed were irresistible as their prime focus because he embodied the most distinctive characteristics of the politics of that era. As Guiteau proved to be the agent at whose hands the status quo met its undoing, he stands immortalized not as a madman but as a "disappointed office seeker," and he has secured the place of trigger man in the death of the very spoils system from which he sought to profit.

Of course, the institution of the spoils and rotation in office survived long past the 10-week death watch over President Garfield; but it did succumb, and Guiteau's crime is more prominent in the story because it energized "public opinion very like a spark on a powder-magazine. It [fell] on a mass of popular indignation all ready to explode" (editorial from the *Nation* quoted in Hoogenboom 1961, 209). The entrenched corruption of the spoils had to end, its opponents proclaimed, because the *people* demanded it. Guiteau's attack showed that the spoils system was so evil that it could lead to homicide. The public outcry revealed that the system also defied the democratic ideals then being given a new and vigorous expression as Reconstruction came to an end and the nation resumed its rapid growth.

The Guiteau story helps to illuminate forces of governmental and social change gathering strength after the Jacksonian era, especially the further growth and bureaucratization of government administrative structures and parallel changes in business organization stemming from industrialization. These forces presented growing challenges to the traditional structures of power, and the public action they spurred is exemplified in two laws widely regarded as original pillars in the edifice of the modern American administrative state: the 1883 Pendleton Act and the 1887 Interstate Commerce Act. The debates accompanying the enactment of these statutes also revealed a new phase of intense struggle with the dilemma that public administration repeatedly presses upon the practice of American government and politics. The collision of democratic ideals, further institutionalization of administration, and increasingly rapid economic and technological change stimulated this new phase, and important chords that were first struck during the resulting dialogues and debates continue to sound today.

Before considering how public administration was conceived in connection with the 1883 and 1887 initiatives, and in the much more searching effort of progressives to reconcile democracy and modernity, it is important to explore further the characteristics of this next stage of democracy's expansionary bent. The civil service reform movement, the effort to alter business-government relations, and other actions signaling a conceptual shift from the negative to the positive state, were manifested in this new stage, evident first in the emergence of a "second state" mentality (Hoffer 2007) and then more forcefully in the progressivism that fully blossomed after 1900.

Morality, Efficiency, and Middle-Class Democracy

The Civil War still stands as the great divide in American political development, even though it closed what is now only the first third of the lengthening history of the United States under the Constitution. In his account of the tension between majority rule and minority rights that undergirds the rise of the

American bureaucratic state, William Nelson (2006) called the Civil War "the great watershed in the nineteenth century" (157), for it marked the realization of reformers seeking to protect minority rights that "moral principles provided little guidance or impediment" by themselves "to a majority's exercise of its authority." These reformers thus sought more robust institutional structures to limit the potential for majority tyranny and preserve "American pluralism" (158). These institutional structures could be built on the foundations of the likes of the bureau structure and regulatory innovations of the Jacksonian era, as well as the early pillars of the "second state" (Hoffer 2007), including the first Morrill Act establishing the land-grant college system, the Freedmen's Bureau of the Reconstruction period, and the short-lived first incarnation of a Department of Education. Beneath this institution building lay shifting conceptions of morality and the political undulations generated by Tocqueville's irresistible democratic tide.

The years from 1860 to the pinnacle of progressivism in 1914 present an extraordinarily complex picture of diverse and sometimes contradictory ideas, organized ventures, and fluid political debates. Nevertheless, one can distinguish certain common causes, especially moral restoration and social justice in politics and society, limitations on the centralization of wealth and power generated by advanced industrialization, government improvement through more efficient and business-like operation, and the intensification and transformation of democratic participation in response to the many challenges the era posed for American self-government. The restoration of proper political morals and ethics through reform of the civil service was the particular province of an older generation of reformers associated with the abolitionist movement. Expanding political power and social justice, through a shift in power to the executive and an increase in government efficiency based on science and technology, was the motivating force of progressives, who were part of an emerging, energetic, and self-conscious middle class. But these areas of concern were not each the exclusive province of one set of reformers. Instead, they were shared with varying emphasis by more established elites, as well as by the Populists and their progressive successors.

MORAL RESTORATION

Over the 230-year course of American political development, each surge in the democratic tide has in essence recreated the original fight for independence. In that fight and its successive recreations, a broad and principled majority goes up against politically distant, entrenched holders of power. An attribute regarded as critical in the popular triumph is the moral superiority of the majority. The elite in power seem exceedingly corrupt and out of touch, while the invigorated majority merely seeks to enshrine such simple virtues as industriousness, honesty, or fair treatment and to realize the principles of democratic rule and individual self-determination. Thus, the patriots of the Revolution had the moral authority of the Declaration of Independence behind them. The Jacksonians sought to restore simple republican virtue and rescue institutions and individuals with crippled moral compasses. Franklin Roosevelt successfully portrayed his opponents as "economic royalists," responsible by their behavior for the political, economic, and social disaster of the Great Depression. Reformers of the 1960s and 1970s successfully affixed a negative connotation to the word "establishment." And from the 1980s on, "career" politicians in consort with "mindless" bureaucrats have become the prime objects of scorn of a diverse collection of reformers, who have sought to exploit broad public frustration with and anxiety about a federal government seemingly out of control and unresponsive to the people's needs.

Although the extent of its crosscutting societal changes make the picture more complicated, the "Republican era" still fits the pattern. In Leonard White's judgment, it "opened in moral chaos" (1958, 365). In response, the reformers who led the fight for civil service reform aimed squarely at the moral degeneracy brought about, they thought, by the controllers of the spoils system the reformers sought to eradicate. In 1868, Julius Bing declared, "At present, there is no organization save that of corruption; no system save that of chaos; no test of integrity save that of partisanship; no test of qualifications save that of intrigue. . . . We have to deal with evil that is manifest here and there and everywhere" (Hoogenboom 1961, 12). Stating it more succinctly, the pre–Pendleton Act Civil Service Commission, in its 1871 report to the president, charged that through the spoils system, "the moral tone of the country is debased. The national character deteriorates" (U.S. Civil Service Commission 1871, 4).

After passage of the Pendleton Act, the message from reform leader and interior secretary Carl Schurz was still the same: "In my opinion, the question of whether the Departments at Washington are managed well or badly, is, in proportion to the whole question an insignificant problem overall. Neither does the question whether our civil service is as efficient as it ought to be cover the whole ground. The most important point to my mind is, how can we remove the element of demoralization which the now prevailing mode of distributing office has introduced into the body-politic" (Crenson 1975, 173–74). Putting it all together with passion and hyperbole, the reformers implicated the spoils in everything from the horrific Union losses in the Civil War, to prostitution, to Guiteau's murderous assault.

The reformers were divided somewhat over how civil service reform would work to restore the nation's moral bearings. Those who saw the *individual* as primary moral agent stressed change and moral restoration through persuasion and "exhortation which could direct citizens and politicians toward paths of honesty and virtue" (Karl 1963, 6). Change through civil service reform, by this approach, would be achieved simply by replacing bad employees with good ones. For reformers who emphasized *organizations* or *institutions* as core moral agents, reform would take "the shape of the redevelopment of political institutions and practices or in supposed reversions to institutions which had degenerated from their pure, original form" (6). Civil service reform from this perspective was, congruent with the Jacksonian view, not just a target of opportunity but the engine for altering the nature of the political system and society at large. The only strategy that civil service reformers ever seriously considered was selection of government personnel not by political affiliation but on the basis of merit, as established by competitive examinations and special qualifications associated with educational attainment. Fortunately for the civil service reform movement, this strategy was conducive to either a simple replacement of the bad with the good or a more "fundamental change in the political system by altering the nature of the civil service" (Rosenbloom 1971, 73).

Progressive reformers would appear to stand in contrast to their predecessors because of their concentration on efficiency over moral restoration in their support for continued administrative reform (e.g., Croly 1914, 397–405). Frederick Mosher designated the period 1883–1906 as "government by the good," followed by the period 1906–1937 as "government by the efficient" (1968, 64–79). In Barry Karl's observation, "the early years of the twentieth century saw a transition taking place—from the older emphasis upon sin and corruption to be investigated by vigilantes armed with public virtue to a new emphasis, now upon 'efficiency and economy,' to be investigated by experts armed with technical training and science" (1963, 51). Robert Wiebe (1967, 171) echoed Karl. "Civil service . . . had once been a negative, absolute goal, self-contained and self-fulfilling. Now the panacea of the patrician had given way to the administrative tool of the expert, with efficiency rather than moral purity its objective." Carl Schurz's commentary quoted above further reinforces the contrast.

Yet the seemingly distinct views of civil service and progressive reformers were significantly intertwined. The social control movement, which sought to "employ governmental power to impose homogenous standards of behavior on the entire population," was a significant component of progressivism (Chambers 1980, 114). Indeed, efficiency and science and technology were enlisted in the moral crusade. William Nelson argued that before turning to institutional structures to protect minorities, reformers first sought to build a new "scientific morality" (2006, ch. 4), stressing specialized expertise and neutral standards like efficiency, on the ruins of an earlier effort to restore morality to government in the immediate post–Civil War period (also see Chambers 1980, 133–36). Reflecting this, Stephen Skowronek observed that the civil service reformers, "during the Civil War . . . had turned the United States Sanitary Commission into a propaganda instrument for espousing new values of professionalism, self-discipline, and science" (Skowronek 1982, 53). As civil service reform advanced, Senator George Pendleton, an Ohio Democrat, in a speech supporting his own civil service reform legislation, argued that "reform would eliminate . . . the twin evils of political corruption and business inefficiency" (Hoogenboom 1961, 217).

Four years after passage of the Pendleton Act, Woodrow Wilson saw moral recovery as preface to more far-reaching administrative and governmental change. "Civil-service reform is thus but a moral preparation for what is to follow. It is clearing the moral atmosphere of official life by establishing the sanctity of public office as a public trust, and . . . opening the way for making it businesslike" (W. Wilson 1887, 210). More emphatically, at the very heart of his treatise on progressive democracy, Herbert Croly declared, "During the last quarter of a century general relaxation of American moral fibre has unquestionably been taking place; and in spite of the increasing use of disciplinary measures, the process of relaxation has not as yet been fairly checked" (1914, 207). It was the ideal and the program of progressive democracy, built on a "democratic political organization" that was "fundamentally educational" but also "organized for efficiency" (378), Croly contended, that would not merely check but would cure that moral decline. The pinnacle of progressive moral fervor, complete with overt religious symbolism, was Theodore Roosevelt's Progressive Party campaign for president in 1912 (Milkis 2009). As Roosevelt declared, "We stand at Armageddon and we battle for the lord" (T. Roosevelt 1912).

Those "who concerned themselves with honesty and efficiency" were the men who "made the Progressive and Populist platforms. They had fought for civil service reform as well as for expanded governmental regulation and control of public services. They had attempted to reform corrupt governments by the introduction of honest men" (Karl 1963, 19). Efficiency was in a very real sense, therefore, itself a moral concept. "The precise meaning of the term was . . . arguable, but its moral significance could hardly be questioned. Efficient administration was 'good'; inefficient administration was 'bad.' . . . The public service, to be good, must be both politically neutral and efficient, and there was more than a little doubt that it could be efficient unless it was also politically neutral" (Mosher 1968, 71).

Democracy for the Modern Age

That the reform efforts stretching across the mid-nineteenth century to early twentieth century were also supported by a robust democratic impulse seems beyond dispute. As Grant's Civil Service Commission declared, civil service reform was "emphatically the people's cause, the people's reform" (U.S. Civil Service Commission 1871, 23). The texture of that impulse was distinctive and important, however. First, beyond the civil service reformers' rhetoric of a people's cause, the reform impulse emanated from the raw, leveling passion of the Populists aimed at concentrations of economic and political power. That passion soon combined with and then was subsumed into and ameliorated by the desire for participation, access, and power of a new professional middle class, the majority core of the progressive movement. More direct democracy—that is, bringing the government and the people closer together—became a special progressive rallying point. This was direct democracy taken out of the hands of the political machines, which progressives saw as dependent on the poor and unschooled urban masses swelled by waves of immigration. Second, however, the drive for participation and access reflected the intention of many reformers, particularly among the diverse professional and economic interests of the middle class, to reinvigorate the pluralist properties of the constitutional system. In William Nelson's account, that reinvigoration is a particularly enduring legacy of this era in American political development, reflecting the desire of the reformers to dampen the political disruptions and even violence caused by raw majority rule, even as, in Arthur Link's judgment, "progressivism . . . was grounded so much on majoritarian principles" (1959, 848).

Third, thrown into the mix was the seeming paradox of an antidemocratic yearning of a "patrician elite" to "resume their natural posts of command" (Wiebe 1967, 61). Seen slightly differently, progressives sought to develop and control a new, professional elite rule that modern mass democracy could accept

(Karl 1987, 29). The civil service reform movement was composed of "lawyers, journalists, academics, and clergy. These professionals controlled the executive committees of the reform associations. . . . As a group, they represented a key link between America's old patrician elite and its new professional sector" (Skowronek 1982, 53). The movement as a whole, moreover, "was fed by fears of a partnership of party and industry that would exclude the 'interests of the great middle classes' from government" (52). Despite the contrasts between older and newer reformers, fundamental links between the two were unmistakable. "The old reformers had sought to expand democracy; the new sought to preserve it within limits now imposed by science and technology. The groups had a common history, even if they did not always remember it the same way" (Karl 1983, 17).

Finally, and equally paradoxically, progressives sought to link greater direct, popular participation in government affairs not filtered through the parties with a more administratively centered state. There was some logic to it, as progressives contended that their brand of democracy "would put the American people directly in touch with the councils of power, thus strengthening the demand for government support, and allow—indeed, require—administrative agencies to play their proper role in the realization of progressive social welfare policy" (Milkis 2009, 15). Still, how would that contact with power be effectuated? The progressive answer was to transform the presidency into the leader, shaper, and conduit for a nationalized public opinion that would counterbalance the parochial biases of a locally based party system that controlled Congress.

The common historical orientation of all the reformers was nevertheless readily evident: The American political and governmental system from the very beginning embodied the promise of democracy, but that promise had been systematically thwarted. Progressive historians stressed the popular origins of American democracy, for example, and depicted American political development as reflecting a succession of selfish elites frustrating the search for social justice by the majority (see Herson 1984, 177). Connections between government and upper-class wealth were signs of corruption of popular control, not of inherent structural defects. The Constitution was fundamentally democratic, they concluded, but it had not been put into operation as its designers intended (Karl 1963, 24).

Certainly, many of the reformers sought "to provide individuals and minorities with protection against what they perceived to be an increased threat of majority tyranny," and thus "to institutionalize pluralism" to address the concern of the founders "that popular power be limited by popular rights" (W. E. Nelson 2006, 5).

Key elements in this push for pluralism may have had their roots in the "more pluralistic" Whig view of American politics (Storing 1980, 110). All of this was consistent, nevertheless, with the growth of a middle class concerned about the realization of its own conceptions of democracy and thus its own political power, a middle class that defined itself on the basis of professional and business interests given concrete form as "associations."

Whether or not public sentiment was increasingly speaking with a pluralist tongue, the central current of reform during the period was unequivocal: the expansion, and refinement, of *popular* government. Populists sought "to achieve a direct intrusion of the majority into government" (Herson 1984, 170), if possible by dispensing with the "artificial barrier" of "formal political structures" (Wiebe 1967, 61), that is, political parties. Progressives pursued a similar attack on the parties through a number of legal and constitutional changes, such as direct election of senators, direct primaries, and ballot reform. Such changes aimed at intensifying direct democracy, but progressives acknowledged the importance of constitutional forms and thus the "boundaries of popular democracy" (Karl 1987, 28). Hence, perhaps their most important contribution to democratic reform came in the guise of reinterpretations of founding principles of executive leadership (see, e.g., Tulis 1987, chs. 4, 5) leading to the concept of "executive government," with its "efficient organization" for the "rule of the majority" (Croly 1914, 305). All of this had major consequences for how public administration was conceived of and situated within the constitutional regime.

Neutral Service to the Popular Will

The insignificance of the absence of the word *administration* anywhere in the text of the U.S. Constitution is now well established. A national administrative system, although modest by modern standards, was central to the state building of Alexander Hamilton and the Federalists. Both the Jeffersonians and the Jacksonians, even as they espoused principles of small government, decentralization, instrumentalism, and subordination, not only expanded administrative structures, but in many of their ideas and actions gave administration a prominent place in efforts to further shape or reshape the American regime. It is not altogether clear that the reformers of the late nineteenth century and early twentieth century fully grasped this historic constancy to their efforts. Their attack on the Jeffersonian-Jacksonian public philosophy, and its Gilded Age political-economic offspring—laissez-faire—suggest that they did not. By the problems on which they fixed their attention and the issues that animated their public actions, however, they, like their predecessors, placed public administration and its conception, articulation, and construction at the center of efforts to remake American constitutionalism. Indeed, in his expressions of support on the Senate floor for civil service reform, Republican Sen. George Hoar of Massachusetts declared that the scheme approved in 1883 "will be regarded in the future by the American people almost as the adoption of a new and better constitution" (quoted in Hoffer 2007, 132).

For the civil service reformers, of course, attention to administration was central, because government at all levels was completely tarnished by patronage, which was *the* insidious evil that had to be exorcised from the body politic. As the reform leader George Curtis put it, "The difficulty is not the abuse of patronage but the patronage itself" (Skowronek 1982, 52). The best way to get at patronage and eliminate it from government and society was to neutralize the civil service, a process Herbert Kaufman described in starkly effective terms. "The assumption imbedded in the [Pendleton] Act—indeed, in the philosophy of civil service reform—is that the civil service is a 'neutral instrument,' without policy preferences of its own (taken as a body) and without any inclination to attempt to impose any policy on the country. For civil service reformers, the civil service was like a hammer or a saw; it would do nothing at all by itself, but it would serve any purpose, wise or unwise, good or bad, to which any user put it" (1965, 39).

The object of the neutralization of the civil service was the dissolution of partisanship, not only in the selection of administrative personnel but also in the behavior and decision making of administrative officials. Did this reflect "only a very mild dichotomy between politics and administration"? It would appear so. The civil service reformers advocated "the partisan but not total political neutrality of the service. Their doctrine of neutrality was that of the British. Career civil servants were forbidden to play any active party role and were protected from partisan removal and assessments, but they were expected to further the lawful policies of the party in power" (Van Riper 1983, 482). American reformers, in other words, wanted American public administrators to follow the doctrine espoused by the British diplomat Robert Gilbert Lord Vansittart: "The soul of our service is the loyalty with which we execute ordained error" (Denhardt 1993, 252).

This assessment is bolstered by some of the more complex characterizations of the effects of reform. Carl Schurz, for example, envisioned "presidents and heads of the executive departments" as "respected officers of state having high duties to fulfill," which demanded "strength and ability" (Skowronek 1982, 55).

In his 1884 address to the annual meeting of the National Civil-Service Reform League, George Curtis argued that "the essential point is not to find coal-heavers who can scan Virgil correctly, but to find coal-heavers who, being properly qualified for heaving coal, are their own masters and not the tools of politicians" (Proceedings 1884, 16). Curtis's statement is especially provocative. By "their own masters" did he mean that these coal heavers were not mere tools of "the people" either but might also seek to shape the purposes for which they were heaving coal? His speech is unclear on that question, but in invoking "the people" numerous times, he intimated that public offices belonged to the people and they, not the parties, could appoint to those offices whomever they so chose.

The characterization of the neutrality sought by civil service reformers is, however, more confirmatory of a strong dichotomy than it appears. A public administration that is political yet nonpartisan might seek to shape the polity, perhaps through its discretionary authority, in ways inconsistent with the policies of the party in power but perfectly congruent with the special values and qualities it embodies as an institution, even as it also carries out its ministerial duties as directed by the president, Congress, or the courts. They would be Curtis's coal heavers who were their own masters and who, for instance, might drop a few chunks of coal along the way to help the poorest of the poor. In contrast, a civil service that was *totally* neutral, in Kaufman's sense of the complete absence of any policy preferences of its own, would be the one that only did the bidding of the party or majority in power. It would surely be engaged only in the ministerial, or nonpolitical, aspects of administration.

And the latter is precisely what the reformers sought. Restrictions on the political character of the public service were "intended to insure its impartiality, and to eliminate the possibility that the civil service, either voluntarily or under coercion, could use partisan political activity to subvert the democratic process" (Rosenbloom 1971, 94). For the civil service reformers, protecting the integrity of the democratic process meant not just washing away partisanship from the civil service but thoroughly expunging politics of any sort from administration as well. The reformers "were anxious to make the best tool possible available to whoever occupied the highest seats in the American governmental system. They conceived of policy and administration as distinct and separate, though related, activities, and they wanted to restrict partisanship to the policy-makers in order to provide a superlative mechanism by which the voters' mandates could be carried out. They perfected the instrument; let the people put it to what use they would" (Kaufman 1965, 39).

This characterization of administration as instrumental by political leaders of this new reform era was as thorough as anything offered by the Jacksonians, with whom they otherwise vehemently parted company. So, too, Kaufman's assessment suggests, was their idea of administration's subordination to the popular will. Issuing an executive order on political neutrality three years after enactment of civil service reform, President Grover Cleveland insisted, "Officeholders are the agents of the people, not their masters" (Richardson 1898, 8:494). So thorough was the acceptance of this conception, in fact, that neither the long rhetorical campaign of civil service reformers nor the congressional debate on the Pendleton Act—the principal concrete initiative of the civil service reform movement—generated anything resembling more expansive thinking about the structure of public administration and its standing in the polity. Indeed, the subordination of the civil service to the people (and, for some, to the party) as a ministerial instrumentality was the dominant image conjured up during the debate. The civil service reform effort mirrored the tensions and contradictions about public administration's place in the polity that had been evident in the Jacksonian attempt at republican restoration, with added strains evident from the ensuing expansion in administrative structures and increasing bureaucratization of government operations.

Moral Restoration and Neutral Obedience: The Pendleton Act

Of the many public debates on civil service reform in this era, the most critical was the one that took place in December 1882 on the floor of the U.S. Senate. Reform forces had finally gathered sufficient strength to push final consideration and enactment of the Pendleton bill. Of the several notable themes that permeated the debate, one oft-repeated argument was that substantial growth in the size and responsibilities of the federal government had made it impossible for the heads of departments and bureaus to know all their subordinates and thus to be able to judge their capabilities and deficiencies. Hence, even if the spoils system was not corrupt and destructive (which of course to the reformers it incontrovertibly was), it was no longer practical. Some impersonal, efficient method for selecting civil servants to meet the government's needs had to be found. Evidently, the problems of "moral hazard" and "adverse selection" prominent today in rational choice theories of public bureaucracy (e.g., Garvey 1993, 25–33; G. Miller 2000) were already recognized.

The most deeply entrenched theme was public administration's subordination and service to the people. Proponents argued that this was best fulfilled by a merit system, which was in keeping with the original principles and practices of government under the Constitution. Opponents argued that party control and rotation in office was the best way to maintain "a people's government." Senator Pendleton offered the reformers' case.

> The bill has for its foundation the simple and single idea that offices of the Government are trusts for the people; that performance of the duties of these offices is to be in the interest of the people. . . . If it be true that offices are trusts for the people, then it is also true that the offices should be filled by those who can perform and discharge the duties in the best possible way. Fidelity, capacity, honesty were the tests established by Mr. Jefferson when he assumed the reins of government in 1801. He said then . . . that these elements were necessary to an honest civil service, and that an honest civil service was essential to the purity and efficiency of administration, necessary to the preservation of republican institutions. (*Congressional Record* [hereafter cited as *CR*] 1882, 206)

Not only did Pendleton tie the new concept of civil service selection by merit to Jeffersonian ideals, presumably for the benefit of his fellow Democrats, but he tried to lessen the threat that merit selection might be seen to pose for party democracy and the sovereignty of the states by further insisting that his proposal was consistent with the "democratic theory of the Federal Constitution and Government; that its powers are all granted; that the subjects on which it can act are very limited; that it should refrain from enlarging its jurisdiction; . . . that it should scrupulously avoid 'undue administration'" (*CR* 1882, 207–08).

Pendleton thus attempted to signal rejection of the worst aspects of the Jacksonian criteria for selection by party loyalty without losing that close linkage of administration to the people that the Jeffersonians and Jacksonians had deeply ensconced in governing philosophy. If administrators are the people's servants, however, should not the people's direct representatives have a say in how those servants are selected? Reform opponent Daniel Voorhees of Indiana made just such a claim later in the debate, arguing that assisting office seekers was one of the duties of elected representatives.

> This is a people's government, a representative government. We are sent here by the people who own this Government. I for one am not ready to say the moment I am in place that nobody shall approach me. I am not ready to say that the people who pay the taxes, till the soil, do the work and the voting, shall not

have the ear of their representatives and access to their presence anywhere and everywhere. We are their servants, not their masters. A different system is growing up here to that in the days of our fathers. The sooner we return to the old principle that we are the servants of the people and not their masters, the better it will be for us and this country. (CR 1882, 355)

Cutting across this major line of division between proponents and antagonists of reform was the impact of reform on the parties. Indeed, in his history of the campaign against the spoils system Ari Hoogenboom concluded that, "concern over the Pendleton bill's effects on the civil service . . . played second place to its calculated effects on either party" (1961, 243). That concern did stretch the senators' thinking just a bit with respect to the structure of the federal administrative establishment. Many legislators from western states, for example, called for a balanced sectional representation in the federal service through continuation of rotation in office, an idea that may be said to have its roots in George Washington's policy of geographic balance in executive appointments (L. D. White 1948, 256). A public administration regarded as a representative institution in this way would surely break out of the bonds of purely instrumental subordination. Alas, the public record of the debate offers no evidence to suggest that advocates of sectional representation, like Nebraska's Senator Charles Van Wyck, had any such a notion in mind. What they mostly sought was their fair share of government jobs.

Even more provocative was the proposal for "the direct election of officers located outside of Washington" (Hoogenboom 1961, 219), a version of which Senator Pendleton himself introduced as a separate bill. Democratic Senator James George of Mississippi added a twist by proposing "a constitutional amendment providing for the local election of all federal officers" (239). In the House, Representative Amasa Norcross (R-MA) proposed a constitutional amendment to create a "house of electors to elect or confirm civil officers" (CR 1882, 16). Direct election of public administrators is hardly foreign to American political and governmental practice. Today, all but a handful of states directly elect at least some administrative officials, such as secretaries of state, attorneys general, and treasurers. Some states also elect agriculture commissioners, auditors, comptrollers, education commissioners, insurance commissioners, and public utility regulators (see *The Book of the States* 2010, Table 4.10).

The election of *federal* administrators would have wide-ranging implications, however. With federal administrators having obvious and identifiable constituencies as the result of elections, could the president or Congress exert any effective control over them? In spite of the Constitution's provision for only three branches, public administration might truly have become the de facto fourth branch of government it has long been touted to be (see Meier 1993). But such far-reaching implications were never addressed in debate on the Pendleton Act. The idea of electing public administrators was pursued by opponents of the Pendleton bill less as a serious alternative than as a political maneuver to undercut the reformers' claim that civil service reform was the better way to achieve fidelity to the people's will.

Finally, an issue that also crossed the line between proponent and antagonist and, more importantly, pushed the senators to think more expansively about public administration under the Constitution, was the structure and status of the commission that would oversee any merit system. Pendleton's bill was essentially written by Dorman Eaton and the legislative committee of the New York Civil Service Reform Association (Hoogenboom 1961, 201). It provided for a five-member examining board, serving the president directly during good behavior. Senators raised objections to both the "good behavior" provision and the absence of Senate confirmation of the commissioners in what became another iteration of the struggle over the removal power.

Senators attacking commissioner tenure during good behavior argued that it amounted to ensuring "life tenures for civil officers" and created "an aristocracy or bureauocracy [*sic*] of a class of men beyond the reach of public opinion" (*CR* 1882, 244). Senator John Ingalls of Kansas strenuously urged that the commission "be limited to a distinct and definite term of office, and . . . be held to the American doctrine of direct responsibility to the people, like all other officials. . . . The theory of our system is that when a man is elected or appointed he shall abandon his functions at the end of a certain term to receive the verdict either of the people or of the appointing power as to whether he has discharged his duties well and is fit to fill the place again" (*CR* 1882, 276). Of course, Sen. Ingalls's suggestion that it was fundamental constitutional doctrine that appointed civil officers should face a specific time limit on tenure in office was disingenuous. Nothing in the Constitution requires it, and tenure of office laws were instituted not only so that Congress could better constrain the presidential removal power, but also to enhance rotation and thus the number of offices a party majority could control.

Arguing in favor of tenure during good behavior, Senator Joseph Hawley (R-CT), having obviously done his homework, sounded remarkably like James Madison in 1789.

Sir, I would leave the chief with the fullest responsibility. . . . I believe he has and ought to have the power of removal, as he has the power of appointment, and let the full judgment of the country then come down upon him for any failure to do his duty. He has the power to do his duty; he can command abundantly excellent service if you let him, but the moment you put up a barrier between him and his subordinates, and shield him from responsibility, you scatter it, divide it, and destroy it. . . .

To protect us from such results we rely on the principle of responsibility of the chief. . . . Hold him to his duty. (CR 1882, 244)

Also opposing fixed terms for the commissioners, and in the process driving home the connection between service to the people, neutralization of civil service, and the dichotomy of politics and administration, Senator Warner Miller (R-NY) argued that the Constitution fixed the terms of elective officials because they made policy, and that required direct responsibility to the people. In contrast, "duties which the appointive officer is called on to discharge are usually simply executive or ministerial; they have nothing whatever to do with the policy of the Government or with the methods of government, but with the administration of affairs which are in almost all cases purely clerical" (CR 1882, 316). That many appointed positions in federal administration had long since moved past the clerical to the policy-oriented and adjudicative did not enter into Sen. Miller's argument.

Senators attacking the design of the commission in the Pendleton bill as a body directly in aid to the president sought to have the appointment of commissioners subject to the advice and consent of the Senate. This effort, combined with moves to fix tenure, not only of the commissioners but of most civil officers, thus centered the debate squarely on the removal power. As Senator John Sherman, Pendleton's Ohio colleague, stated it, "the power of removal ought to be checked in some better way than is proposed in this bill" (CR 1882, 210). Charles Thach's question thus was again the focus of contention. "Was the new merit system ultimately an arm of the President or an arm of the Congress?" (Skowronek 1982, 61). By one estimation, merit protection ultimately diminished congressional power in favor of the president (Mashaw 2010).

The outcome of the debate on the commission was its reduction in size from five to three commissioners, to be appointed by the president and confirmed by the Senate, and serving for fixed, staggered terms. These conditions subjected the commission to the push and pull of presidential-congressional struggles over most of its existence (C. G. Hall 1965). Remarkably, however, the commission gained increasing control over the removal power (Kaufman 1965, 53–56), which all the reformers in 1882 had proclaimed was part of the president's basic executive authority, not to be diminished by the creation of a neutral civil service. This consequence would contribute in its own way to the rift between the rhetoric of an ideally subordinate, instrumental administration and the reality of a public administration with constitutive qualities, as evidenced in actual political and governmental practice.

The civil service reform debate of 1882–83 was another in the concentric waves on the surface of American political and administrative development, broadcast out from the impact of the Decision of 1789. A significant portion of the debate centered on which side could prove that its approach to filling federal offices would keep administration obedient to the popular will and avoid bureaucracy. Unlike those in 1789 or 1834–35, the discussions in 1882–83 did not stimulate the kind of thinking that grasped the constitutive dimension in administration in a way that might have led to an alternative conceptualization and design for public administration in the American regime. One reason for the narrow focus of the debate may have been the reformers' single-minded attention to only one method of reform. "There was not very much original thought about the best kind of substitute for spoils beyond competitive entrance examinations and security of tenure" (Mosher 1968, 65). More generally, the Pendleton Act was a reform of the "second state" rather than of the progressive effort to bring a true administrative, regulatory state into being. As George Pendleton's arguments made clear, Congress "could aggrandize the state administrative apparatus of the federal government if they could cloak their proposals in the language of the old republican synthesis: government growth to secure liberty and democratic government" (Hoffer 2007, 107). The Pendleton Act debates proceeded "in familiar coded terms" of second state logic: "simple need, a set of problems requiring practical solutions, and . . . reform the least intrusive and American solution" (135).

Like the 1834–35 removal power discussions, however, the Pendleton Act debate and the more general civil service reform effort did reinforce the incongruity of the Jacksonian reforms. Reformers and political leaders trumpeted the idea of public administration as purely instrumental and subordinate, in connection with a new and spirited surge of demands for popular control and participation. Yet they also pushed for a neutral, expert administration, because they understood and publicly proclaimed it a vital constituent in the moral and democratic transformation of the regime. Along with the distinctive governing style of the second state, "to encode novelty as the most conservative possible response to absolute exigency or as the most practical housekeeping measure to deal with pesky inefficiencies," the result also showed a "disconnect" between the ideas espoused and "acts of enlarging the government" (Hoffer 2007, 197). For a new generation of reflective citizens, the questions they might have been driven to ask, albeit more complicated, were essentially the same as that of their forebears. How could administration be purely neutral, and remain a subordinate instrument of popular will, if it was expanding its authority and reach? With a new set of values at its core—merit and professionalism—would it not have a hand in reshaping the moral pillars of that will?

Representation and Management of Societal Interests: The Interstate Commerce Act

The sharpest counterpoint to the continuing dominance of the instrumental conception of administration came with the struggle over the regulation of interstate commerce and the establishment of a commission to wield that regulatory power. The debate occasioned a spirited exchange of views and ideas among congressmen, other public officials, and prominent private citizens about the proper structure and character, and potential, for public administration in the American system.

The railroads had posed a problem for the American political economy for nearly a decade before Congressman John Reagan of Texas, a Democrat, brought focused legislative attention to it in 1878. A version of the story, grounded in economic theory and claiming that the railroads were behind the push for federal regulation (Kolko 1965), remains a key part of the scholarship on the establishment of interstate commerce regulation. Certainly, because the initial law was only weakly restrictive of the railroads, "some [railroad] executives actually welcomed it as protective cover" (Wiebe 1967, 53). Regulatory initiatives in several states had preceded passage of the Interstate Commerce Act (ICA), however, fomented largely by the Granger movement, with its blend of moral outrage, naked majoritarianism, and the pitting of agrarian versus industrial interests. A diverse cross section of economic interests closed ranks to push for federal regulation (Purcell 1967), and the railroads by and large opposed the final result (Fiorina 1986). Responding to the populist origins of demands for regulation, Reagan told his constituents in 1877 upon leaving for his second post–Civil War term in Congress, "There were no beggars till Vanderbilts and Stewarts and Goulds . . .

shaped the action of Congress and moulded the purposes of government. Then the few became fabulously rich, and the many wretchedly poor . . . and the poorer we are the poorer they would make us" (Wiebe 1967, 8).

Reagan had served two terms in the House of Representatives before the war. He resigned from the House to participate actively in Texas's secession from the Union, and he became postmaster general of the Confederacy. After serving a short prison term at the war's end, he was elected to the House again in 1874. Bringing with him a background as both railway entrepreneur and harsh critic of the railroads, and having broad interests in interstate and foreign trade, he assumed the chairmanship of the House Commerce Committee. In the spring of 1878, he successfully steered his committee to favorable action on his own bill "to regulate interstate commerce and to prohibit unjust discrimination by common carriers" (quoted in Fiorina 1986, 33). The bill languished for seven years, through Senate inaction and the Democrats' loss of control of the House in the Forty-seventh Congress (1881–83). Activity and debate reignited at the end of the Forty-eighth Congress and the beginning of the Forty-ninth, sparked by the Supreme Court decision in *Wabash, St Louis, & Pacific Railway Co. v. Illinois* (118 U.S. 557) declaring state railroad regulation unconstitutional. The legislative reaction to the court's decision came to fruition in the passage of the Interstate Commerce Act of 1887 and the establishment of the Interstate Commerce Commission (ICC) that same year. Originally placed as a bureau of the Interior Department, the ICC gained its status as an independent regulatory commission two years later (Rohr 1986, 95).

A critical aspect of this debate concerned what form the regulation of interstate commerce should take. Illinois senator Shelby Cullom was the principal proponent of a commission. The alternative was reliance on the "common law" and the courts, which Reagan advocated. Reagan defended his approach on the simple populist terms that the courts "were close to the people, and familiar to them" (Rohr 1986, 95) and that as regulatory entities they better fulfilled the fundamentals of constitutional design. In "the best Madisonian tradition Reagan argued that courts were so numerous and dealt with such a wide variety of issues that no single interest would find it practical or possible to control them, though isolated instances of corruption certainly were possible, and indeed were matters of record" (Fiorina 1986, 38 n. 10).

In earlier assessments, the commission idea "had appeared to Reagan an instrument designed to impress the railroad point of view on Congress and the people" (Skowronek 1982, 144). Congressman Reagan and his supporters pressed this and other points of attack as the debate reached its zenith in 1886–87. They expressed concern that a commission could not in practice do what it was being asked to do. This concern reflected in part the enormity of the task, with respect to both geography and the extent of the demand for relief. Yet it was also an insistence that the commission could not do its job well because it could not avoid falling under the influence of the railroads ("agency capture" in current parlance), no matter how pure, competent, and well intentioned the commissioners. With respect to appointments to the commission, Reagan observed that the "vast resources" of the railroads enabled them "to control the best legal and business talent of the country, and would enable them to procure influential men in their interest to appeal to the President in the name of justice and on account of capacity to name such men as would serve their purposes" (CR 1886, 7283).

Reagan and his colleagues pressed the attack still further, however, arguing that even if "clothed with a limited discretion," as promised by commission advocates, regulation by commission placed an unwarranted administrative body between the legislature and the judiciary and between the people and the legislature. This would be a body that, if not wholly unconstitutional, was certainly a foreign threat to the American system. "The American people have as a rule great respect for law and for the action of the judiciary, but they are not accustomed to the administration of the civil law through bureau orders. This system belongs in fact to despotic governments; not to free republics" (CR 1886, 7283).

Congressman Reagan's commentary on this point is really quite remarkable, because, most likely unbeknownst to him, at nearly the same moment Woodrow Wilson was struggling with precisely the problem of how to adapt administrative methods used by despotic governments and employ them to help modernize American democracy. Wilson described the situation vividly in a famous passage in his groundbreaking 1887 essay: "If I see a murderous fellow sharpening a knife cleverly, I can borrow his way of sharpening the knife without borrowing his probable intention to commit murder with it" (1887, 220). Reagan's contention, however, might have served as a warning to Wilson and others that their efforts would face stiff resistance. Thus, in the view of one commission opponent, Representative Charles O'Ferrall of Virginia, it was better to keep it simple and direct. "The Congress of the United States is the commission created by the people for the enactment of laws, and the courts of the country the tribunals for their enforcement. . . . Let those who have been accredited as the representatives of the people here prove themselves equal to the high duties they have assumed. Let them not stand appalled and paralyzed in the face of corporate power; let them give the relief demanded, assume responsibilities, and not throw them off upon a commission that will be responsible to nobody" (CR 1886, 7296).

The reasoning behind the anticommission view in the debate was quite clearly instrumental in its foundations. The people were calling for regulation of the railroads, and the appropriate means had to be found to reach that end; but a commission was too dangerous an instrument to employ, because it could too easily be seized by the railroads for their own purposes. The courts could better serve the public goal of regulation and, like every other political institution, were essential instrumentalities of the popular will. Indeed, as Representative O'Ferrall proclaimed, even the railroads were instruments of the people. "In a word, sir, they are in the intendment of the law the servants and not the masters of the people, and I would act toward them in that fair, just, and equitable manner that should characterize the treatment of a servant, and in return demand of them that consideration due from a servant" (CR 1886, 7293).

Commission opponents seemed to be claiming something more, however. Pursuing "administration of the civil law through bureau orders," they contended, would alter the regime. The introduction of bureaucratic structures and the actions of unaccountable bureaucrats would transform the very essence of the American republic. This appears to have been a much more profound concern for commission opponents than which institution would prove the most effective, but their commentary makes it clear that the two concerns could not be severed and considered separately.

Supporters of the commission idea were hardly unified in their conceptions of what the commission should be, but in their diversity, they managed to articulate images of the proposed ICC that, among other things, had it fulfilling critical niches in modern American governance beyond what the Congress, presidency, or the courts did, while still expressing and embodying important features of American constitutional structure. Senator Cullom regarded the administrative authority embodied in the ICC "as a way to compensate for the deficiencies of a representative body in formulating a regulatory policy" (Skowronek 1982, 146). Hence, Cullom and other commission supporters sought broad, vague delegations of authority to the ICC so that the expertise and deliberative reasoning of the commissioners would lead to the most rational regulatory policy.

In written testimony submitted to Senator Cullom's special investigative committee, the constitutional scholar and jurist Thomas Cooley, who would become the first ICC chairman, envisioned the commission as "combining in its management" the interests of the railroads, "constituting . . . a section by itself of the political community," with "the State representing the popular will and general interests" (quoted in Rohr 1986, 104). Cooley's idea contained a hierarchical aspect, because Cooley used the analogy of municipal government to explain his idea. Municipalities combine state and local power, but the "states are the constitutional masters of local government" (Rohr 1986, 105). Moreover, Cooley, like Representative O'Ferrall, also viewed "corporations as instruments of the state—at least when the state chooses to treat them as instruments" (105). Yet Cooley's conception of the ICC as operating to commingle significant interests in American society seemed to stretch beyond the idea of an administrative entity as simply an instrument of the popular will or of elected representatives. Cooley's subsequent behavior as ICC chairman "carried the clear implication that [the ICC] was ultimately responsible to the Constitution, rather than to the will of elected officials" (110). Indeed, the ICC under Cooley "sought to build administrative authority in order to conserve, protect, reconcile, guide, and educate" (Skowronek 1982, 151), which are activities much more expansive than those one would associate with a neutral, subordinate instrument.

Other commission proponents advocated the idea that the ICC would mediate between key interests in American society, thus performing a representative function. A. T. Hadley, a professor of economics at Yale, envisioned the commission as an intermediary body between the legislature and the railroads (precisely one of John Reagan's principal fears). In Hadley's view, the commission's function would be "publicity"; that is, the commission would represent the interests of the railroads to the public, and the interests of the public to the railroads (Rohr 1986, 97). Similarly, railroad executive Albert Fink pushed for the ICC as "a mediator and counsellor between the railroads and the public" (quoted in Rohr 1986, 97). New York representative Charles B. Baker saw the commission "representing at once public sentiment and the law" (quoted in Rohr 1986, 99). Baker's views suggested that the ICC possessed "its own peculiar constituency, national public sentiment" (99). Indeed, notable in the debate on the ICC is the "remarkable frequency with which the members of the proposed commission were referred to as 'representatives'" (100).

An administrative body that fills a key governing niche, that represents distinctive societal interests, and that, furthermore, commingles core societal interests, not just passively as in an open field of play, but actively as in Cooley's idea of "managing," would appear to be constitutive in its essential nature. This would especially be the case to the extent that it helped to shape the outcome of that interest interaction by defining or redefining what those interests were.

Whether any of those debating the creation of the ICC were at all conscious of the implications for such constitutive impacts that lay in the future is unclear. The debate on the powers the commission would actually wield may have allayed any resulting concerns about the commission's "despotic" potential. The emphasis on a common law remedy for the interstate commerce problem brought many participants in the debate to the conclusion that the commission had to be some kind of court (Rohr 1986). Similarly, the "commission plan avoided an extensive bureaucracy and existed in harmony with a lawyer's model of court-centered administration of public policy" (Hoffer 2007, 160). Others engaged in the debate saw the commission as a more complex institution (Rohr 1986, 97), wielding a mix of legislative, judicial, and executive powers (Hoffer 2007, 161). Senator John Morgan of Alabama observed, "My judgment is that we have combined very skillfully powers derived from each of these departments of the Government in the hands of these commissioners" (CR 1886, 4422). This mixing of powers concerned Morgan. He did not want executive officers wielding legislative and judicial powers, and he offered a cautionary amendment. He warned that failure to clarify the nature of the commissioners' powers would result in the creation of a body of "autocrats."

A concern for the powers that administrative agencies exercise goes to the very heart of the question of public administration's status under the Constitution. The record of the brief debate on Senator Morgan's amendment suggests, however, that senators understood, or at least accepted, the mix of powers they were granting the ICC. Senator Samuel Maxey of Texas rang down the curtain on Morgan's amendment by stating, "It is not a matter of the slightest consequence to me whether the powers are called executive, judicial, legislative, or ministerial. We have defined on the face of the bill the powers which are to be exercised by the commissioners" (CR 1886, 4422). The senators seemed willing, then, to accept that the commission might exercise substantial authority and influence, under the control of a limited grant of discretion, a formula that Theodore Lowi (1979, 96) held up as a model of proper administrative structure and delegation.

In many ways, the debate on the establishment of the ICC stimulated extraordinary thinking and deliberation about administration and its proper character and place in the American governmental and political system. That deliberation was especially important because it took place in public, in exchanges among public officials, scholars, and businesspeople. Indeed, the ICC debate elicited most of the major points subsequently advanced in support of independent regulatory commissions as solutions to the administrative dilemma by progressives like Herbert Croly (1914, 363–66; also see Chambers 1980, 242) and by New Dealer James Landis (1938). The developed argument promoted the idea that commissions should operate with substantial discretion, but only within the narrow sphere defined by their mission and expertise. They should exercise a mix of legislative, executive, and judicial powers, but again only within a narrow sphere, and they should be representative of significant societal interests. The debate associated with these claims also elicited the two central criticisms that have come to dominate both politics and scholarship concerning independent commissions: the threat of interest-group capture (Barkow 2010; M. H. Bernstein 1955; Huntington 1952; Posner 1974) and the problem of vague delegations of power (Lowi 1979).

Despite the impressive content of the ICC debate, its immediate impact on the administrative dilemma was relatively inconsequential. The principal public focus at the time was still on civil service reform—the transformation of the character of the entire executive establishment into a wholly neutral, subordinate instrument. In the long run, moreover, the debate on the creation of the ICC probably contributed more to public disdain for bureaucracy than to construction of an alternative conceptual foundation for public administration. Although the formula for proper delegation of power that Lowi pointed to did emerge during the debate, it did not encompass a coherent conception of administration, clearly articulated and anchored in recognition of its instrumental and constitutive qualities and the tensions between them. Several conceptions of the commission that merit categorization as constitutive thinking did surface, but they did not fit together into some overarching idea, nor did the thinkers attempt to make them fit together. If anything, the court-like conception that dominated thinking about the nature of the commission during the debate inhibited more than it facilitated more expansive thinking about the constitutional status of a growing administrative establishment.

With a chairman of Thomas Cooley's background, the early years of the ICC might have generated a conception of the commission as having a constitutive role in American governance, but Cooley's tenure was cut short by poor health (Rohr 1986, 106–10). Of course, the Supreme Court, working through its own version of the dominant instrumental conception, undermined Cooley's efforts anyway (Skowronek 1982, 154–60). Cooley had advanced concept-stretching ideas, to be sure, but he seems never to have tied the ideas together with a unifying argument. The ICC would eventually function in a representative capacity and not only serve but also shape policy aims through its expertise and mix of powers, but this autonomy and policy-making authority went beyond any justification that the founding legislation could have provided (see Lowi 1979, 101–4). When in subsequent decades that autonomy and authority appeared to fulfill John Reagan's prophecy of agency capture, experience reinforced acceptance of the importance of regarding administrative agencies as subordinate instruments, to be tightly controlled by the people through their elected representatives.

The establishment of the ICC thus presents a prime opportunity for observing the consequences of the tensions between an ideology of administrative instrumentalism and subordination and the reality of public bureaucracies functioning in ways that noticeably influence the character of the polity. It also provides a prime lesson in the necessity of designing both the parts and the whole of public administration with its essential constitutiveness recognized. This lesson was reinforced when intensive debate flared again in Congress over railroad regulation and the powers of the ICC in connection with the Hepburn Act. The legislation sought to empower the ICC to set "just and reasonable" maximum shipping rates and to establish a uniform system of railroad industry accounting, including the authority to review railroad company financial records. President Theodore Roosevelt forcefully promoted the legislation in his famous speaking tour in the spring and fall of 1905 (Milkis and Nelson 2003, 206; also see Tulis 1987, 97–101, 108–110).

From a twenty-first-century vantage point, the intense focus on the railroads may seem misplaced, but the public concerns about and harsh criticisms of the railroads were both important and far reaching. "Public concern about the corrupting influence of business corporations on the nation's political life naturally picked out the railroads as a prime target. As vast arterial systems, reaching into every corner of the land and wielding immense economic and political power, they [posed threats] that went to the heart of a republican political culture. They thereby raised important 'constitutive issues' about the relationship between private power and public welfare" (Harrison 2004, 56). Proponents of expanding ICC authority again had to confront, and sought to disparage, judicial alternatives to address the continued problems of unfair rate structures. Recourse to the courts was expensive, inefficient, and thus a "futile remedy," argued Illinois Republican Rep. James Robert Mann (CR 59.1:2242–8). Proponents further argued that no court review of ICC rate setting decisions was necessary, as rates fixed by the ICC were the legitimate exercise of Congress's commerce power. Although there were again various expressions of the threats to the republic that concentrations of bureaucratic power posed, primarily from Democrats still adhering to Jeffersonian-Jacksonian ideology, the Hepburn Act debate centered primarily on the same central concern as the original ICC debates, namely, what constitutes true administrative functions, given the mingling of legislative, executive, and judicial powers in the ICC authorizations. Theodore Roosevelt insisted that the function of supervising railroad rates was "unequivocally administrative" (quoted in Harrison 2004, 67). There was, however, a new, more sweeping worry expressed by opponents, that, as Augustus Bacon warned, power was shifting and "the controlling factor in national legislation is not in Congress . . . but in the President" (quoted in Harrison 2004, 249).

The grant of authority to the ICC in the Hepburn Act "constituted a radical advance" (Harrison 2004, 81) that made it a "landmark in the history of federal regulation of private industry" (Milkis and Nelson 2003, 207). Yet this was still only the beginning of new efforts stretching across more than 50 years to come to grips with the nation's growth and expansion and the administrative demands such development generated. These developments intensified the political dilemma an active, formative administrative establishment poses for American aspirations to self-government. Congresses of the last two decades of the nineteenth century "laid the groundwork for supplanting the second state mind-set with the third state approach" (Hoffer 2007, 167). That third state approach of the progressives meant confronting the demands of modernity across a much broader front. As the new century arrived, progressive political leaders wrestled with the tensions and contradictions posed by administration in a liberal democratic regime in new confrontations with powerful business interests, as in the Hepburn Act, but also in other areas of the rapidly changing political economy, such as the reconstruction of the banking system and improvements to the purity of foods and drugs. As Senator Bacon's warnings intimated, however, nowhere was the dilemma more dramatic than in the effort to redefine executive power.

Presidents, Popular Will, and Public Administration

President William Howard Taft sent a special message to Congress in June 1912 addressing "the need for a national budget." In his message, Taft argued that "the executive, as the one officer of the government who represents the people as a whole, lacks the means for keeping in touch with public opinion with respect to administrative proposals" (Skowronek 1982, 188). President Taft's point was that a national budget would provide the appropriate vehicle for reinforcing the link between the president and the people, particularly in connection with "a well-considered executive program for governmental activity" (188). In a subsequent letter to the secretary of the treasury with copies to all department heads, Taft claimed authority to require department heads to provide information to him in a form that could be the basis of a national budget. "Under the Constitution the President is intrusted with the executive power and is responsible for the acts of heads of departments and their subordinates as his agents, and can use them to assist him in his constitutional duties" (Weber 1919, 90). That Taft had to assert such authority seems remarkable today. At the time, however, the relationship between the president and the executive departments was still fluid, and it would remain so until well into the New Deal.

Scholars have judged Taft harshly as president, particularly in comparison with his more celebrated presidential contemporaries. He was demonstrably weak because of his lack of political skills in the face of extraordinary public demands and because of his pursuit of an untenable mix of progressivism and conservatism (e.g., Chambers 1980, 154–60; Milkis and Nelson 2003, 219–24). He consequently suffered complete repudiation in the 1912 election as the regular Republican candidate and incumbent president, winning the electoral votes of only two small states.

Nevertheless, in his efforts to attain more centralized and coordinated budgeting under presidential control, and in the emphasis on the interconnections among the president, public opinion, and public administration that those efforts signified, Taft demonstrated that his progressive thinking was eminently consistent with the answers Theodore Roosevelt and Woodrow Wilson offered to the central political question of the era: how to bring about the governmental centralization and expansion of national administration required by the rapidly accelerating social, economic, and political demands of modernity. Too late for his presidency, Taft did present a thorough and forceful answer in the "managerial view of the presidency" (Rohr 1989a, 17) that he rendered as chief justice in *Myers v. U.S.* (272 U.S. 52 [1926]). As Taft declared at the heart of his majority opinion, "There is nothing in the Constitution which permits a distinction between the removal of the head of a department or a bureau, when he discharges a political duty of the President or exercises his discretion, and the removal of executive officers engaged in the discharge of their other normal duties. The imperative reasons requiring an unrestricted power to remove the most important of his subordinates in their most important duties must, therefore, control the interpretation of the Constitution as to all appointed by him" (134). Thus, Taft took the link connecting the Decision of 1789 and the Jacksonian presidency and extended it to establish the constitutional-legal basis for the progressive presidency. But by the time of his decision, Roosevelt, and, even more so, Wilson, had already undertaken most of the heavy lifting required for the political reconstruction of the presidency. That reconstruction centered on leadership of public opinion, leadership of Congress through policy initiative, and raising the visibility and expanding the reach of national administration, making it the primary institutional structure for national governance.

THE RHETORICAL PRESIDENCY

Theodore Roosevelt established the foundation for "progressive" speech and practice concerning the relationship between the president and the public by making direct yet moderate appeals to the public on issues, especially railroad regulation, that he thought posed dangers for the nation. He thus "ushered in the 'rhetorical presidency'—that is, the use of popular rhetoric as a principal technique of presidential leadership" (Milkis and Nelson 2003, 204; see, more generally, Tulis 1987, ch. 4). Roosevelt portrayed his transformation of presidential behavior as an effort to synthesize the Hamiltonian emphasis on a strong executive with the Jeffersonian emphasis on popular rule. Roosevelt argued that Abraham Lincoln's leadership perfectly embodied this synthesis but that it ought to apply in day-to-day governing and not just during national crises. Consistent with progressive reform aims, Roosevelt portrayed the synthesis as remaking the presidency into the "steward of the public welfare" (quoted in Milkis 2009, 182). This enabled the progressives, especially by the time they reached the pinnacle of their political strength in the 1912 election, to solve the riddle of their twin aspirations toward a national form of direct democracy, and a more centralized, executive-centered government with administrative agencies playing an ever more expansive role. By pushing the legitimation of direct, popular appeals by presidents in times not amounting to national emergencies, Roosevelt showed Americans that the popular will had a conduit to the corridors of power, not through the now suspect and corrupt parties, but through more direct and even personal connections to the president.

In tune with his redefinition of the president's relationship with the public and its role as steward of national welfare through social and economic reform,

Roosevelt sought to solidify the role of a growing, more expert, and distinctly nonpartisan administration as central to guiding the development of United States as a modern industrial nation. However, Roosevelt faced a fragmented administrative establishment that had grown largely outside of, and with little influence from, the presidency. Thus, with the popular support and electoral stability he enjoyed as president, Roosevelt attempted "to forge an executive-centered reconstitution of civil administration. . . . The neutral civil service was to be transformed into a separate class of citizens, a state caste insulated from party and Congress and dependent in all its interests on executive officers and the President's [civil service] commission" (Skowronek 1982, 179). This portrayal suggests that Roosevelt might have envisioned administration in constitutive terms, as a fundamental component in the reshaping of national governance. For the most part, however, Roosevelt's actions, although taking "support for civil service reform . . . beyond a moralistic statement against the spoils system" and "[g]iving teeth to the authority granted the President under the Pendleton Act," were largely tactical, aiming to make "the merit civil service into an instrument of executive-centered government" (180).

As president, Roosevelt went no further than this instrumental orientation in his rhetoric and actions regarding administration's governing status. By 1912, however, during his Progressive Party campaign, Roosevelt envisioned the progressive transformation of American industrial society in service to national welfare primarily, albeit not exclusively, in administrative terms. The party platform, "A Contract With the People," included calls for a national health service, national social insurance, a federal securities commission, and a federal interstate trade commission ("Panaceas Offered by the New Party," 1912). It clearly anticipated the full-blown administrative state, and even the welfare state that came fully into being during the New Deal. Indeed, one might say that Roosevelt and the Progressive Party would have administered the government into what they wished it to be, to paraphrase Madison's swipe at Hamilton, a denunciation that Roosevelt might have been proud to receive.

Yet Roosevelt, although a voracious reader and prolific author, did not confront these tensions and conflicts publicly in a way that suggested sustained thoughtfulness about their systemic implications. It was left to the likes of Herbert Croly, progenitor of the political synthesis of the progressives, and Woodrow Wilson, the first prominent American to give sustained attention to the role of public administration in constitutional governance, to probe more deeply these tensions and how the formative power of administration might be legitimated.

Administrative Stability and Social Improvement: Herbert Croly

Herbert Croly appeared out of relative obscurity to become one of the major intellectual drivers of progressivism. This was no accident, as Croly set out with his first and most influential book, *The Promise of American Life* (1909), to reshape the philosophical foundations of American governance in the direction of what would become modern liberalism. Like Roosevelt, Croly was a proponent of Hamiltonian nationalism and executive power fused with Jeffersonian commitment to popular rule. Croly expanded and deepened the synthesis, promoting a new political order in which the bonds of the old Jeffersonian-Jacksonian constitutionalism and political tradition would be broken, releasing in government a necessary energy to tackle the formidable social problems of modernity. He envisioned "a democracy devoted to the welfare of the whole people by means of a conscious labor of individual and social improvement . . . [,] precisely the sort of democracy which demands for its realization the aid of the Hamiltonian nationalistic organization and principle" (214). Consistent with Hamilton's ideas, Croly saw this principle as requiring that an energetic national executive take charge of protecting and promoting the national welfare, by taking the lead on initiating policy.

Croly's attention to administration in *The Promise of American Life* centered almost exclusively on the need for further civil service reform, and for reorganization of the executive to ensure greater unity of command and the proper vesting of authority and responsibility that went with it. It was not until he published *Progressive Democracy* (1914) that Croly attempted to define more thoroughly the role of public administration in the new progressive social and political order. In doing so, he wrestled with the question of how to conceptualize administration and properly situate it in the regime given its instrumental and formative qualities. Croly pursued the matter extensively in a chapter revealingly titled "The Administration as an Agent of Democracy." Croly began by explaining how traditional American two-party democracy had not only interfered with genuine popular rule but had also enfeebled administration. He then addressed the deeprooted American revulsion toward powerful administrative officials. He argued that progressive democracy did not seek "ordinary bureaucratic government" (351) based on coercion, the sort of government prevalent in Europe. Instead, because progressive democracy was based on popular political power and "the consent of public opinion, administrative action cannot very well become an agency of oppression" (353).

Croly then drew a sharp distinction between "the administration and the executive" (1914, 354). Under progressive democracy, the executive is "essentially a representative agency," whose "primary business is that of organizing a temporary majority of the electorate, and of carrying its will into effect." The executive is "primarily a law-giver and only secondarily an agency for carrying out existing laws" (355), thus offering a definition of the executive in parallel to Woodrow Wilson's description of the role of the president in *Constitutional Government* (1908). Croly proceeded to argue that because the "organization of majority rule" by the executive is temporary and "fluid," it "might degenerate into a succession of meaningless and unprofitable experiments, which would not get enough continuity either to accomplish stable results or to teach significant lessons" (359). Hence, a critical role is defined for public administration. It assists the executive "in converting his program into well-framed and well-administered laws" (356), and it serves "as an agency of political continuity and stability" (358).

It is no surprise that Croly would build on Alexander Hamilton's ideas about the role of public administration in maintaining regime stability. Many scholars have since developed the idea further (see, for example, Long 1952; Marx 1957; Terry 1990; B. D. Wood 1988), and I examine it in more depth in chapter 7. As did Hamilton, Croly's characterization of administration as an agency of stability captures both its instrumental and its constitutive qualities. He saw the stability and permanence of administration as providing it the opportunity to gain knowledge and experience from the much greater programmatic experimentation likely to be seen in progressive democracy with policy initiative in energetic executive hands. The knowledge and experience administration would gain could then guide the popular will and the policy initiatives of temporary executives away from stalemate and toward the goal of real, permanent social improvement. In short, despite the shifting passions of the electorate, especially as expressed in presidential elections, administration would ensure long-term continuity in progressive program development. Again, this is almost exactly what Hamilton argued (Bailey 2008), and it would moderate the energetic executive that even Taft was keen on promoting. More important, as part of this process, Croly saw administration having a teaching function to perform requiring "an element of independent authority." Croly argued that the "conscientious and competent administrator of an official social program would need and be entitled to the same kind of independence and authority in respect to public opinion as that which has been traditionally granted to a common law judge" (361). Like the Whigs, then, Croly drew parallels between the administrator and the judge.

As John Rohr expressed the idea, "the skills of the administrator who listens to the public in some sort of open forum, however informal, are not altogether unlike those of the judge" (1986, 53).

Thus, Croly conceived of public administration as instrumental because it functions as an agent of the popular will expressed through elected representation. Administration is an agent specifically in pursuit of the end of enlightened social improvement, an end "demanded by prevailing political and economic conditions and ideals" (1914, 358). But Croly also argued that administration, through its stability, knowledge, scientific expertise, and experience, would play a vital part in defining the exact meaning of that enlightened social improvement. Although he characterized administration "as the instrument of a social program," it therefore, "must have a hand in creating the social experience which it is also recording" (371). Finally, Croly argued that the "administrator must manage to be representative" (372), by keeping "articulate with the democracy, not by voting expedients, but by its own essential nature" (373). Thus, administration properly understood would embody the long-run essence of progressive democracy.

Croly clearly sought to reconcile the constitutional need for administration to remain subordinate to the elected executive with administration's own need for the authorization and capability to operate with sufficient autonomy to function as a distinctive political institution within the regime. It is not clear, however, to what extent either political leaders or attentive citizens took seriously Croly's conception of public administration's status and role. In contrast, neither leaders nor ordinary citizens could completely ignore the much more extensively developed ideas of Woodrow Wilson, who enjoyed much greater prominence as public intellectual and national educational leader, and who carried his ideas onto the most visible national stage as candidate and president.

POLITICS, ADMINISTRATION, AND STATESMANSHIP: WOODROW WILSON

In major European countries during much of the nineteenth century, scholars and public officials alike undertook a substantial effort to develop public administration as a distinct institutional exercise of public power. Tocqueville's visit to the United States, ostensibly to study the administration of the American prison system, was an early sign of the serious attention to the administrative art that he would exhibit in his political career (L. Smith 1942). A distinctive facet of the developmental effort Tocqueville's American adventure signaled was the conceptualization of "multiple differentiations among judicial, legislative, executive, and administrative power. . . . All were different forms of power, and all had separate contributions to make to the polity" (Martin 1988, 632). This suggests that acceptance of a separate institutional sphere for the exercise of a distinct power deemed *administrative* must be part of the basis for recognizing administration's constitutiveness.

On the western side of the Atlantic, scholarship began to bristle with activity regarding the development of public administration in the latter three decades of the century. This was happening in conjunction, of course, with civil service reform and interstate commerce regulation, as well as municipal government reform and national budget reform. Scholars and reform activists were fairly well versed on European thinking (see Karl 1987; Martin 1988; Van Riper 1983), although it is not altogether clear to what extent the developing American thinking self-consciously followed that of the Europeans. Certainly, Woodrow Wilson had read widely, including the work of Lorenz von Stein, whose 1887 *Handbuch der Verwaltungslehre* provided much of the foundation for Wilson's essay "The Study of Administration." Yet the driving imperative behind his first direct treatment of the subject was to create a clear distinction between European thinking on administration and American political values. This distinction would prove central to Wilson's theorizing about administration and by extension his eventual embrace of the presidency as the solution to the conundrum administration posed for the American constitutional system.

In the first section of his essay, for example, Wilson admitted that administrative *methods* must be borrowed from the Europeans, because Europe is where the science of administration developed. But borrowed methods had to be grafted onto new roots, "adapted, not to a simple and compact, but to a complex and multiform state, and made to fit highly decentralized forms of government" (W. Wilson 1887, 202). John Reagan's position on this question, articulated during the debate on interstate commerce regulation, strongly implied that the prospects for such adaptation might not be favorable. Wilson anticipated the difficulty, acknowledging that the methods had to be "radically" Americanized, "in thought, principle, and aim" (202).

Such an adaptation of methods seemed plausible to Wilson, for he was willing to adopt the neutralization strategy of the civil service reformers that sought to separate administration from politics. "Most important to be observed is the truth already so much and so fortunately insisted upon by our civil service reformers; namely, that administration lies outside the proper sphere of *politics*. Administrative questions are not political questions" (W. Wilson 1887, 210; em-

phasis in original). Wilson had also addressed the separation of politics and administration in his treatise *Congressional Government* (1885), wherein he insisted
on "the drawing of a sharp line of distinction between those offices which are
political and those which are non-political" (W. Wilson [1885] 1981, 180).

Thus, in his exploration of the politics-administration dichotomy, Wilson initially cast public administration in distinctively instrumental terms. He compared administration to the "methods of the counting house" and to "machinery" (W. Wilson 1887, 210). John Rohr connects Wilson's instrumental conception
of administration to his preference for the parliamentary form of government
(1986, 75). "An instrumental view of administration fits neatly into a model of
government that rests on legislative supremacy. The people elect their representatives, who, acting in their sovereign capacity, pass laws which are duly
carried out by the Public Administration" (85). Wilson's treatment of the instrumental dimension of administration was not as simplistic as it initially appeared, however. In his final written work of a distinctly scholarly nature, *Constitutional Government*, Wilson acknowledged that the executive was regarded
"as little more than an instrumentality for carrying into effect the laws which
our representative assemblies originate." But he went on to insist that "it is by
no means a necessary inference that [those who administer the law] shall be
in leading strings and shall be reduced to be the mere ministerial agents of a
representative assembly" (1908, 15). Moreover, Wilson proceeded to point out
that "no part of any government is better than the men to whom that part is
entrusted. The gauge of excellence is not the law under which the officers act,
but the conscience and intelligence with which they apply it, if they apply it at
all" (17). In short, citizen experience of the law, whether good or bad, is constituted as much by the actions of administrators as by the statutory designs of
legislators.

Even in his early disquisitions on the politics-administration dichotomy,
Wilson did not just give expression to an instrumental conception of public administration as the simple and safe solution to the problem of importing and
adapting the methods of "despotic governments" to American circumstances.
He accepted that it would be necessary to place those methods into the hands of
a well-trained administrative cadre, although not in quite the same form as Roosevelt's "state caste," and giving those hands sufficient space to operate without
violating the principle of popular sovereignty. In doing so, Wilson began to wres-
tle with delineating the place of public administration, with its instrumental *and*
constitutive dimensions, in an American democracy facing "those enormous

burdens of administration which the needs of this industrial and trading age are so fast accumulating" (W. Wilson 1887, 218).

Unsatisfied with his first attempt at defining the full scope of public administration's role in the rapidly modernizing American polity, over the course of the following two decades, Wilson developed a conception of administration that sought to reconcile the profound importance to and impact of administration on a still relatively immature regime with the dominant ideology of administrative subservience to popular will. This conception emerged piecemeal, and Wilson was unable to bring all the pieces together into a grand treatise—the "Philosophy of Politics"—he envisioned. Nevertheless, from his classroom lectures, his text *The State* (1890), and numerous essays and public talks, four primary elements of his effort to delineate and legitimate public administration's status and role are clearly evident.

First, Wilson made clear his view that administration did not consist of the mere instrumental function of carrying formal, written law into effect. It went beyond "mere executive management" and a concern only with "the mechanism of government" (Link et al., 1966–1994, 7:114–15). Administration was grounded in fundamental political principles and the historical development of constitutions, and thus not merely a matter of applying business principles to government. Far more, administration was a part of what constituted the vitality of the state and the living, breathing commotion of public endeavor. Public administration thus had to embody the peculiarities—the "national habit and national sentiment" (116)—of a given nation-state and its origins, growth, and likely future developmental directions.

As part of this first component of his conception of administration, Wilson put great weight on what he called administrative integration. As an institution—an organ of the state—and as the premier form of modern power—the power of "coordinations of organizations" and "the irresistible energy and efficiency of harmony and cooperation" (Link et al., 1966–1994, 17:135–36)—Wilson did not accept that administration could be casually, or worse, theoretically, divided into multilevel spheres. Administration had to be understood as an organic whole to enhance its effectiveness in aiding national development and adaptation to modernity. Connecting administration to such imperative yet practical aims was central to Wilson's legitimation effort.

Second, Wilson identified administration as the realm of the pragmatic, of what it was possible for the state to do. It concerned the practical and workable, the sphere of action. It "sees government in contact with the people" and "touches, directly or indirectly, the whole practical side of social endeavor" (116). Wilson thus argued that the scope of administrative power was "considerably wider and much more inclusive" than the executive power of classical liberal theory. "Besides the duty of executing positive law, there rest upon the administrative organs of every State those duties of provident protection and wise cooperation and assistance," whether "explicitly enjoined by [legislative] enactment" or not, that enable the government to fulfill its functions of ministering to the welfare of its citizens (130).

Third, Wilson articulated a particular notion about the relationship between law and administration, portraying it as tethered to law but not encircled by it. As an appendage of the state, administration by necessity had to confront "that great question" concerning the proper functions of government, because "the functions of government are in a very real sense independent of legislation, and even of constitutions." They are "as old as government and inherent in its very nature." Furthermore, the volume and detail of positive law masked the reality that "administration cannot wait upon legislation, but must be given leave, or take it, to proceed without specific warrant in giving effect to the characteristic life of the State" (Link et al., 1966–1994, 7:121). By doing so, administration was "indirectly a constant source of public law. It is through Administration that the State makes a test of its own powers and of the public needs,—makes [a] test also of law, its efficiency, suitability, etc." (138). Law exerted a pull on administrative action that defined a "sphere of administrative authority . . . as wide as the sphere in which it may move without infringing the laws, statutory or customary, either in their letter or in their reasonable inferential meaning" (150). The need for law to define as precisely as possible the nature and extent of its pull on administration was a central theme of Wilson's 1912 presidential campaign speeches as he sought to contrast his idea of "regulated competition" with Roosevelt's "regulated monopoly" in dealing with concentrations of economic power (Cook 2002).

Given these first three components, one way of understanding Wilson's conception of public administration's role in a democratic polity is that he saw administration as occupying the social and temporal space where dynamic social life was translated into knowledge—sometimes incomplete, sometimes inaccurate—and in turn into the raw material for the deliberative and often wrenching process of formalizing and codifying social habits and experience in written laws. Public administration does not just carry out such formal law, nor does it just fill in many of the gaps left by law. It also seeks to learn what it is practical for the state to do in the face of continuing change in habits and forms of social interchange growing out of such forces as economic growth and expanding racial, ethnic, and cultural interaction. Because of its special position in the polity, administration can more systematically assemble abundant material on which to base the reform of existing law, the shaping of new law, and even the reform or reconstruction of constitutions.

From this conception, Wilson went one step further, and the fourth component in his analysis was the most extensive and complex aspect of his conception of the place of administration in a democratic regime. Wilson portrayed administration as playing the vital role in a liberal democracy of balancing public and private on a daily basis. Through its actions, administration defines in continuously recurring fashion what does and does not constitute governmental interference in private life, particularly private economic activity. Administration "rests its whole front along the line which is drawn in each State between Interference and Laissez faire" (116). As a result of this aspect of its role, added to its more general station as continuing observer of and participant in governmental contact with social life, administration is "the State's experiencing organ" (138). By testing laws already on the books, by taking action on cases for which no law directly and obviously applies, and by repeatedly probing for what is practical in terms of the state's involvement in the private sphere, the "Real Functions of the Administration are not merely ministerial: they are also adaptive, guiding, discretionary" (Link et al., 1966–1994, 9:31).

Although he did not express it in quite this way, Wilson clearly argued that administration was fundamentally engaged in the signature dynamic of modern democratic politics: the ongoing reconstitution of the regime. Wilson accepted that the bulk of public administration's work and obligations did lie with the instrumental task of policy management, but he regarded public administration's engagement in policy development—the making or remaking of laws, and even constitutions—as its most far-reaching and vital task. Wilson's thinking in this regard superseded his initial association with the axiomatic division between administration and policy-making politics that became enshrined in orthodox public administration theory. Wilson did insist that for the more instrumental and mechanistic aspects of policy management and day-to-day governing, the political maneuvering and blatant party biases acceptable in the policy formulation process ought not to interfere. Yet viewing governance in a liberal democratic state more broadly, Wilson saw administration continuously and deeply intertwined with policy making. Indeed, if public administration was to function as Wilson envisioned it in his most expansive thinking, administrative entities and the public servants who staff them could not avoid being engaged in the continuously evolving endeavor to articulate the aims and aspirations of a national polity.

Wilson recognized, however, that this work of public administration was the most difficult to legitimate in regimes of popular sovereignty. It was this realization that led him to expand on Roosevelt's stewardship presidency and refashion it into a full-blown reconception of the presidency in the constitutional system. This reconception envisioned the presidency as bridging the Constitution's separation-of-powers divide between the legislative and executive spheres, shaping and harnessing public opinion to guide both policy design and policy management, and thus ensuring the legitimacy of administration's expansive role by binding it to both statutory design and popular will. Using the newly emergent rhetorical techniques, and the expanded range of public forums the president could access, Wilson signaled as both candidate and president his assurance of the safety and legitimacy of administrative entities continuously and substantially engaged in the experiencing, informing, policy-shaping functions he envisioned. He did so by combining party leadership with the art of direct popular appeals to create the primary vehicle for closing the constitutional gulf. Wilson sought to shift the party system away from functioning principally as the means by which state and local politicians, and hence Congress, would place shackles on executive power. Instead, the party system would be the primary conduit by which the president could link leadership of public opinion and leadership of policy making in Congress in service to national purposes and national development.

Wilson fully accepted the progressive shift of primary control over administration from Congress to the presidency, although he envisioned the president as primarily leader of opinion and policy, not as chief administrator. This "dictated his working theory of executive organization and devolution. It was the simple and cogent theory of reliance upon the heads of departments" (Macmahon 1958, 113). He thus granted wide latitude over administration to his department heads while retaining tight control over policy development and articulation. The result is that Wilson laid on top of the already well-established interest-based character of the federal government's administrative structure the foundation for what in subsequent decades would be called "vertical functional autocracies," generating "picket-fence federalism" (Seidman and Gilmour 1986, 197) reflecting that national policy and national control had expanded into realms that were formerly the nearly exclusive province of the states. Most of Wilson's successors would adopt his rhetorical techniques and leadership practices in some form, but save for Franklin Roosevelt, none of them would do so with a conscious recognition of administration's formative effects and the need therefore to tend continuously to its legitimacy. Indeed, to expand their power through the plebiscitary elements implicit in the rhetorical presidency, they would give voice to new versions of the dominant claim of administration's instrumental subservience.

The Paradox of Progressive Reform

As the writings of Woodrow Wilson and Herbert Croly suggest, the Progressive Era was incontrovertibly a great intellectual watershed for public administration in American government and politics. At no time before or since have scholars and intellectuals who were also public figures and political leaders engaged in such a broadly and deeply searching enterprise to understand the nature of public administration and situate it properly within the constitutional system. Because political leaders were involved, a great deal of the enterprise was conducted in public view. Among their greatest insights, the progressives recognized and were willing to act on what the Jeffersonians and Jacksonians had, somewhat surprisingly, resisted, namely, that democratic politics by definition would remake the regime of the Constitution, almost continuously in small ways, and on occasion in big and dramatic ways. It was an insight that Tocqueville had tried to convey, but which many casual followers of the Frenchman have missed in their celebration of his discovery that the regime had some built-in safeguards against the tendency of democracy toward administrative centralization. In an important way, the progressives sought to preserve and even enhance those safeguards while harnessing the advantages of centralization. One consequence of that enterprise is that the progressives laid the groundwork for changes in the public philosophy with respect to public administration's constitutional and political role that would fully emerge in the New Deal.

Progressive thinkers and political leaders left their project of political reordering unfinished, however, struggling as they did with both the staying power of the Jeffersonian-Jacksonian ideology and their own internal disagreements about how best to reconcile their commitments to a new kind of popular rule with the need for expansion of national administrative capacity. Thus, in their impact on public thinking and political action, the progressives reinforced more than they altered the prevailing conception of administration as purely instrumental and subordinate to the popular will. To appreciate fully the possibilities and limitations on public administration's contributions to American self-government, it is critical to understand why the efforts of the progressives produced this paradoxical result.

During the Gilded Age the spoils system and the consequent political competition and political corruption obscured the continuing development of new administrative structures and practices (Mashaw 2010, 1381). No national political leader would have touted such development as heralding a new political order, for under the sway of the party system and the old republican ideology, the best that those promoting a stronger national state could muster were "second state" arguments about the need for practical and limited administrative responses to newly emergent social problems, especially the suffering of particular groups. The continued growth of these administrative structures and the expanded opportunities for corruption that such growth offered under the control of the spoils precipitated the attack on that system of party control of administration. In turn, that attack forced a confrontation over what or who represented the national state in everyday governance. Unfortunately, for a proper understanding of the nature of public administration and its role under the Constitution, the mix of reform aims, ideas, and interests at play in this confrontation resulted in a debate that primarily centered on whether the parties, or a "new bureaucratic class" (Mashaw 2010, 1391), properly represented the state.

Surely some political leaders among those expressing fear of rule by bureaucrats realized that such fear was unwarranted, as the growing administrative complex of the federal government was largely a disjointed set of formally organized government clientele, the administrators of which would never amount to an all-encompassing bureaucratic class. Indeed, reformers touted a new breed of administrator based on specialized professionalism and expertise that dovetailed nicely with the increasingly interest-based structure of national administration, producing a strong orientation of administrators to the interest-based missions of their agencies and not to some overarching norm of service to the state. Nevertheless, opponents of reform and the growth of a more vigorous national state, whether through passion or cunning, deftly delivered their anti-bureaucracy jeremiads, well-grounded in the old republican ideology with its roots in Whiggish fears of the power of the ministries to undermine both liberty and popular rule.

To achieve their goal of displacing the parties as the primary vehicle of representation and the primary constraint on the reach of national administrative power, civil service reformers had to argue that nonpartisan, politically neutral administrators were in fact even more subservient to the popular will than they had been under tight party control. When they actually began to achieve their aims via the Pendleton Act and the political imperatives that drove presidents to expand rapidly federal administrative positions covered by the merit system, reformers had to scramble to devise a substitute source of political control over administration that would demonstrate the neutral subservience they claimed. That substitute had to sufficiently reassure their many fellow citizens still honestly fearful of administrative power, and it had to successfully counter the attacks of those in national office who, still committed to the old ideology, were antagonistic toward the new, neutralized, professionalized civil service as a threat to their own power. Despite the more expansive thinking of the likes of Croly and Wilson, the reformers' commitment to their conception of a politically neutral, professional, and subservient administration left them with no constitutionally and politically coherent alternative conception of public administration's role in the regime that could capture and effectively convey its dual instrumental and constitutive qualities. Thus, the progressive response to their success in displacing the parties was a strategy of continuing to build on the existing interest-based foundation for administrative expansion while trying to bring it under the control of a reconceived national political executive, although neither the parties nor Congress were ready to capitulate (Skowronek 1982, 211, 247, 284).

Roosevelt and Taft initiated an effort to construct an "administrative presidency" to go along with the rhetorical one (Milkis 2007). Yet their initial efforts faltered because of worries about Roosevelt's aims for a new administrative caste that Wilson ably exploited in the 1912 election campaign. Wilson's attack on Roosevelt's "regulated monopoly" notion was rooted in his fundamental concern for the need to carefully legitimate an expanded role for administration in governing, a concern dictating that he articulate a plausible constraint on the scope of administration's governing role to limit the risk of the rise of bureaucracy in the true sense of the word—rule by bureaucrats. This Wilson tried to do in the form of his advocacy for "definite law" (Cook 2007, 170–75), because he regarded bureaucracy in that true sense as the greatest threat to harnessing the power of administration to make a truly modern form of American self-government. Hence, Wilson's conception of the president as party and national leader, combined with his extended scholarly examination of the nature of administration, led him to be more ambivalent about the notion that administration was strictly subordinate to and the instrument solely of the president. The consequence was "abandonment of the idea that administrative control required independent and imposing executive machinery . . . [and a] turn toward a cooperative system that would join President and Congress through reliance on party and department heads" (Skowronek 1982, 195).

It is important to reiterate that such action was not inconsistent with Wilson's ideals, since in his attempt to see a way around the debilitating effects of separation of powers, Wilson "preferred that the president and Congress be fully integrated into, and implicated in, each others' activities. . . . Cooperation was especially necessary because the president lacked the energy he needed, energy that could be provided only by policy backed by Congress and its majority" (Tulis 1987, 123). By 1916, however, "Wilson's cooperative partnership of President and Congress in administrative affairs had turned into an aggressive congressional counteroffensive for control over civil administration" (Skowronek 1982, 198). That counteroffensive reached a fevered pitch in the debate over the Lever Food and Fuel Control Act of 1917. Opponents of the legislation's grant of sweeping presidential powers over the core necessities of life and economic functions, which would be directly delegated to the heads of the specially created food and fuel administrations, warned of food and fuel dictators with a power that was "vicious and unconstitutional" ("Assails Food Bill as Dictatorial," 1917). By the end of the First World War, an "institutional stalemate" prevailed, "with administrators themselves being asked to make policy decisions in a political system defiant of authoritative controls" (Skowronek 1982, 209).

Given the progressive claims for a neutral civil not under party control yet still under political control and thus subordinate to the people's will, this stalemate and its consequences could not have had a positive effect on popular regard for public administration. Moreover, the situation was exacerbated by the character of progressivism itself. The movement consisted of a wide array of groups with interests and agendas that often overlapped but were nonetheless distinct. Many of these were already well organized and professionally managed and so were well primed for engagement in political action. When civil service and progressive reforms sufficiently disengaged the political parties from control of administration, many of these groups moved in to fill the vacuum. With the overall structure as well as individual agency design of federal administration already reflecting extensive group influence, progressivism extended and regularized group influence still further, making interest groups one of the new masters of administration. The result of this group influence was to involve agencies in policy making in a way that flew in the face of the dominant ideology and rhetoric of instrumental, subordinate administration.

The progressives offered a conception of public administration's role under the Constitution that was far more sweeping in its reliance on neutral expertise and extended tenure in office than Hamilton's vision and the more general Federalist notion of fitness of character. It was, however, all too easily crystalized into the now infamous politics-administration dichotomy that has bedeviled public administration scholars ever since (see Overeem 2012; Rohr 1986, 183). Whatever its merits as a legitimating device for an expanded role for administration in the American regime in the face of the demands of modernity, the dichotomy as both normative theory and operational prescription further reduced the likelihood that political leaders and an attentive public would arrive at an understanding of public administration that embraced its constitutive bearing. This in turn perpetuated the tensions and contradictions generated in the lengthening history of the American struggle with the administrative dilemma, intensifying their corrosive effects on public support for a recognizably coherent public administration that could contribute effectively to the maintenance and improvement of the regime. Fortunately, for the progressives, events global in scope soon gave them one more run at the problem.

Chapter Five

Serving the Liberal State

Administration and the Rise of the New Deal
Political Order

Despite a 12-year interregnum (Schwarz 1970) of conservative Republican control in Washington, the progressive reform impulse had not come to an end. Progressive ideas continued to be honed, particularly in universities and research institutes, including the emergence of the pragmatist school in legal studies (Wang 2005) that would play a central role in the articulation of the New Deal conception of the national state, the role of administration, and the need to centralize control of policy and administration in the presidency. Although many progressive reform efforts were blunted and even reversed in national policy, the effects on the presidency remained, evident even in the presidencies of Warren G. Harding and Calvin Coolidge.

Although both Harding and Coolidge sought to widen the separation-of-powers divide between the executive and legislative spheres and had little in the way of programmatic ambitions, Harding approved national budget legislation in the form of the Budget and Accounting Act of 1921. The act created the Bureau of the Budget, located in the Treasury Department but "intended to serve as a presidential staff agency" (Milkis and Nelson 2003, 254), and the act gave the president the "legal authority to oversee the allocation of expenditures in the executive branch" (255) that Roosevelt, Taft, and Wilson had all sought. (Wilson had vetoed the legislation because it limited the president's removal power over new officers who would oversee the audit functions designated by the act.) As secretary of commerce, Harding appointed Herbert Hoover, who had served

Wilson as food administrator during World War I, and brought ideas from the newly emerging science of economic management to the Commerce Department assignment. Harding also appointed Taft chief justice, leading to the reinforcement of presidential removal power in the *Myers* decision of 1926. Even "Silent Cal" Coolidge, advocate of greatly diminished government intrusion in the national economy, capitalized on the emergence of the rhetorical presidency to sustain the popular basis of presidential power by expanding the close personal relationship of the president and the people through artful use of mass media, particularly press conferences and radio broadcasts (Milkis and Nelson 2003, 259–60).

Herbert Hoover was even more of a personification of the staying power of progressivism in the face of Republican political and policy control. He was "the leading political innovator of the 1920s and a worthy heir of the progressive legacy of Roosevelt and Wilson" (Skowronek 1997, 261). Indeed, it might be said that Hoover was the first, and maybe the only, president cast in the progressive mold of the neutral, technical expert. He gravitated toward "an extrapartisan, pluralist politics where executive officers, armed with the authority of expert knowledge and the power of public opinion" (268) in what proved to be his increasingly forceful response to the crash of 1929 and the onset of the Great Depression. Hoover confronted the stubbornness of the economic collapse with increasingly radical devices that reflected his status at the time as "master administrator of the modern age" (269). His experimentation "anticipated much of what would occur during the early years of the New Deal" (261). Still, Hoover denied the one dimension of progressive thought that most distinguished it: the commitment to a fundamental reordering of the political and social order. Thus, neither he nor any other political leader of the interregnum sought to probe further the questions about public administration's status and role in the regime that the progressives had raised, or the answers they had offered.

Before the crash, the period of "healing" and "normalcy" that Harding had promised did not mean a complete lack of attention to public administration in the public realm. The development of public administration as a distinct, practice-oriented field of study had begun to emerge by this time, as represented by Leonard D. White's textbook *Introduction to the Study of Public Administration* (1926). In the preface to his text, White defined public administration as "a single process, substantially uniform in its essential characteristics wherever observed." It's study "should start from the base of management rather than the foundation of law," and thus should not be primarily concerned with "the decisions of the courts." Finally, White saw that administration had "become, and will continue to be the heart of the problem of modern government" (quoted in Gaus 1958, 233), carrying forward Woodrow Wilson's assessment of four decades earlier. Similarly, William F. Willoughby of the Institute for Government Research, one of the predecessors of the Brookings Institution, saw public administration, "viewed broadly," as encompassing "all matters having to do with the organization and operation of the machinery of government." It's study concerned "the manner in which the several branches of government, the legislative, the executive, the judicial, and the electoral, are organized and conduct their business," with particular focus on "the modifications that can be made therein with a view to making them more efficient" (1930, 39).

As the views of White and Willoughby suggest, those in the emerging scholarly field regarded public administration both broadly and narrowly: concerned with all the structural components of government across the constitutional branches and the levels of American federalism—capturing in a sense Wilson's idea of thinking integratively about administration in the American regime. Yet this broad compass was accompanied by a focus almost exclusively on organization and management for increased efficiency. This focus on management and efficiency did not stand completely divorced from larger questions of democratic governance, however, since underlying the scholarly view was the progressive consensus that increased efficiency served modern American democracy by making government less susceptible to special interest control and more effective in marshaling resources to advance social welfare. In a very real sense, then, the progressives had triumphed by separating legitimating arguments about the importance of public administration to the regime from questions about the size and scope of government generally and the federal administrative establishment specifically. The politics of the conservative Republican interregnum did not reject the progressive focus on neutral expertise applied to improvements in management across government writ large; they only contested how far-reaching government's writ should be. Indeed, the efficiency aspect of the progressive orientation fit nicely with old notions of economy and retrenchment to which conservative Republicans and Democrats alike adhered.

Worries about bureaucracy and about threats to the separation of powers and other constitutional bulwarks from an expansive conception of executive power moved to the fore again by the centralizing actions deemed necessary for total mobilization and war fighting during America's involvement in World War I. Yet the instrumental orientation for thinking administratively that focused on management and efficiency made the accompanying conception of a broad reach for an administrative orientation to government from the likes of White and Willoughby appear safe as long as it remained abstract. When the Great Depression forced the nation to consider again calls for far-reaching, intrusive government action, Franklin Roosevelt's New Deal made questions about the status and function of public administration in American government and politics central to the political debates of a renewed and even more sweeping effort at systemic reordering and reform. Indeed, FDR's fundamental intention by the beginning of his second term was to place public administration at the heart of a new American political system.

Characterizations of the New Deal

For general interpretive purposes, scholarly characterizations suggest that the New Deal can be understood in one of two ways. Either it was reactive, that is, an extemporary response to the Great Depression and the threats it posed for the American system; or it was purposive, that is, a substantial structural and functional alteration of American government, politics, and economics with a relatively clear aim and at least a rough plan of action. The interpretation of the New Deal as reaction has its locus in impressive mid-twentieth century historical research. The depiction of the New Deal that emerged from this research was that of a pragmatic response to the evils of the Depression. By some accounts it was an opportunistic, stumbling, groping response, and by others a more coherent pragmatism (Kessler 1989, 160). Carrying the reactive characterization a step further, Russell Kirk, a chronicler of American conservatism, argued that it was not FDR who swayed the mass of Americans to follow him in the course he chose to preserve American constitutionalism but instead FDR who "was swayed [by the public] to adopt the course he took." Hence, Americans "were not thrown far out of the course of their established political and moral habits," nor "stampeded out of their sound civil habits by the hardships of the depression" (quoted in Eden 1989a, 24).

It is no secret that FDR brought to his administration a fairly loose and improvisational style. Among other things, he sometimes had aides working at cross-purposes, and he preferred to allow cabinet members and close advisors to debate and disagree openly in his presence. This improved the chances that he could witness a full venting of views on any important issue. It also weakened potential rivals to his power (see, for example, Arnold 1986, 89–91).

Also often cited is FDR's reference to "bold, persistent experimentation" in a 1932 speech at Oglethorpe University, and his insistence that it is common sense, if one fails when attacking a problem, to try one method after another. "But above all," he exhorted, "try something" (quoted in Kessler 1989, 160). But a careful reading of the speech reveals that FDR was referring to "experimentation in means, not in ends (if such a thing were possible)" (Kessler 1989, 161). Indeed, although the New Deal contained plenty of improvisation and experimentation, and certainly not all of it successful, it was far from a wild, unguided, purposeless experimentation. Herbert Hoover had resorted to increasingly radical experimentation of means, but with the aim of preserving his notion of the traditional "American System" (Skowronek 1997, 281–85). If the New Deal was similarly purposive and only experimental in means, then FDR must have had fundamental principles and aims in mind. He centered those aims on transforming presidential administration fundamentally (Karl 1989, 187–88).

In reality, the New Deal was both reactive and purposive. The purposive New Deal was a consequence of the improvisational New Deal. "Roosevelt was like a juggler with a dozen balls in the air. Initially he wowed the electorate with his boldness. . . . Coordinating his creations was the President's next task" (Arnold 1986, 89). Furthermore, FDR came to regard the improvisations as "makeshift necessities, not virtues" (Karl 1983, 156), leading him to seek the help of experts in formulating new and more rational forms of administrative organization. More broadly, the lack of "any single principle" about the relationship between the state and capitalism, combined with the shock of the recession of 1937–38, "forced a serious reevaluation among American liberals of the policies and philosophy of the New Deal" in search of "a coherent vision" (Brinkley 1989, 86, 87; also see Karl 1983, 158–61). Viewed from an operational perspective, the New Deal's dual character was evident in "the pragmatic style of the New Dealers, who were busy running real government institutions as they thought and wrote about the new order of American politics they were creating" (Rohr 1986, 55).

Both the improvisation and the purpose must be kept in view when considering the New Deal and its legacy, but the latter must draw the lion's share of attention in an assessment of the impact of the New Deal on the conception and treatment of public administration in American politics. Like the American founders and the generations of reformers before him, Roosevelt expressed relatively consistent intents and purposes for his reforms, and public administration was a central element of them. These intents and purposes emerged in their most complete expression in the initiatives of the so-called Third New Deal, FDR's plans for his second term. FDR intended the initiatives to go far beyond the more improvisational efforts of his first term (see Karl 1988). Consistent with the efforts of his predecessors, FDR's objectives encompassed the refinement and advancement of democracy, and—a distinct but not entirely separate goal—the definition, institutionalization, and perpetuation of a modern liberal program.

The Democratic Meaning of the New Deal

In a speech delivered at Roanoke Island, North Carolina, on August 18, 1937, Franklin Roosevelt excoriated opponents of the New Deal. He accused them of attempting to undermine the will of the people as expressed in the landslide 1936 election, and he labeled them "American Lord Macaulays." By likening them to the Tory leader who had disparaged American popular government, FDR portrayed these opponents as seeing their "anchor for salvation of the Ship of State" in a select class of educated men who were deeply interested in the security of property and the maintenance of order. Roosevelt then declared, "Mine is a different anchor. They do not believe in democracy—I do. My anchor is democracy—*and more democracy.*" As he began to draw the speech to a close, he claimed that his opponents rejected "the principle of the greater good for the greater number, which is the cornerstone of democratic government." Roosevelt then assured his audience, "I seek no change in the form of American government. Majority rule must be preserved as the safeguard of both liberty and civilization" (1938, 331, 333; emphasis added). Such was the tumult of the 1930s that Roosevelt could safely defend himself against charges that he was engaged in an effort at formal change, when one could only conclude that formal change is exactly what he was attempting. Later that same year, in the introduction to the first volume of his public papers, FDR reiterated that the New Deal meant "a new order of things designed to benefit the great mass of our farmers, workers, and businessmen" (quoted in Skowronek 1997, 292). Appreciating the peculiar nature of the democratic foundations of FDR's attempt at a sweeping political reordering is crucial to understanding the role of public administration in the New Deal transformation.

FDR "was the first statesman to 'appropriate' the term *liberalism* and make it part of the common political vocabulary. In doing so, however, he reworked—some claimed perverted—the elements of the old faith into modern form" (Milkis 1993, 49). It is easy to see from the Roanoke Island speech why Roosevelt could be regarded as perverting the American liberal creed. For many, that creed entailed liberty and individual rights as first principles. Democracy, understood as broad popular participation in the choice of leaders, meant nothing if individual liberties were seriously restricted. Indeed, implied in one's civil rights was not only the right to vote but also to otherwise influence the government. The liberal creed held, in short, that individual rights were the foundation of democratic government. Yet here was FDR declaring nearly the converse, that democracy was the protector of individual liberty. As inverted—or perverted—as that sounded to many, FDR was in fact tapping into a powerful and venerable sentiment. As Charles Lindblom stated it, "historically, people have turned to democracy primarily as a guarantor of personal liberty" (1980, 1). Indeed, some scholarly interpretations portray the intentions of many of the founders in almost precisely the manner stated by FDR: they chose a constitutional design based on popular sovereignty to serve as guardian of the liberty they held so dear (see, for example, M. Diamond 1975; Rohr 1986, 78–79).

Philosophically, the New Deal was democratic to its core. Taking the long view, the political energy of the New Deal was readily reconcilable with Tocqueville's vision of an irresistible democratic tide pushing on through the generations. Whereas the progressives represented the first attempt to reconcile this inexorable democratic expansion with the realities of advanced industrialization and a more populous, more interdependent world, the Great Depression gave FDR—the most thoughtful and ambitious progressive inheritor—the opportunity to advance much farther, if not to complete, that reconciliation. For FDR, as much as for the American people, the Depression was "a blessing in disguise" that allowed for the adjustment, and then the application, of founding principles to the altered conditions of the day (Kessler 1989, 163). The adjustment involved the modernization of American democracy by further centering it on the presidency. This was consistent with the efforts of FDR's progressive forerunners. But the New Deal also encompassed two dimensions more distinctly Rooseveltian: reworking standards of honor for great social achievement and thereby distributing them more widely and expanding the definition of political liberty to include a broader range of rights.

A New Majority Consensus

The most experimental stage of the New Deal culminated in the National Recovery Act, in which Congress delegated authority to the president to set industry standards in conjunction with business associations. In a real sense, then, FDR first tried to build his response to the Depression and his larger reordering project on the basis of cooperation with business and industry in a way not very different from Hoover's efforts. When the U.S. Supreme Court found the NRA unconstitutional for its extraordinary delegation of authority, Roosevelt was forced to clarify and reenergize the core reordering aims of his New Deal (Skowronek 1997, 310–12). From then on, more than ever, the New Deal "mounted a sustained challenge to the ruling ethos of the preceding Republican era" (Eden 1989b, 55). At the heart of this challenge was a choice "between hatred of *arbitrary executives* and love of free and solitary enterprise" that FDR tried to force the Democratic Party in particular—the party of Thomas Jefferson—to make "once and for all" (55; emphasis added). Roosevelt set about the task of building a new majority consensus on the basis of a new standard of "democratic honor," a standard that included placing "arbitrary executives" in positions of leadership.

Franklin Roosevelt's essential task was to transform the deeply rooted conception of democratic honor that prevailed at the beginning of the New Deal, a conception of honor embodied in the Horatio Alger stories: a solitary, courageous individual overcoming incredible obstacles and even multiple failures to obtain wealth and comfort and the admiration of the community. These were (and still are) the sorts of people honored with public acclaim by the Republican ruling ethos. But FDR was convinced that this conception of honor and its accompanying majoritarian consensus on values was at the root of the mess that was the Great Depression. Thus, Roosevelt sought a change in the accepted conception of democratic honor that would mean a newly inclusive ruling ethos and a broad changing of the guard signifying that new types of people were being granted public laurels and the honor of ruling.

Roosevelt's alternative conception of democratic honor incorporated a "civil or social courage in guiding complex enterprises," not "stoically, minimally, or unobtrusively," but with dashing good cheer (Eden 1989b, 59; also see Wills 1994, 70–79). This was, of course, precisely what FDR personified, and it led logically to making the president the guardian of the new conception of democratic honor, thus binding the "organized electorate" to the national government and, thereby, registering its acceptance of New Deal centralization (Eden 1989b, 60). The traditional conception of honor reflected the task of taming a wild and mostly uninhabited continent and saw this as primarily the work of solitary entrepreneurs. "Roosevelt reinterpreted the task of subduing nature as a cooperative task in which the main actors were not individual entrepreneurs but, rather, organized groups" (59). Part of the reinterpretation involved redefining the task. It was no longer taming the wilderness but managing "tamed" resources effectively (e.g., Brinkley 1989, 99, 109; Kessler 1989, 163). The fundamental, culturally ingrained American struggle to control nature to promote the general welfare and attain relief from want was to be in the hands of a more broadly inclusive cast.

The New Deal bestowed the honor of recognition and support as public leaders not only on the likes of corporate executives but also on union leaders, farm association representatives, reformers, social activists, and professionals—including liberal lawyers and management experts, *and*, although to only a limited extent when compared with today's standards, to the African Americans and women among them. Indeed, the establishment in the Democratic Party of "special divisions" for women, blacks, and labor (Milkis 1993, 62–68), and FDR's reliance on ostensibly nonpartisan groups in his campaigns represent well this dimension of the New Deal conception of democratic honor. Such efforts had their roots in the similar drive of the progressives to democratize American politics by expanding the sphere of participation to more economic and social interests. The associational or corporatist structures of both "New Era" progressivism and the early New Deal (see Balogh 2009, ch. 9; Eisner 1993) were one distinctive manifestation of this modern pluralist orientation. All of this came together to form one of the central features of postwar politics, famously interpreted by Theodore Lowi in his near epithet of "interest-group liberalism."

Although seemingly quite disparate, these several elements of a new code of democratic honor were consistent with Tocqueville's general conception of democratic honor (see esp. Tocqueville 1988, 616–27). They reflected Roosevelt's effort to alter and reinvigorate the *spirit* of the American people and to establish a new majoritarian consensus on basic values—a new "moral authority" built on "the morale of a political majority" (Eden 1989b, 61). Hence, the New Deal represented a very powerful democratic current. But what of the nature and focus of that current with respect to American constitutional and political foundations?

PRESIDENTS, MAJORITIES, AND ECONOMIC RIGHTS

An inkling of the answer can be seen in Roosevelt's positioning of the president at the center of the new conception of honor, an indication that FDR drew upon progressive, and even Jacksonian Democratic, roots (Skowronek 1997, 292). Furthermore, like "most progressive reformers during the first three decades of the twentieth century," FDR believed that Thomas Jefferson and Alexander

Hamilton "stood for two contending theories of government that animated later political controversies in American history and still lay unresolved before them" (Milkis 1993, 21). Jefferson, along with James Madison, represented and had carried out in 1800 the construction of barriers against governmental consolidation and strengthening of the executive. Hamilton, in contrast, sought a strong, even dominant executive, to check an overreaching republicanism. Roosevelt's response, born in part of his ambition to lead the country, was to recognize "that Jeffersonian ideals would have to be applied to modern problems in such a way that these ideas were respectful of Hamilton's 'genius' for sound administrative practices" (22). FDR articulated his effort to do just that in his address to the Commonwealth Club in San Francisco on September 23, 1932 (see Milkis 1993, 38–40, on its origins).

The "seriousness of the Commonwealth Club address is apparent from the beginning" (Kessler 1989, 161), when FDR declares that he intends to speak "not of politics but of Government," and "not of parties, but of universal principles." What FDR then proceeded to do, consistent with his and his advisors' reformation of progressive thought, was to "give new meaning to the Hamiltonian tradition by infusing it with a democratic purpose" (Milkis 1993, 41). This democratic purpose was the energetic definition and advancement of individual rights—not the traditional rights, particularly property rights, understood by both Hamilton and Jefferson—but *economic* rights, particularly "the economic freedom of individuals to earn a living" (quoted in Milkis 1993, 41). Thus, FDR offered both a modernization of Jeffersonian ideals through an "economic declaration of rights" and a democratization of Hamilton's energetic, executive-led nationalism. This democratization would come about by tying the "enlightened administration" necessary to ensure the sustenance and protection of the people's economic rights to the presidency, which, as Andrew Jackson, Theodore Roosevelt, Woodrow Wilson, and even William Howard Taft had argued, enjoyed a direct link to the people and the support of a national electoral majority.

Like his progressive forebears, then, and like Jackson as well, FDR sought to use the presidency, and public administration, to give shape, substance, and guidance to the inevitable democratic tide. Throughout the construction, refinement, and defense of the New Deal, Roosevelt labored continuously to "establish a government responsive to the needs of the majority" and a presidency "with authority over [its] domain" (Milkis 1993, 111) to ensure that such responsiveness was in service to the reordering of the regime newly redefined as liberal.

The New Deal's Programmatic Liberalism

For the "economic constitutional order" announced by Roosevelt in the Commonwealth Club speech to come to fruition, however, several other things had to happen. First, FDR had to convince Americans that his brand of progressivism and his plans for governing were consistent with the values and principles they held dear. He accomplished this by drawing forward Jeffersonian ideals and using the language of rights to portray his objectives. By doing so, he linked his progressivism to constitutionalism and interpreted it as "an *expansion* rather than a *subversion* of the natural rights tradition" (Milkis 1993, 43; emphasis in original). The outcomes of the 1932 and 1936 elections confirmed, at least to FDR, that the American electorate was indeed convinced.

Second, Roosevelt had to label his program distinctively and banish to the political wilderness any opponents who might claim the same label. FDR achieved this by adopting the title "liberal" and forcing his opponents to accept the designation "conservative." As long as the American people valued the ideas of progress and upward mobility, *conservative* would spell political difficulties for those who bore that label (Patterson 1967; Rossiter 1962). This was an especially meaningful achievement, for the American political creed was fundamentally liberal. According to John Dewey, the creed consisted of two strains of liberalism—laissez-faire and humanitarian—with the former dominant and the latter associated with personal and voluntary effort (Dewey 1936, as cited in Milkis 1993, 304–5). FDR successfully raised the political status of humanitarian liberalism and redefined it in connection with government activism, generating a sharp competition between the two streams of liberal thought—now in the guise of liberalism and conservatism—that has continued and increased in intensity (Milkis 1993, 305).

The combination of these two achievements was the construction and political legitimation of "programmatic liberalism" (Harris and Milkis 1986; Milkis 1993, 38–51), which encompassed an expanded list of rights—mostly concerned with economic security—that were defined, delivered, and protected by positive government action, particularly executive initiative. Such an idea of rights stood in contrast to the more traditional conception of rights as "natural" and requiring protection *from* government interference. Because FDR sought to put his stamp on the American polity, a stamp of historic proportions that would reduce the likelihood of recurrence of something like the Great Depression, and because his expanded conception of rights was predicated on programmatic

initiatives by government, placing it at the whim of electoral politics and a democracy of localized parties, his brand of humanitarian liberalism had to be protected in ways that would sustain it beyond the time in which he could reasonably expect to serve in office. Safeguarding programmatic liberalism in this way
required additional achievements.

Because of the party tradition in American politics, which was strongest at
the local level, New Deal liberalism had to be attached to a political party or, to
be more precise, one of the parties had to become the programmatic liberal
party. Equally important, the party of liberalism had to become and remain the
majority party, through a true partisan realignment. However, the American
party system was far too decentralized to be easily controlled from Washington.
It was also strongly ensconced in Congress, which, by virtue of the Constitution's
design, made it relatively resistant to long-term presidential control. Party government, FDR came to conclude, was simply too fickle and unpredictable to be
the anchor of the New Deal. Hence, the preservation and even extension of programmatic liberalism had to be entrusted to an institution that would be relatively immune to changes in electoral fortunes and party control. That institution was public administration.

This strategic assessment only added to the importance of administration's
role in the New Deal scheme, a role already central because the rights defined by
FDR were programs, not "formally ratified as amendments to the Constitution,
nor . . . fully codified in statutes and policies" (Milkis 1993, 50). They required
"enlightened administration" not only for their fulfillment but for their long-
term upkeep and repair as well. FDR's expanded definition of rights thus reoriented the role of the national government and placed executive-led administration at the core of that reoriented role. Roosevelt's pursuit of a protected
humanitarian liberalism led to the emergence of an "administrative constitution" (Milkis 1993, 145), an overlay of redistributed powers and newly defined
rights that did not depend on formal amendment of the original document.

To understand the more general impact of the New Deal on the status of public administration under the constitution, it is important to recognize that under
the emerging administrative constitution, public administration was an *instrument of partisanship*, and it was so in a manner not very different from the Jacksonian conception. The nature of the partisanship under the New Deal transformation was, however, notably different.

Woodrow Wilson's complex and probing examination of the appropriate role
for public administration in the American regime, interconnected as it was to

his extensive and more subtle development of Theodore Roosevelt's rhetorical presidency, led Wilson to conclude that expert professional administrators could safely be left with responsibility for the details of running the government, while the president was to attend to politics and political leadership, that is, the development of basic principles and policies and the mustering of public support for them. This was at the root of Wilson's commitment to party leadership and to governance by a party majority in Congress. Franklin Roosevelt served in Wilson's administration as assistant navy secretary, and he was a serious student of Wilson's presidency. Like Wilson, FDR faced the problem of how best to exercise party leadership and to govern through the party system. Intending to bring about a transformation to a progressive social program, he opted for vigorous party leadership in the short run, both to transform the Democratic Party into the party of liberalism and to achieve a true partisan realignment that would make the Democratic Party the majority party. This realignment, however, was intended to *end* party politics and partisan realignments (Milkis 1993, 110), because, as FDR suspected and as it was fully confirmed during his fight to liberalize the Democratic Party, the party system would in the end only stand in the way of achieving and sustaining a liberal social program.

Realizing this, FDR sought to make the president the center of national electoral politics *and* the engine for the programmatic liberal transformation of American government and politics outside the parties. Public administration, so vital to the creation and sustenance of that liberal program, would replace party as the institutional home for programmatic liberalism because it could be more easily and permanently attached to the president. Through the New Deal, in other words, FDR sought "a blending of partisanship and administration, one in which administration would become a vehicle for partisan objectives; for liberal partisanship" (Milkis 1993, 51). Bringing about this administrative partisanship and keeping it in check required "tying the administrative state to the presidency" (103). At the heart of Roosevelt's endeavor in this regard was his attempt at executive reorganization, pursued with the help of the President's Committee on Administrative Management (PCAM), the Brownlow Committee.

Executive Reorganization and the New Deal Conception of Administration

Amid minor disagreements about how it all started, scholars of the presidency and public administration agree that executive reorganization, which eventually shifted control over administration far more to the president's side, was critical to adjusting the American constitutional scheme to twentieth-century conditions. For progressive reformers the Constitution posed a problem, because it "had not been written to cope with large-scale administration" of the kind the modern world seemed to demand (Arnold 1986, 10). That problem required a shift in "the proper locus of administrative authority in the American regime" from Congress to the president (3), to reconcile expansion of government capacities with basic constitutional structure, particularly separation of powers (see Arnold 1994, 6–13). Similar arguments portray the "traditional" regime as Congress centered, as intended by the Constitution (Lowi 1985). The traditional system was not overturned until the New Deal. The "President's Committee on Administrative Management was the first of many efforts to adjust an eighteenth-century constitution to the twentieth century" (Lowi 1985, 2; also see Mosher 1968, 80). The central theme of the committee was that the new powers of the national government had to be centralized in the hands of the president to ensure that administrators would exercise those powers responsibly and the democratic character of the regime would be preserved.

Along the lines of Alexander Hamilton's effort to define under the Constitution an energetic, independent executive with substantial—although not exclusive—authority over administration, the New Deal pursued a constitutional political science regarding administration like that in *The Federalist*—pragmatic and adaptive (Rohr 1986, ch. 9). The focus of the pragmatism and adaptation was the constitutional legitimacy of the modern welfare state that emerged under the banner of the New Deal. The New Dealers secured a substantial well of legitimacy for the expanded administrative power they sought (Milkis 1993, 102–4). However, to leaven the administrative power backed by popular will through the president that the New Deal achieved, additional procedural safeguards for individual rights—primarily in the form of the Administrative Procedure Act—subsequently had to be put in place (see, for example, Rohr 1986, ch. 10).

THE BROWNLOW REPORT'S CONCEPTION OF ADMINISTRATION

As a number of scholarly analyses stress, the report of the President's Committee on Administrative Management was influenced by the ideas of all three members of the committee that wrote it—Louis Brownlow, Luther Gulick, and Charles Merriam. Yet the report was perhaps most strongly shaped by the ideas of Gulick (Stillman 1991, 116). Indeed, it was Gulick and Urwick's *Papers on the Science of Administration* (1937) that served "to provide a common language for the [PCAM] staff," and a "tool kit of administrative principles" (Arnold 1986, 97) and might also lend scientific legitimacy to the committee's analyses (but see A. Roberts 1996, 30–33).

If Luther Gulick's ideas formed the technical core of the Brownlow Committee's report and the executive reorganization legislation that followed, they reinforced the more general focus on the president's need for help in governing through a more tightly structured, more effectively controlled, and thus more efficient administrative apparatus. Under Gulick's "new Nationalist" progressive creed, the president was the chief political leader *and* the chief administrator and as such was the elected official most likely to revitalize the American system of government through more centralized "administrative management" (President's Committee 1937). More precisely, the modernization of American democracy would occur through more effective public administration. The solution to the problem of responsible government in the twentieth century rested with administrative reform, meaning, primarily, more centralized presidential control (Milkis 1993, 109; President's Committee 1937, 1–3).

This idea that administrative reform and the tightening of presidential power and control through executive reorganization was in service to American democracy permeates the Brownlow Committee's report (Newbold and Terry 2006; Rohr 1986, 147, 252 n. 54). At the close of the report's introduction, the committee forthrightly states, "There is but one grand purpose, namely, to make democracy work today in our National Government; that is, to make our Government an efficient, up-to-date, and effective instrument for carrying out the will of the Nation" (President's Committee 1937, 4). The nature of that national will, moreover, was quite clear to them: "the constant raising of the level of the happiness and dignity of human life, the steady sharing of the gains of our Nation, whether material or spiritual, among those who make the Nation what it is" (President's Committee 1937, 1).

Both committee pronouncements were quite consistent with the New Deal notion, articulated as far back as FDR's Commonwealth Club address, that the principal task of government was the effective management of the nation's resources to prevent destitution and want. Making the point more emphatically later, the committee insisted that the "whole basis of reorganization must not be the superficial appearance but the integrity of the social services underneath, *which are the end of government*" (President's Committee 1937, 38; emphasis added).

The "explicit mention of the purpose of government as something other than the protection of individual rights" in the Brownlow Report is "a textbook example of the triumph of administrative means over liberal ends" (Rohr 1986, 148). It is inconsistent with American constitutional tradition (149; also see Newbold and Rosenbloom 2007) but wholly consistent with the New Deal redefinition of that liberal constitutional tradition. If this marginalization of individual rights required a corrective, which "thoughtful" New Dealers provided in the 1941 attorney general's report on administrative procedure (Rohr 1986, 112, 149, and ch. 10), it is important to stress nevertheless that not all those involved thought the correctives were advanced thoughtfully, or that they were grounded in core principles rather than ideological conflict (Bertelli 2010; Gellhorn 1986; McNollgast 1999). It is even more important to reiterate that through the New Deal, FDR and his supporters sought and achieved a transformation in the *conception of rights* and integrated it into a social services or welfare conception of the positive state. In other words, ensuring the delivery of basic social services, now often referred to as the social "safety net," was the same as protecting and advancing individual rights. "With the advent of the New Deal political order, an understanding of rights dedicated to limited government gradually gave way to a more expansive understanding of rights, requiring a relentless government identification of problems and the search for methods by which these problems might be solved" (Milkis 1993, 131). This identification of problems began with FDR's articulation of a "Second Bill of Rights," addressing economic security. By the 1960s and 1970s it had expanded much further, to encompass broad health, welfare, and "quality-of-life" problems that reformers argued required delineation of additional basic rights as part of their resolution. Like the most recent effort to guarantee affordable health care in the Patient Protection and Affordable Care Act of 2010 (PL 111–148), each of these efforts has met stiff resistance from re-branded "conservatives."

Underlying the final Brownlow report were struggles over its aims and the partisan orientation of the committee (A. Roberts 1996) and, more profoundly, over the exact vision of how administration would fulfill its role as servant to the democratic will of the nation and the nation's demand for services. Historian Alan Brinkley (1989) describes a struggle between two contending liberal conceptions of the state that was carried on from the late 1930s to the end of World War II (also see Karl 1988). A regulatory state view promoted relatively extensive government intervention in the economy through actual management of economic institutions, to correct the problems of capitalism and protect the interests of the public. A compensatory government view advocated much less state intervention, relying instead on programs that would stimulate demand and thus economic growth, and on welfare programs that would appropriately distribute the fruits of that growth. The compensatory government view, built on a core of Keynesian economics, prevailed, partly as a result of the bad experiences of state management during World War II (Brinkley 1989, 100–111). These two conceptions of the state, it is nevertheless clear, were consistent with the Brownlow report's idea of administration as serving the people best by being under the close, coordinated control of the president.

The conception of public administration in the Brownlow report was, then, decisively instrumental. Administration was to be the principal device with which to meet the demand for the "effective delivery of promised services" in the positive state (Rohr 1986, 137). This instrumental conception was expressed quite explicitly, as in the passage from the report's introduction quoted above, and in its later insistence that the "national will must be expressed not merely in a brief, exultant moment of electoral decision, but in persistent, determined, competent day-to-day administration of what the nation has decided to do" (President's Committee 1937, 58). The instrumentalism was also manifested subtly yet perhaps most fundamentally, however, by the committee's reference to "those who make the Nation what it is." This phrase signaled that the committee saw the public, or more specifically the majority, as defining or *constituting* the polity. The committee clearly did not include public administration and public administrators here. Instead, administration and administrators are to serve those who define and redefine the character of the nation. Administration is to do this particularly by ensuring the "steady sharing" of mostly material "gains" under the direction of the president, who can most coherently articulate the aspirations of "those who make the Nation what it is." In this characterization and in other passages in the report, the committee sustained, and even intensified, the progressive separation of politics and administration and the instrumental image of public administration it entailed.

CIVIL SERVICE REFORM AND THE NATURE
OF THE ADMINISTRATIVE INSTRUMENT

Luther Gulick denied that the Brownlow Committee's works was co-opted by FDR, leading Peri Arnold to conclude that any presumption about "the specific details of the committee's recommendations [being] specified by Roosevelt beforehand conflicts with the facts of his past record in administrative coordination" (1986, 107). Yet the general scholarly consensus is that the product of the committee's labors reflected Franklin Roosevelt's ideas and intentions. FDR found "in the members of the President's Committee on Administrative Management . . . steadfast loyalty and a shared vision of presidential government" (Milkis 1993, 108). Roosevelt's "personal influence on the recommendations [of the committee] was great" (Karl 1983, 157), and "the president helped to shape the content of the report to an unprecedented degree" (A. Roberts 1996, 23).

What FDR shared with Brownlow, Gulick, and Merriam at the most basic level was a conception of the American regime, and of public administration's role in it, which was necessitated by the stresses they saw imposed on democracy by modern society. "FDR was committed to moving the political system from a government order based on *constitutionalism* to one emphasizing *public administration*. Or, more accurately, FDR hoped to transmute constitutionalism, so that it was less legalistic and more open to centralized planning. Planning would not be directed at efficiency for its own sake; rather, the goal was to make American democracy more directly responsive to the developing interest in government-provided social services" (Milkis 1993, 110; emphasis in original; also see Karl 1988). Each of the five principal recommendations in the Brownlow report, constituting the core of the executive reorganization plan FDR proposed in 1937 and pursued in one way or another even after the bill's defeat, gave concrete expression to the New Deal conception of administration. Public administration moved to a central place in the regime, but it became, more fundamentally than ever before, an instrument in service to an externally defined purpose. The Brownlow Committee's recommendation regarding civil service reform, and subsequent actions taken in this area, are particularly illuminating on this score.

The Brownlow report is famous for its recommendation that the merit system be extended "upward, outward, and downward" to cover most of the positions in executive agencies not responsible for policy determinations; the committee also pressed for separating personnel administration from the merit system by the creation of a single administrator responsible to the president (President's Committee 1937, 4, 7–12). The committee further recommended the creation of a citizen board to serve as a watchdog over the merit system. The interpretation of these proposals by (mostly Republican) critics of the New Deal was that they were intended largely as a patronage effort to reward loyal Democrats with permanent federal jobs. Many feared that FDR was bent on creating a national political machine. The Hatch Act of 1939, which sharply curtailed the involvement of federal administrators in presidential and congressional election campaigns, was the response.

This worry, while not surprising, was largely misplaced, however. FDR "was more interested in orienting the Executive Department for the formation of liberal public policy than he was in developing a national political machine, and the insulation of federal officials from party politics was not incompatible with such a task" (Milkis 1993, 138). Indeed, Louis Brownlow defended these proposed actions as a necessary part of moving from the "negative, protective" phases of civil service reform associated with the patronage abuses of the spoils system to the "positive," progressive phase. The latter could be expected to bring with it a federal administration and administrators dedicated to the programmatic liberalism of the New Deal political order (Milkis 1993, 116).

The consequence of a totally neutral, instrumental public administration, as conceived by nineteenth-century reformers, was to relegate administration to ministerial, nonpolitical tasks. The New Dealers realized, however, that this attempt at complete separation of politics from administration simply could not be sustained in practice. The Jacksonian strategy, attaching public administration as instrument to the president and thus the parties, is relevant for understanding the New Dealers' problem. The Jacksonian approach served the parties' interests, because administration could be democratized through the parties, as well as serving as a source of party sustenance through patronage. It also served the Jacksonian objective of restoring republican virtue and, in keeping with Jeffersonian tradition, kept public administration's political and governing role circumscribed. The Jacksonian conception nevertheless posed its own dilemma, for the quest to restore republican virtue meant that public administration would have some role in shaping citizen qualities and sensibilities despite the claims of strict subordination and control. That the Jacksonian method—the spoils—seemed to produce exceedingly immoral and corrupt results in the public service, and politics more generally, seemed only to reinforce the notion that the bureaucracy could never legitimately contribute to the character of the polity in ways consistent with fundamental ideals and principles.

Like both their mid- and late-nineteenth-century predecessors, the New Dealers conceived of public administration as an instrument in service of democracy. Unlike the civil service reformers but like the Jacksonians, New Dealers sought not a neutral but a dedicated instrument. Rather than simply neutralizing administration so that it served whatever master sought to use it, New Deal reformers specified the master of the administrative instrument. The New Deal reforms thereby brought politics and administration back together within the presidential sphere but outside the regular party apparatus, in recognition of

Roosevelt's vision that "the line between lawmaking and administration would grow fuzzier," with the president assuming "an expanded role in the more 'streamlined' democracy of post-Depression America" (Milkis 1993, 121). The balance of power and authority shifted, in short, and the presidency became more influential in both policy and administration while also becoming more detached from the parties. Unable to restore party control of administration, New Deal opponents nevertheless succeeded in placing constraints on the political aspects of administration, and thus on its capacity to advance a programmatic liberal agenda under direction of the president, by imposing such safeguards as the Hatch Act, and eventually the Administrative Procedure Act. New Deal Democrats acquiesced in these constraints as a way to protect the programmatic liberal bureaucracy from falling under the control of future presidents who might not be so favorably inclined toward that programmatic liberalism (Bertelli 2010; McNollgast 1999). Albeit with subsequent modifications and subject very recently to more furious attacks, this New Deal conception of public administration as the central instrument of a programmatic liberal state has proved quite robust.

Congressional Debate on Executive Reorganization

Like the initial installation of an administrative structure under the Constitution, and the Jacksonian and progressive reforms, the New Deal reform effort sparked a major congressional debate centered at least in part on questions about the status and role of public administration in American government and politics. Not surprisingly, the Brownlow recommendations, as they were pronounced in the legislation FDR submitted in January 1937, became the principal field of battle, particularly during deliberation on the floor of the Senate. The reorganization initiatives, even as modified by supporters of executive reorganization, prominently Senate floor manager James P. Byrnes of South Carolina, generated sometimes heated exchanges and substantial opposition. The initiatives encompassed expanded presidential support staff, improved executive planning and management capabilities, merit system extension and civil service system reorganization, extension of the president's reorganization powers, consolidation of various extra-departmental agencies, boards, and commissions under closer presidential control within 12 executive departments, and auditing function reconfiguration to improve the fiscal accountability of executive agencies to Congress. The exchanges in floor debate were sufficiently vehement and the opposition substantial enough that the Brownlow recommendations in their original legislative form went down to defeat when the House voted 204–196 to recommit the legislation in early April 1938. This happened despite House passage the preceding December of legislation granting the president six new assistants and renewing reorganization authority that had lapsed in 1935, and despite Senate passage of the full, albeit modified, reorganization bill by a 49–42 vote in March.

Scholars have examined the steady crescendo of trouble and eventual collapse of the initial push for executive reorganization of the Third New Deal, both immediately after the fact (Altman 1938; Rogers 1938) and more recently (Arnold 1986; Karl 1963, 1983; Milkis 1993; Polenberg 1966; A. Roberts 1996). It is worth recounting some of the contextual factors they have pointed to in explaining the defeat of the 1937 reorganization bill, because doing so also sets the stage for characterizing the congressional debate over how public administration and its proper role in politics and government was treated by supporters and opponents of executive reorganization.

Foremost among these contextual factors was that reorganization got tangled up in the political battles over other "big ticket" items FDR pushed the Seventy-fifth Congress to consider. This included, especially, the so-called court-packing plan, in which FDR sought authority to reorganize the judiciary, particularly an expansion of the number of justices on the Supreme Court, to allow better response to the increasing demands for judicial review spurred by New Deal programs. Also included was a proposal to create seven regional natural resource planning authorities, an idea consistent with the New Deal emphasis on economic security through proper resource management rather than new exploration and exploitation. FDR launched both of these in February 1937, a month after introducing the executive reorganization legislation, and the latter was pushed back on the congressional calendar, as the House and Senate took up the seemingly more far-reaching proposals first.

That these initiatives somehow interfered politically with the reorganization effort is not altogether surprising. Although the court reform proposal "prepared the constitutional ground" for the proposals made by the Brownlow Committee (Milkis 1993, 113), it is also clear that the rhetoric and substance of arguments against the court-packing plan, and important elements of the opposition coalition, were readily transferable to the fight over executive reorganization. Similarly, the proposed regional planning system and FDR's reorganization effort were inextricably linked, but this linkage made the fears of centralized power raised by the former generically applicable to the Brownlow report's recommendations as well (Karl 1983, 166). Indeed, in crucial respects, court reorganization, regional planning, and executive reorganization were all parts of FDR's endeavor to remake the presidency and establish an "administrative constitution" to fulfill the tenets of modern liberalism (Karl 1983, ch. 8; Milkis 1993, ch. 5). The congressional debate over executive reorganization thus was destined to recapitulate the substance and rhetoric of the contests over court packing and regional planning. The latter two went down to defeat in July 1937 and March 1938, respectively. The achievements of the Third New Deal should not be completely discounted despite these defeats (Milkis 1993, ch. 6).

Two other factors contributed noticeably to the character of the congressional debate on executive reorganization. First, sensing that reorganization was a sensitive issue, the Democratic leadership in both chambers delayed bringing the legislation to the floor for debate. This allowed opposition outside Washington to build and sharpen. Also, the vagaries of congressional scheduling brought legislation to the floor that tied up activity still further. A prominent example was the filibuster by some southern senators against an antilynching bill (Patterson 1967, 193). Second, the economy slipped into recession in August 1937. By the time FDR returned his attention fully to congressional action on his executive reorganization plan, it was in the context of a special congressional session he had called in November to deal with the recession. The effect was to create "a new atmosphere of mistrust, since it raised doubts about Roosevelt's economic policies, and these doubts, in turn, evoked defensive language from the administration" (Karl 1983, 157).

Finally, the efforts of the Brownlow Committee itself in preparing the ground for the reorganization plan have come into question. The "prospects for adoption of the report were dim to start with, . . . this was clear in 1936, and . . . the committee did little to anticipate the looming controversy" (A. Roberts 1996, 5). The committee exhibited a "pervasive ambivalence about the purpose of its work," and placed constraints on its commitment to FDR's aims by the "need to protect the field of public administration by making a show of their independence and neutrality" (6).

In most respects, then, the parameters for congressional deliberation on executive reorganization had already been established by the time floor debate finally began in earnest at the end of January 1938. The major themes and stratagems had been honed during the debates on other issues that had occurred throughout the previous year. One important feature of the established terrain for the debate was the increasingly coherent and effective conservative counterattack on the New Deal. Although it would have been fallacious to speak of this opposition to the New Deal as "an inflexible conservative coalition voting as a bloc on every issue" (Patterson 1967, 220), at its core were the "irreconcilables," conservative congressmen of both parties in both houses who considered themselves "the bulwark against the New Deal" (212). Throughout the nearly three months of full floor debate, it is clear, opposition to the executive reorganization bill was in part energized by the drive simply to stop Roosevelt and the New Deal, so as "to 'conserve' an America which [the opponents] believed to have existed before 1933" (viii).

During the lengthy and complex debate senators advanced a wide variety of arguments. Particularly noteworthy for the reorganization debate was the continuation of the traditional distinction between legislative and executive views on the purpose of reorganization. In a March 1 speech, Senator Harry F. Byrd of Virginia expressed the legislative view precisely, by laying down certain "fundamental principles," the first of which was that "Congress [should] go clearly on record that *economy* is one of the main objectives of any reorganization of the Government" (*Congressional Record* [hereafter cited as *CR*) 1938, 2590; emphasis added). In anticipation of this argument, Senator Byrnes tried to dispel the notion that reorganization would result in substantial savings, unless, he declared, "we . . . stop appropriating money for functions." He contended that no senator should believe "that by regrouping Government organizations, by consolidating them, and by abolishing a few of the existing commissions, a large percentage of the total appropriations can be saved. It cannot be done" (*CR* 1938, 2506). Instead, such restructuring would provide "that the President can know what is going on in this organization or that organization" (*CR* 1938, 2502), or, as FDR stated it to Louis Brownlow, the "reason for reorganization is good management" (Milkis 1993, 107).

Also plainly evident in the debate were the numerous but not untypical attempts by congressmen to protect their pet programs and key constituencies by exempting particular agencies from the president's reorganization power. This activity was encouraged in part by the modifications, specifically exempting certain units, which FDR allowed Byrnes to make. It also reflected an opposition tactic to "eventually . . . amend the bill beyond recognition" (Patterson 1967, 221) with a relentless series of proposals to exempt additional agencies, rooted in "a near universal drive among institutional actors to secure independence from presidential controls" (Skowronek 1997, 318).

James Patterson's description of the anti-reorganization forces in the Senate and the tie that bound them points, however, to the most pervasive substantive themes in the reorganization debate. These forces, led by Sen. Burton K. Wheeler of Montana, a "tried and true progressive veteran" who viewed himself as "the true defender of liberalism in the [Democratic] party" (Patterson 1967, 114, 115) and who thus became "a consistent foe of the Third New Deal" (Milkis 1993, 126), consisted of "Republicans, conservative Democrats, and moderate Democrats fearful of excessive centralization of power" (Patterson 1967, 221). The question of whether executive reorganization as proposed by FDR presented too great a threat of centralizing power in the executive emerged time and time again during the debate on reorganization.

In a fascinating exchange between Republican senator William Borah of Idaho and the majority leader, Alben Barkley of Kentucky, on March 15, Borah proclaimed, "A democracy is a peculiar institution. It does move slowly and it necessarily moves with great deliberation. . . . A democracy moves slowly in order to present the views of the masses whom we represent. I would infinitely rather take some time and obtain the judgment of those whom we represent than to move with the celerity which we are witnessing in other parts of the world" (CR 1938, 3400). In response, Barkley stated, in part, "One of the things which it seems to me will preserve democracy is for democracy to be efficient, responsive, and ready to serve the people. I do not think there is any question of democracy or autocracy involved in simply authorizing the President to transfer a bureau from one department to another" (3400).

Everyone at the time understood, of course, that Borah's reference to "other parts of the world" meant the dictatorships that had arisen in the crippled democracies of Germany, Italy, and perhaps even Russia. Eleven days earlier, Senator Arthur Vandenberg had similarly argued, "The intended creation of a civil-service dictator," and the "creation of Executive control over public expenditures," were "unfortunate and ill-advised concentrations of Executive authority under any circumstances. They are particularly unfortunate and ill-advised at a difficult moment in our history when the crying need of the hour is an assurance to America that we are not going farther down the road toward authoritarian, centralized, one-man government in the United States" (CR 1938, 2813). Other senators voiced similar warnings before, after, and in between Vandenberg's and Borah's statements, but the conflict in views about the essential character of American democracy given voice in the Borah-Barkley exchange proved to be behind most of the expressions of fear of an authoritarian threat.

Barkley's response to Borah was the very incarnation of the progressive struggle against "traditional" democracy. In the progressive conception articulated by

Senator Barkley, American democracy should be efficient, responsive, and oriented toward serving the very basic needs and wants of the American public generally. This was Herbert Croly's argument, that such basic public wants and needs were distinctively different in a modern, industrial age. As Democratic senator Joseph C. O'Mahoney of Wyoming similarly argued with clarity during the reorganization debate, "the people of the United States . . . are not content with a government which merely restrains the inhabitants of the land from injuring one another. They want a government which helps them to do the things they want to do, and helps them to live the sort of lives they want to live; and the pressure never ceases" (CR 1938, 2826). The appropriate response to this unceasing pressure, argued Croly, the progressives, and their New Deal progeny, was a less fettered, more energetic executive, which would formulate the most rationally organized, efficient, and thus most effective actions. It was the modern, democratic Hamiltonianism expressed in FDR's Commonwealth Club address.

Borah's contention that American democracy needed to be appreciated as slow, deliberative, and founded on popular opinion expressed through representatives, symbolized most of what the progressive movement had battled to overcome, and it showed how difficult the task of importing the methods of "despotic governments" and adapting them to American needs really was. The anti-reorganization forces held to a legislative-centered rather than an executive-centered view of American democracy, emphasizing decentralization and a clearly delimited executive power. As Senator Vandenberg stated it, "the gravest errors—in terms of hazard to the administration's own objectives—usually have found root in the departure from democracy and in the substitution of government by Executive decree for our traditional processes of representative and decentralized government" (CR 1938, 2813).

The reorganization debate was, therefore, the occasion for a vigorous public probing of that fundamental Jeffersonian-Hamiltonian tension that interlaces the structure and conceptual foundations of the American regime. This should not come as a complete surprise, since FDR's efforts, particularly with respect to the Third New Deal, were aimed precisely at resolving that tension in favor of a progressive vision. But the Borah-Barkley exchange hints at another fundamental point of contention in the reorganization debate: the relative powers of the president versus the Congress in the constitutional system, specifically as manifested in control over administration. FDR's reorganization proposal "touched very centrally" on what had evolved into a "delicate balance of power" (Milkis 1993, 121).

Senator Byrd addressed this issue head on during his principal speech against the reorganization bill. He argued that "to give the President the authority to abolish or modify, in whole or in part, a function of government, involves a great surrender of power by the Congress. A function of government is a policy of government. Congress is the sole agency to determine a policy of government" (*CR* 1938, 2592). Similarly, Senator Josiah Bailey of North Carolina argued that the time had come "for Members of Congress . . . to assert their power in order that it may be known in the United States, and particularly in [the] departments, that the power is ours and not theirs; that the responsibility for the Government and its policies [is] upon the elective and the constitutional representatives of the people and not upon those whose offices we create and to whom we give public funds for distribution for the public benefit" (2710). Finally, Burton Wheeler, in a lengthy speech and exchange with Alben Barkley that served as a bridge between the two main areas of contention, argued, "If we are to have a democratic republic . . . we are going to have inefficiency in government, but the answer to those who are saying we cannot function under a democratic government . . . is not delegating our powers to a President . . . or to the executive branch. The answer to the evils of democracy is more democracy, and have it intelligently and honestly applied" (3023).

Undergirding these invocations of congressional authority, opponents "saw reorganization as weakening their own power and prerogatives in relation to those of the president. They did not want Roosevelt to gain firmer control over his own administration" (Freidel 1990, 276; also Skowronek 1997, 318–19). Alternatively, reorganization opponents were not just expressing "irrational fears" but acting on an institutionally based partisanship, grounded in tradition and the Constitution, in response to the very real threat that policy and administration would be reunited under the president's control (Milkis 1993, 121). If this was to be the case, Burton Wheeler argued, "let us adjourn the Congress and let the departments do the legislating for the people of the United States" (*CR* 1938, 3023).

It is not just coincidence that the battle over executive reorganization is reminiscent of the contest between Andrew Jackson and Senate Whigs (Skowronek 1997, 295). Both confrontations involved very popular presidents leading a wave of democratic sentiment toward systemic reform in congruence with a particular conception of the regime. Both involved efforts to attain greater presidential control over administration and to restructure administration so that it would be an effective instrument in service to the conception of the regime being pursued.

Both saw a vigorous congressional counterresponse, embodying contending ideas about the nature of American democracy and a struggle over the relative power and authority of the president and Congress under the Constitution, especially with respect to the control of administration. The executive reorganization debate even involved the issue of presidential removals from office, several actually exercised by FDR, as well as the threat of such action in connection with the proposed creation of a single civil service administrator to replace the civil service commission.

Nevertheless, one feature of the executive reorganization debate made it different from the 1835 confrontation and the similar debates probing basic regime questions during other times of political change, reform, and development. That feature is the stunning absence of any attempt to articulate alternative ideas about public administration and its place in the regime. To be sure, there was the occasional glimmer, such as Representative Noah Mason's characterization of "government administration" as "vital activities affecting the welfare and the very destiny of this Nation" in his attack on the proposal to abolish the Civil Service Commission in favor of a single administrator (CR 1938, 1232). Such glimmers never grew much brighter, however, and the ideas behind them were not developed more systematically or coherently.

The reorganization debate also probed distinctions between strictly executive officers and those who performed quasi-legislative and quasi-judicial functions, in connection with the proposed civil service administrator and the proposed auditor general to replace the existing comptroller general. This probing followed the Supreme Court decision in *Humphrey's Executor v. U.S.* (295 U.S. 602 [1935]), however, and thus was dominated by its reasoning. In the end, then, the representatives and senators of the Seventy-fifth Congress never actually confronted the challenge of trying to define for themselves what constituted an executive officer.

Overall, the only conception of public administration apparently given any credence in the reorganization debate was that of an instrumental, subordinate institution. Indeed, in the records of the debate the two most prominent words used to characterize administration and administrative agencies are *mechanism* and *instrumentality*. Although considerable debate ensued over the extent to which administrative agencies were instruments of the president or the Congress, or perhaps more precisely, what administrative units were the instruments of which branch, at least a plurality of representatives and senators even accepted the notion that administration was solely the tool of the president. The several debates, beginning with those in 1789, on the status of public administration in the American regime, and especially the very powerful progressive and New Deal conception of administration as the president's foremost tool for the management of a modern democracy, seem to have squeezed out of public thinking any glint of an idea that public administration might have any other role in the regime than servant to popular demands.

The 1939 reorganization legislation that Congress passed and FDR signed, although a "shadow form" of the original, nevertheless represented congressional acceptance of the president as "first among equals in tackling the problems of administrative management" (Skowronek 1997, 319). The Third New Deal thus succeeded in securing the acceptance of an executive-centered administrative hierarchy, one that the president was responsible for managing, but control over which would be a constant source of contention with Congress and a host of other interested actors. Since the New Deal, Congress has engaged in some fascinating debates about the design of and political control over administration, in connection, for example, with the passage of the Atomic Energy Act and the Administrative Procedure Act, both in 1946, with post-Watergate reforms, such as the Civil Service Reform Act and the Ethics in Government Act, both passed in 1978, and the Government Performance and Results Act of 1993, associated with the reinventing government craze. As the principal forum for public debate about the nature of public administration and its place in the regime, Congress would never again quite measure up (but see Rosenbloom 2000). To the extent that debates about the status and design of administration occurred later in the New Deal and during the post–New Deal political order, they were confined mostly *within* the executive branch, often in connection with the work of presidential commissions like the first and second Hoover Commissions, following the precedent of the Brownlow Committee (e.g., Arnold 1976; Pemberton 1986), and they unleashed a veritable frenzy of reorganizations that only rarely threatened congressional sensibilities about control of the administrative apparatus. The high-level, searching, concentrated debate about the design and placement of administration in the regime evident in the congressional debates of 1789, 1835, 1883, and 1887 has never reappeared even as the questions have persisted to the present day.

The New Deal in Perspective

In his unprecedented effort to make his refashioned liberalism the core public philosophy and to realize the benefits of an active social program of progressive democracy, Franklin Roosevelt of necessity confronted the dilemma that public administration as a political institution poses for the constitutional system. His response was to take completion of the progressive enterprise as far as he could, principally by more firmly linking administration to presidential management and increased, but not complete, presidential control. This FDR intended as a way to ensure that the expanding administrative apparatus remained responsive and accountable to the public will. FDR also furthered the intentions of the progressives by accelerating the transcendence of party politics. Again, this was principally connected with the effort to establish, protect, and sustain programmatic liberalism by making administration, rather than the party, its institutional platform and moving it further into the presidential sphere. Another of the consequences, however, was a strengthening of the ties that bound administrative agencies to organized interests, especially those of a liberal persuasion that were part of the New Deal coalition. Those ties transcended liberal ideology, however, reflecting in part the response of interests with well-established organizational representation in the administrative state, a response that served to constrain the presidential control aspirations of the Third New Deal (Skowronek 2011, 183–84).

The New Deal did not, therefore, resolve the dilemma administration poses for the regime. Indeed, in significant ways, it intensified the tensions and contradictions created by the progressive reformation project by broadening the gap between perception and reality, between the conception of administration that had come to dominate American political ideology and rhetoric and how administration actually functioned. Two contradictions are most clearly evident in the New Deal reforms.

First, although an administration conceived of as the instrument of modern liberalism would not be involved in designating the purposes of the liberal state—those would come primarily from the president, as leader and interpreter of the public will—such a distinction could not be sustained in practice. By making public administration the custodian of liberal partisanship, FDR really did meld politics with administration, perhaps to a greater extent than he realized. "Many of the objectives of governments . . . were social, not readily measurable, and difficult for [an elected] legislature or executive to define with any degree of exactitude" (Mosher 1968, 76). This left to the discretion of bureaucrats not just the identification and development of means to achieve given public policy objectives, but the designation, or at least refinement, of those objectives themselves. Thus, "during the New Deal period and the war which followed it most new policies and programs were initiated in the executive branch, often, if not usually, well below the levels of political appointees" (82). Policy subgovernments linking interest groups, agencies, and congressional committees formed in response to this reality, and they were soon thereafter attacked as perversions of popular control of government. In particular, they clearly violated the understanding of a subordinate, instrumental public administration.

Second, and perhaps even more profound, FDR seemed to conceive of administration—the institutional platform he chose as the means to sustain and even extend modern liberalism—as also having a hand in shaping the liberal aspirations of American citizens. This is implicit in the notion that administrative agencies would be responsible for the upkeep and repair of the liberal programs that they administered. This concept was taken even further, however. "Roosevelt and the architects of administrative reform hoped to cultivate a federal work force dedicated to advancing the cause of New Deal reform" (Milkis 1993, 116). Part of that cause would be "to cultivate amongst the American citizenry an appreciation of government planning and extensive public service" (110). In other words, to perpetuate programmatic liberalism, administration would have a central role in fashioning and fortifying the public's liberal sensibilities. It would help create a more liberal polity.

Recall that the Jacksonians had a similar conception of the role administration would play in their reform endeavor. The public service would be the instrument of a republican restoration, but in that earlier case, the federal workforce would also help to cultivate in the populace the simple values and virtues that were at the heart of the republic's origin myth. It is in just such a conceptualization as this that the distinct but interconnected qualities of public administration, the instrumental and the constitutive, clearly surface. Andrew Jackson does not appear to have grasped this. Woodrow Wilson did, however, and Franklin Roosevelt may have also. Both Wilson and FDR sought to convey in their public speech the legitimacy of an expansive governing role for administration in a large, complex, modern industrial nation. In FDR's case, however, at just the point when such speech was most needed both he (Skowronek 1997, 320–21) and his expert committee (A. Roberts 1996) faltered, relying on technocratic rationales and falling back on progressive claims about administrative neutrality to sell a governmental reconstruction that went far beyond "executive reorganization." Wilson's expansive conception of administration that FDR appeared to have embraced was hidden behind the façade of management and the portrayal of administration as simply the tool of the public's social service and economic security aspirations. The president, in turn, was to be the personal and organizational embodiment of those aspirations, but would only have to manage the administrative instrument in the quest to realize them.

The reality, again, was quite different. An administratively centered state was now well established, with administrative agencies at all levels of the federal system actively and extensively involved in defining policy goals and the interactions with citizens that would give shape and substance to those goals. The president gained some control, but it would take governors several more decades to follow suit (Sabato 1976). In subsequent efforts, first Congress, and then the more professionalized state legislators, endeavored to enhance their control as well. Administrative agencies of various sorts retained considerable autonomy, power, and discretion, however, and the subsequent battles between future presidents and Congresses, and future governors and state legislatures (Rosenthal 1990), over the next 60 years would be fought over control of that power and discretion to serve contrasting programmatic ends. It would not entail fundamentally different conceptions of government and administration, however.

By expanding public administration, increasing its capacity and competence, placing it at the center of a reformed political and governmental system, and linking it to great works—restoring an economy to health, establishing the rudiments of broad-based economic security, and defeating fascism across the globe—Franklin Roosevelt generated for American public administration a great well of legitimacy and public support that would last a generation. The price for his accomplishment was very high, however, as subsequent challenges to the New Deal would reveal.

Chapter Six

Politics and Administration after the New Deal

Liberal Orthodoxy and Its Challenges

"How shall the 'public sector' be made public and not the arena of a ruling bureaucracy of 'public servants'?" The Students for a Democratic Society (SDS) posed this question in their manifesto, *The Port Huron Statement* (1962). The authors of the document went on to answer their own question by calling for "steadfast opposition to bureaucratic coagulation." More revealingly, however, they advocated minimizing "the bureaucratic pileups . . . by local, regional, and national economic planning—responding to the interconnection of public problems by comprehensive programs," while also promoting "experiments in decentralization" that would restore to people the "personal capacity to cope with life." The tension between the desire for centralized efforts to dispel chaos and overcome inaction and the desire to keep government closely tied to people in their everyday lives is unmistakable in this "New Left" statement of aspirations. It was a clear manifestation of another rise in the democratic tide, one particularly intense in its orientation to what it called "participatory democracy," and in the tensions and even contradictions that idea entailed.

The post–New Deal political order is distinguished by the spirit of the New Left and two other ideologies—neoconservatism and neoliberalism—contending for control of the public philosophy and, by extension, the administrative state. All three sprang from the turbulent politics of the Cold War, the civil rights movement, and the generational change associated with the postwar "baby boom." They have overlapped, collided, and oscillated across political time in their influences on how Americans think, talk, and act regarding politics and government. The concepts, language, and reform measures of all three movements, in a dizzying mix, have become accepted, even deeply ingrained, elements of American politics and government in the nation's third century. Advocates of all three, moreover, have in one way or another characterized their efforts as countermoves against progressive and New Deal politics and governance. The focus on bureaucracy in the passage from the SDS declaration presaged subsequent neoconservative and neoliberal lines of attack on the administrative core of the progressive and New Deal state. Such attacks again placed public administration in the bull's-eye of self-proclaimed reform efforts tied to claims about the restoration of fundamental American values. None of these erstwhile counterreformations have (yet) succeeded in dismantling the administrative state, although it does bear the scars of the pummeling it has taken from their efforts. Understanding the nature and aims of those attacks and why the administrative state has survived the onslaught is vital for appreciating the current state of public thinking about administration and its place in the regime. A good place to start toward that understanding is to return to the story of the New Deal and briefly trace its fate during and after World War II.

The New Deal and Cold War Liberalism

Franklin Roosevelt's ambitions for the creation of a liberal polity, guided and sustained by a liberal public administration, were blunted by the "institutional thickening" he confronted as a "reconstructive" leader (Skowronek 1997, 31). The prime consequence of his battles with Congress over executive reorganization, the so-called court packing plan, and his failed effort to purge conservatives from the Democratic Party, seemed to be that despite gaining "the institutional independence he needed" to manage the new liberal administrative regime, "everyone else got the independence they needed to prevent him from controlling it" (319). Yet FDR was not wholly deterred in his ambitions for liberalism by the political and economic setbacks in 1937 and 1938. In his annual message to Congress in January 1941, delivered after he won election to an unprecedented third term, FDR wove his liberal vision into his message about the nation's aims in the face of the rapidly spreading reality of a second global war in less than a generation. This was Roosevelt's "four freedoms" speech, in which he sought to project the rights-based roots of American liberalism into the worldwide struggle against totalitarianism. The third of the four freedoms—freedom from want— encapsulated the bulk of the New Deal's social welfare aims centered on controlling economic forces through positive government for the benefit of all people, not just a special and powerful few.

The nation's entry into the war and the vast industrial and governmental expansion that came with it ended the worst depredations of the Great Depression, but Roosevelt was not yet finished in his efforts to advance his vision of a liberal age. In his 1944 State of the Union address, FDR enumerated an "economic bill of rights," greatly expanding the economic security orientation of the "freedom from want" in the 1941 speech. The rights to economic security that Roosevelt listed, including housing, health care, employment, fair prices for farm products, and fair competition for small businesses, essentially charted the boundaries of what would come to be regarded as the modern American welfare state. This was a structure of programs and protections to be overseen by public administrators, although not necessarily directly delivered by them. Both the welfare state edifice itself and those primarily tasked with operating, analyzing, preserving, and, in some respects, expanding it, rested in part on significant anchors in the private sector. Nevertheless, they both would also be a constant target of political conflict over the ensuing decades as a threat to American tenets of small government and laissez-faire.

The end of the war and victory brought the nation superpower status but also unprecedented economic power and a prosperity of a sort that seemed to signal the end of widespread need for government controls on the economy and continued expansion of efforts toward greater economic equality. Yet the war "had also thrown into relief new problems of industrial economy and social policy that strengthened the hand of liberal political actors and pressure groups" (Bell 2004, 2). This led to "the development of a social democratic network of activists inside and outside Congress whose ideological frame of reference was not simply, or even primarily, the New Deal," but also a further extension and embodiment of FDR's economic security rights and freedoms, in "a politics of equality of opportunity and social welfare that transcended national boundaries" (4).

This left-of-center political thrust and further extension of the spirit of FDR's ambitions for a liberal polity failed to set down roots broad and deep enough to ensure its supremacy, however. The principal cause of this failure and the consequent withering of the most far-reaching of the social democratic impulses of progressivism was the Cold War. The small state, localistic ideology of Jefferson had taken a beating in the face of modernity, a modernity that brought with it horrific challenges in the form of a worldwide depression and two world wars. A resurgence of the ideology on which FDR had forced the name "conservative" began with interest alliances, primarily between Republicans and southern Democrats, that helped fend off the most far-reaching of Roosevelt's reform efforts of the Third New Deal. An anti–New Deal conservative opposition gained further strength from the relative economic prosperity the nation experienced immediately following the war, further aided by public sentiment, perhaps more apparent than real (see Parmelee 2000), that it was time to cast off the wartime economic and social constraints. If "powerful social democratic forces and significant anti-statist interests" (Bell 2004, 1) had reached a sort of parity immediately after the war, the closing of the iron curtain, the emergence of aggressive Soviet espionage, and the consequent second Red Scare tipped the balance rightward in significant ways.

Most important for present purposes, the panic over the ideological and, to many, the existential threat the Soviet Union seemed to pose led, first, to a fracturing within the New Deal and larger left-liberal coalition in American politics. The communist threat prompted many prominent public figures to adopt a "Cold War liberalism," a staunch anti-communism blended with a more modest but still relatively substantial social welfare policy orientation, albeit one tied even more closely to private sector rather than public sector solutions to persistent social ills. In its worst manifestations, this ideological reorientation encompassed a willingness to curtail civil liberties in pursuit of Soviet infiltrators and the more general communist threat (Grossman 2002). Second, and more profoundly, the second Red Scare prompted the launching of a series of so-called loyalty investigations of federal civil servants that went far beyond the primary aim of ferreting out communist spies and sympathizers. What came to be synonymous with the hotheaded single-mindedness of Sen. Joseph McCarthy actually preceded McCarthy and originated under the auspices of the White House as well as Congress. Whatever residual wisdom there may have been in looking out for real Soviet infiltration turned into a far more sweeping and ruthless purge in the hands of conservative political leaders and institutional power players such as FBI Director J. Edgar Hoover. Their aim was to chase out or neutralize public servants who at one time or another strongly favored social welfare and social justice aims and a commitment to the use of government authority and power to expand economic opportunity and constrain the worst excesses of corporate capitalism and to a lesser extent racial and gender discrimination (Storrs 2013).

In short, the second Red Scare and the loyalty programs empowered the forces aligned against New Deal liberalism, enabling them to undermine FDR's original aim of cementing a future liberal polity by housing its guardians in the bureaucracy. The attacks on American civil servants in this period reached surprisingly deeply into American public administration, especially at the federal level, targeting many men and women whose only transgression was to support policies for expanding political equality, economic opportunity, and constraints on capitalism's excesses. The effect was to seriously degrade the intended institutional haven of FDR's new liberalism by dismissing or severely restraining or neutralizing the efforts of many of those public administrators mostly likely to preserve and sustain it, thus "stunt[ing] the development of the American welfare state" (Storrs 2013, 1).

The New Deal philosophy was not destroyed, nor was the administrative state dismantled, by the effects of the second Red Scare. Indeed, in one important respect the administrative state was strengthened in this period by the appendage of a national security apparatus that would eventually prove far more resistant to overhead political control than its milder domestic counterpart and perhaps more far-reaching in its formative effects on the regime. Still, the effects of the Cold War and a resurgent political coalition of small-state ideologues, corporate leaders, and southern Democrats succeeded in curtailing the most far-reaching social welfare and social justice potentialities of the New Deal, pushing the institutional support structure for FDR's aims—a public administration suffused with the spirit of modern liberalism—onto much shakier ground. Both the forces of modernity and the reality of the effectiveness of the administrative state in responding to those forces would, however, convince even implacable foes of the New Deal in Congress to preserve its organizational forms.

Institutionalization of the Administrative State

It is not altogether surprising that Congress would prove to be the prime motive force behind a reasonably complete institutionalization and even rationalization of FDR's improvised and relatively unsystematic New Deal– and war-driven expansion of the progressive administrative state. After each wave of reform and reconstruction over the course of the nation's development, "the positive and constructive task of fleshing out [a] new regime has fallen to Congress" (Skowronek 2011, 97). In the case of the New Deal, of course, the initial constructive task was primarily undertaken in the midst of a global economic emergency, and the construction was a wild and wooly affair with new agencies scattered across the institutional landscape. This is what prompted the work of the Brownlow Committee in the first place. The war brought further, explosive federal administrative growth, but the continuing threats arising in many parts of the world from insurgent movements unleashed by the war, as well as communist expansionary aims, blunted the traditional demobilization and institutional dismantling that had traditionally followed American engagement in war. Congress faced the need to rationalize the institutional structure for an apparently more permanent state of national security threats and military readiness alongside a continuing stream of internal socioeconomic problems that seemed to require a large institutional edifice of technical expertise to manage national responses to those problems on a continuous basis.

With the help of the courts, the nation's legislators accepted the constitutional legitimacy of broad delegations of legislative and judicial authority to administrative agencies but sought to infuse the use of that authority with a set of values that privileged legislative over executive or managerial values. Beginning with the Administrative Procedure Act and Legislative Reorganization Act, both enacted in 1946, Congress accepted the reality of a substantial administratively centered American state, reorganized itself internally in response, and positioned itself to exert both broad and finely tailored control over the exercise of administrative power as a counterweight to the continued development of executive management in the presidency.

Congress's fashioning of this "legislative-centered public administration" (Rosenbloom 2000), "relied heavily on the idea that agencies should operate and be treated as extensions of the legislature" (23), an orientation differing "substantially from the traditional constitutional and public administrative treatment of them as Congress's *agents*. As extensions, agencies are essentially fused to the legislature. They exercise its core constitutional responsibility—legislation." Therefore, "Congress may constitutionally direct administration by specifying its procedures and values" (24). Those values stress "open participation in rulemaking, transparency, and reduced intrusiveness" (59). Congress's internal reorganization to adapt to the reality of an administrative state, and its vigorous efforts, ongoing up to the present day, to keep control over administration balanced in its favor, is a remarkable phenomenon in which Congress reconstituted itself in ways that have had profound formative effects on the lives and careers of its members, and on American politics as a result (see Rosenbloom 2000, ch. 4). It also strongly suggests that Congress, if only implicitly at an institutional level, held and may still hold a deep appreciation for the constitutiveness of political institutions. Indeed, it is hard to deny that Congress recognized, at least implicitly, the constitutiveness of public administration itself. Why would members have sought to instill a particular set of values in agencies and the administrative state as a whole if they did not recognize the formative influence of political institutions based on the values they carry?

As much as this is exciting to contemplate, in the end Congress's construction of a legislatively centered administrative state does not appear to have helped American citizens acknowledge public administration's constitutive dimension or to consider the implications of administration's formative effects given its primarily instrumental role in the regime. Instead, along with the process values of open participation and transparency Congress sought to inculcate in the administrative state, legislators also sought to bend and sculpt the administrative state to suit the particularistic interests of individual members, turning agencies into modern patronage machines through casework demands, earmarks, and other levers (Fiorina 1989). Accompanying the structural adjustments that have proved a boon to career aspirations and improved reelection chances, those seeking congressional office, incumbents and challengers alike, discovered the additional benefit of employing a rhetorical and symbolic politics centered on denouncing the "Washington establishment." Over time, the rhetoric has trended toward increasingly shrill attacks on alleged bureaucratic incompetence, wastefulness, intrusiveness, and threats to liberty that would make any Whig proud. By the 1980s, this rhetoric had become standard political fare in electoral campaigns and policy debates (Garrett et al. 2006; T. Hall 2002; Hubbell 1991).

Some of the congressional uses of administration have served legitimate constitutional purposes, at least in the eyes of Congress's members. Likewise, some of the harsh rhetoric has served legitimate policy aims, although the damage to administrative effectiveness is all the same, in the form of impediments to effective policy implementation and "recruitment, retention, and training difficulties" affecting the competency of both career administrators and the critical political appointee positions below the senior level (Garrett et al. 2006, 236). Yet the most significant results by far have been to reinforce not only the instrumental imagery but also the underlying instrumental conception of administration. That conception's contradiction with the obvious constitutive effects of administrative action has provided plenty of fodder for more sweeping and more strident attacks as the contradiction between rhetoric and reality made the intrusiveness and bureaucratic tyranny seem all the more starkly real in the public mind. More profoundly still, the growth and maturation of the administrative state and the attempts by all three constitutional branches to exert control over it has initiated the American political equivalent of the Thirty Years War, with armies battling back and forth over control of the administrative edifice for particular political aims, offering little new in how to think about administration in American constitutional governance, and all the while undermining the capacity of agencies to meet even the instrumental expectations proclaimed for them. The attacks have occurred in waves of ideological ferment. The first of such attacks, following the success of conservative forces in blunting the most far-reaching social welfare and social justice tendencies of the New Deal, came from the left.

A New Liberalism and Its Instrument

The effect of curtailing the most far-reaching social welfare tendencies of the New Deal in the late 1940s and 1950s was to privatize those tendencies, aided in part by the social insurance programmatic choices of New Deal reformers (Bell 2004). Without a large institutional edifice wholly committed to pursuing those social justice and social welfare aims, progressivism fragmented further into incremental efforts to advance, or protect, the welfare of discreet groups. Those groups best organized were the most successful beneficiaries, a dynamic captured by the "iron triangle" model and eventually given the more sweeping moniker "interest-group liberalism" (Lowi 1979). These developments were the targets of the New Left activists who emerged in the late 1950s and began to assert themselves by the early 1960s (see Miller 1987). The New Left reform drive reached its ascendancy in the late 1960s and then broke apart. A brief review of its short history is essential for understanding how a movement so determined to be anti-bureaucratic only served in the end to reinforce the bureaucracy-affirming instrumental orientation to administration that not only continues to prevail but also has intensified in the past 30 years.

The New Left had its roots in the philosophy of American pragmatism, especially the work of John Dewey, as further modified and in some ways radicalized by C. Wright Mills and Arnold Kaufman (Lacey 2008). Its central aim, pursued primarily through the network of student activists initially centered in the SDS, was "not only . . . the desire to create a sense of wholeness and communication in social relationships, but . . . to create noncapitalist and communitarian institutions that embodied such relationships." Its politics "attempted to develop the seeds of liberation and the new society (prior to and in the process of revolution) through notions of participatory democracy grounded in counter-institutions; this meant building community" (Breines 1980, 421). The movement's politics was also, therefore, "hostile to bureaucracy, hierarchy and leadership, and it took form as a revulsion against large-scale centralized and inhuman institutions; its most acute concern was to avoid duplication of the hierarchical and manipulative relationships characteristic of society" (422). Central to its critique was that hierarchy and bureaucracy depoliticized society, stripping citizens of their inherent power in a democracy to reshape, that is, *reconstitute* that society. Those who articulated the movement's tenets imagined the fusion of public and private life so that making and remaking the polity was an ongoing, almost everyday function of community relationships. " 'Being political' meant participation of everyone in decision making and action, in building community—often through direct action. It was a dedication to the means as well as the goal, and a way of circumventing the passivity and hierarchy of electoral politics" (426).

It is difficult to deny that the New Left critics of post–New Deal American politics and society understood, at least implicitly, the constitutive effect of administration. They saw their society as dominated by large, thoroughly bureaucratized public and private institutions that not only failed to perform their instrumental functions well and for the good of all, but also, harkening back to Tocqueville's reflections on administrative centralization, had the formative effect of sapping the political energy from citizens, leaving them demoralized and isolated from their fellow citizens. A sympathetic reading of the Port Huron Statement and the subsequent history of the movement suggests that the core of New Left thinkers and activists may even have recognized both the instrumental and formative value of administrative power, if not in contributing directly to self-government in a large, complex, advanced industrial society, at least in facilitating a more humane society. Yet the core substance of the concrete actions the SDS called for in the Port Huron Statement, to "abolish squalor, terminate neglect, and establish an environment for people to live in with dignity and creativeness" is a recitation of programmatic actions that reads very much like what might have followed FDR's articulation of his economic bill of rights, including expansion of housing assistance, universal medical care, and a living wage.

The New Left and its action arm were dismissed by many contemporaries and later critics as merely a temporarily rebellious movement of affluent, spoiled college students. Being centered in a relatively affluent cohort of university students, however, did not diminish the sweep and power of the New Left critique of interest-group liberalism and privatized social welfare because the activists were in many respects in the vanguard of the new knowledge-based economy emerging in the United States and other advanced industrial nations (Malecki 1977, 49). The problem the New Left faced, however, was that to circumvent the existing structures of politics and power required organizational efforts that were antithetical to the deeply participatory, antihierarchical tenets of the movement. Whether it chose to fail and dissolve rather than sacrifice its means to achieve its ends (Breines 1980), or it chose to abandon its means—truly participatory, communal democracy— to shift "to a position of fighting power with power" (Malecki 1977, 56), the New Left broke apart into several clashing groups. What became dominant were radical and largely destructive elements attempting to follow Marxist-Leninist revolutionary strategies that contradicted both the means and the ends the SDS and New Left thinkers had conceived. That the New Left effort to repoliticize American society through ideals of community on the smallest scale ended in a paroxysm of mass demonstrations and political violence could have been a disaster of epic proportions for the political legitimacy of the New Left's critiques of hierarchical, bureaucratic forms of governance. Instead, those in the movement who eschewed the radicalized strategy of violent confrontation managed to funnel some of the movement's energies toward further expansion and institutionalization of the programmatic liberal elements evident at the start of the movement (Milkis 1993, chs. 8, 9). These elements of the New Left succeeded in achieving political legitimacy and power within the established structures of American politics. They also gained control of and altered fundamentally the character of the Democratic Party, but their primary organizational vehicle became, and remains, a peculiar manifestation of the special-interest group—the "public interest group" or "public lobby" (Berry 1977; Harris and Milkis 1989; Tichenor and Harris 2002–2003).

The "New Politics" of these reformers who reached the apogee of their influence in the early 1970s still stressed participatory democracy, territorial and functional decentralization of government, an expanded panoply of rights, legal formalism, suspicion of administrative discretion, and rejection of interest-group pluralism and the self-interested basis of its political activity (Brand 1989). The intersection of this agenda with the organizational and institutional infrastructure established under the New Deal political order generated a dialectical synthesis (Harris and Milkis 1989, 56) that expanded and radicalized the legal and institutional edifice of the New Deal (Milkis 1993, 195).

Following the sentiments conveyed in the Port Huron Statement, this synthesis is best understood as an expansion of the New Deal welfare state to include "quality of life." Concerns for quality of life beyond the economic security provided by the New Deal was growing among the increasingly affluent, suburban, white middle class of the 1960s and 1970s (Hays 1987), and it was part of Lyndon Johnson's vision of a Great Society (Milkis 1993, 181). Although it reflected an emerging "post-affluent" society in which the primacy of materialist concerns seemed to be waning, it did not embrace the most far-reaching critiques of the New Left regarding the necessity for a complete dismantling of the organizational and institutional structures of the American political economy that true participatory democracy required as part of the communal self-development of every individual. Reformers thus concentrated much of their effort on defining an expanded panoply of rights that included the "collective" rights associated with protection against the dangers of industrial capitalism, the "civil" rights and entitlements associated with the special circumstances and needs of "discreet and insular minorities," and the "procedural" rights associated with the care and exercise of collective rights and entitlements (Melnick 1989, 195–201). The procedural rights also reinforced the drive to expand citizens' influence in the governmental process. The result was a reinterpretation of democracy "as a policy-making process [or a] process for popular control of policy making" (Lindblom 1980, 1). This was a far more limited version of the participatory democracy originally conceived and pursued by the New Left.

All of the new rights required, at a minimum, the same kinds of positive programmatic actions and protections as the New Deal economic security rights, especially expanded agency missions, new agencies, and even new organizational designs for agencies (e.g., Ackerman and Hassler 1981). The conception of and regard for public administration in this context is therefore illuminating. Lyndon Johnson's Vietnam betrayal and Richard Nixon's election convinced the new liberal activists that the presidency could no longer be trusted as the institutional expression of public opinion and the faithful overseer of an administration that was the institutional home for programmatic liberalism. Moreover, administration as an institution was itself suspect, because it was fully implicated in the subgovernment arrangements driven by the self-interested politics of interest-group pluralism. Wary of both the presidency and public administration, these new liberal activists who came to prominence in the 1970s fashioned "a new institutional coalition" (Milkis 1993, 227; also see Melnick 1989) of congressional subcommittees, courts, and public-interest groups. This new arrangement better embodied the vision of democracy the activists sought and more effectively controlled the administrative power deployed in the name of programmatic rights. The latter result was to a considerable extent realized, moreover, because under its "reformation of administrative law" (Stewart 1975), and the "legislative-centered public administration" that was continuing to develop, congressional subcommittees, the courts, and citizen groups became (and remain) more extensively involved in the details of administration. Such an "enhancement" of the "representative character of government action" was not meant "to restrain administrative power but, rather, . . . to reshape it as an agent of democracy" (Milkis 1993, 211). Or, to state it more starkly, through Congress, the courts, and interest-group structures, activists extended their influence over the details of administration "to reduce the independence and discretionary scope of a mistrusted bureaucracy and to subordinate it to more control by the regulated, the beneficiaries of regulation, and the public at large" (Shapiro 1986, 461–62).

The conception and treatment of public administration in politics and government by the new liberalism was, therefore, hardly much different than under the old liberalism of the New Deal. Administration remained a dedicated instrument of programmatic liberalism, although its institutional master was expanded, or transformed, to encompass those coalitions of congressional subcommittees, public-interest groups, and courts the New Left's successors built. Administrative agencies were sometimes working partners in these coalitions (Milkis 1993, 240, 282), but the heightened legal formalism imposed by statute and judicial opinion and restrictions on administrative discretion that the coalitions put in place made it clear that public administrators were to regard themselves and their agencies as simply the delivery vehicles for the will of the people as given expression in the liberal programmatic desires of group activists, judges, and members of Congress and their staffs.

Needless to say, many political actors did not take kindly to this new and more liberalized version of the iron triangle, presidents in particular. Temporarily hobbled by the fallout from Watergate, presidential power and presidential control of public administration received a boost from proponents of what would come to be called neoconservatism, a loosely coherent orientation aimed at restoring traditional sources of authority and traditional institutions of power in the American regime. Neoconservatism and its mirrored twin, neoliberalism, supplanted the New Left as the primary idea complexes in opposition to the progressive–New Deal liberal state.

Neoliberalism, Neoconservatism, and the Rise of Postmodern Politics

Neoliberalism began among European liberals in the 1930s as a "third way," marrying market and strong state in opposition to both laissez-faire and centrally planned economies. In this first incarnation, it was very much akin to American progressive–New Deal liberalism, but without the rights-based orientation that distinguished the social justice and social welfare emphases of the latter. Reborn in opposition to state-centered programmatic liberalism in the late 1970s and early 1980s, neoliberalism essentially sought to carry forward the hegemony of economizing rationality that Paul Diesing (1962) had prophesized. Although heavily stressing free markets, a smaller or at least more decentralized state, and fewer state-controlled restrictions on both economic and cultural activity, neoliberalism still required a strong enough state to ensure the spread of economic rationality to all corners of politics, society, and culture. In political theorist Wendy Brown's assessment, "neoliberalism casts the political and social spheres both as appropriately dominated by market concerns and as themselves organized by market rationality. That is, more than simply facilitating the economy, the state itself must construct and construe itself in market terms, as well as develop policies and promulgate a political culture that figures citizens exhaustively as rational economic actors in every sphere of life." In its orientation to citizens, neoliberalism strives for public actions that "produce citizens as individual entrepreneurs and consumers whose moral autonomy is measured by their capacity for 'self-care'—their ability to provide for their own needs and service their own ambitions, whether as welfare recipients, medical patients, consumers of pharmaceuticals, university students, or workers in ephemeral occupations." In its orientation to governance, neoliberalism stresses the "criteria of productivity and profitability, with the consequence that governance talk increasingly becomes marketspeak, businesspersons replace lawyers as the governing class in liberal democracies, and business norms replace juridical principles" (Brown 2006, 694).

Neoconservatism also gives the market a special place in its orientation, but less so as the means and end of an economically rational polity and more so as one of the institutional sources of traditional power and authority—that of material wealth. Neoconservatism is less coherent than neoliberalism because it has more disparate roots, encompassing anticommunist Cold War liberals, academics who were disgusted by the excesses of the student protests that grew out of the New Left movement, and intellectuals who sought moral clarity in the traditionalism of Christian hierarchy and the social mores that grew out of Christian teachings, although severely modified by the power aims of the organized church. The neoconservative state is more muscular, as it is involved in both enforcing traditional mores internally, protecting those values from external threats, and projecting its power to spread those values beyond state borders. Neoconservatives desire "a strong state and a state that will put its strength to use." They see large, hierarchically organized corporations and churches as allies in the exercise of this strength, particularly with respect to the traditional family unit and "older forms of family life, where women occupy themselves with children, cooking and the church, and men take on the burdens of manliness." Neoconservatives also "see in war and the preparation for war the restoration of private virtue and public spirit" (Norton 2004, 178, quoted in Brown 2006, 697; see also Halper and Clarke 2004).

There are significant tensions within neoconservatism and between neoconservative and neoliberal orientations to citizen roles and the role of the state. Neoconservatives, for example, do not hesitate to support expansion of the national state and central state power at the expense of other levels of American federalism if that state expansion serves traditional values or the national security and quasi-imperial aims of preserving and disseminating those values. These two ideologies are united, however, in their opposition to political liberalism as modified and advanced by progressive–New Deal programmatic liberalism. They have clashed and mixed in their opposition in a number of ways in American politics, at the national level most visibly, but also in state capitals and local government since 1980.

CONSERVATIVE RESURGENCE AND CONTROL OF THE ADMINISTRATIVE STATE

There were hints of the battles to come during the Nixon presidency, manifested especially in Nixon's "southern strategy," which was based on appeals to whites in the states of the Confederate rebellion mixing visions of a "New South" of sunbelt advantages and business entrepreneurship with subtle messages about further threats to the old racial hierarchy that the civil rights movement had attacked head-on. The Nixon strategy built on the inroads Republicans had begun making into the "solid" Democratic south after the Truman embrace of civil rights and the "Dixiecrat" gambit of 1948 (K. Frederickson 2001), but the Nixon campaign focused its messages in response to the increasingly Democratic electoral orientation of African Americans (Boyd 1970). The campaign gave primacy to appeals to law and order to harness racial animosity and generate white flight into the Republican fold.

With his election in 1968, Richard Nixon brought conservatives and Republicans to power at a time when post–New Deal liberalism was still coalescing and gaining strength and momentum. He thus had a chance to stem the tide, and, indeed, he intended to reform the executive branch in such a way as to distance it from the liberalism of the Kennedy-Johnson years. Nixon expected his reform effort—the "administrative presidency" (Nathan 1975, 1983)—"to reconstitute the executive [branch] into a more centralized and independent instrument of government" (Milkis 1993, 233). His margin of victory in the 1968 election was razor thin, however, and, despite his 1972 landslide reelection, Nixon faced a Democratic Congress during his entire presidency. This, it turned out, was just part of the long stretch of divided party control of the federal government that is now the norm, with only 5 out of the past 23 Congresses since 1969 seeing unified party control of the presidency and Congress. Under those limiting conditions, Nixon envisioned himself as "Disraeli to the Great Society," managing rather than departing from or undoing programmatic liberalism (Milkis 1993, 223, 224).

A much clearer marker for the shift in American politics toward a true clash over the nature of the state and the role of administration between programmatic liberalism and the neoconservative-neoliberal nexus, then, was the election of Ronald Reagan and the rise of a "New Right." The latter emerged as a political force by emulating the organizational and political strategies and tactics of liberal public-interest groups, reaching its first plateau of power in the 1980s, and a second in the mid-1990s that has continued with only minor fluctuations since then.

The New Right is an odd mixture that nevertheless manages to cohere. It stresses governmental decentralization and deregulation in most economic regulatory areas and selected social regulatory areas, consistent with neoliberalism, not to mention the old Jeffersonian ideology. Consistent with neoconservatism, however, it also seeks greater governmental influence and regulation of behavior in highly volatile areas of social relations, especially in areas related to marriage, family, and reproduction, where threats to traditional values from a liberal welfare state seemed most acute.

Freedom and liberty were central themes in Ronald Reagan's public speech as both candidate and president, and he sharply questioned, as he had done since his 1964 nomination speech for Barry Goldwater, whether a vast edifice of government programs, representing a wide array of group-based rights, truly meant greater freedom and personal autonomy. Reagan questioned fundamentally both the philosophy and the organizational and institutional infrastructure of programmatic liberalism, as created by the New Deal and elaborated by the reformers of the 1960s and 1970s.

The conservative movement that Reagan led featured a three-pronged attack based on both neoliberal and neoconservative elements that included *defunding*, through tax cuts and shifting of budget priorities from domestic welfare to national security and defense; *devolution* of programs to states and localities (with reductions in fiscal support); and *deregulation*, picking up on initiatives of the Carter years in economic regulation and extending the thrust to important areas of social regulation, including environmental quality and workplace health and safety (Benda and Levine 1988). After an initial spate of legislative successes, this path to reform proved increasingly difficult because of divided party control of the federal government. For this reason, and because the infrastructure of programmatic liberalism was so extensive and deeply rooted, Reagan turned to his own more aggressive and effective version of the administrative presidency.

The essence of the Reagan administrative presidency strategy was to make the federal bureaucracy a more manageable and obedient servant of the conservative agenda. An important tactic centered on shrinking the size of the domestic programmatic and regulatory bureaucracy. But more important was the effort at tightening overall control through budget and regulatory review and clearance procedures and through personnel policies that placed political appointees deep into the career civil service. These policies ensured that all appointees, even at the cabinet level, remained loyal to the Reagan agenda rather than to the agenda of program advocates inside the agencies or among allied activist groups (Benda and Levine 1988; also Durant 1992, ch. 2). While the battle to "debureaucratize" the federal government and dismantle the infrastructure of programmatic liberalism was being fought largely to a draw, the Reagan effort to impose tighter control and even reshape the policy outlook of the federal administrative establishment realized much greater success. The result was the return of the presidency to a mastery over administration similar to what FDR had fashioned (Milkis 1993, 262), and with that return came the reimposition, with a vengeance, of the "administrative orthodoxy" of hierarchically organized controls on administration (Durant 1992).

Despite significant successes, the conservative Reagan "revolution" failed to fully vanquish programmatic liberalism, however. Reagan's attempt at repudiation of progressive–New Deal liberalism was "more rhetorical than institutional," and it "did not actually dismantle any liberal program of significance, nor . . . dislodge any institution vital to the support of progressive government" (Skowronek 2011, 98, 188). Indeed, in some respects, it "actually extended in important respects the *institutional* inheritance of liberal reforms" (Milkis 1993, 262; emphasis added) in such areas as social security and education (see, for example, Glenn 2010–11).

From the perspective of how public administration is conceived and treated, the outcome was an even more sharply honed instrumental status. The Reagan efforts placed administrative agencies in a more complex web of formal controls initiated by both statute and presidential executive order that complemented the informal pressures exerted by a constellation of political masters inside and outside government. The understanding that public administration is simply a mechanism for the delivery of benefits and services (and often judged a very ineffective one at that) became even more pronounced. The political engagement of administrative agencies became even more sharply focused on defending the programs they operated. The idea that administrative agencies might effectively engage in deliberation on, and thus help define, the central purposes of the regime and, further, guide the formulation of appropriate public actions, seemed increasingly absurd (Rourke 1991).

The governmental and political arrangements put in place by the liberal activist successors of the New Deal and the New Left, and by Reagan conservatism, proved to be a highly volatile yet resilient mix. The opposing orientations built on and extended a system of "modern factionalism" (Heclo 1989, 311), marked by "greater autonomy of all political institutions and actors, the tighter integration of administrative services and supports into interest networks of social and economic power, and the consequent weakening of collective, cross-institutional resolve at the political center" (Skowronek 2011, 98). In such a system, it seemed increasingly likely "for activists to win and lose in their struggles over the levers of government without really engaging the general public in a decisive argument about the choices" (Heclo 1989, 314). Thus, American government and politics not in touch with the real troubles of American citizens and not engaged in tackling those troubles (and too ineffectual to succeed at it anyway) became the animating critique of a varied collection of public officials and intellectuals calling for a new way of thinking about government—what they considered a new model or paradigm of governance. Much of the criticism, and much of the interest in taking government in a new direction, arose among the nation's governors, including Bill Clinton, who further pursued his affinity for the ideas of this movement once he reached the White House.

Reinventing Administrative Instrumentalism

President Clinton and Vice President Al Gore, self-proclaimed "New Democrats" (Hale 1995), injected additional energy into the system with a more overtly neoliberal orientation than Ronald Reagan. That orientation emphasized less what modern American government should do, instead focusing on how it should do it. The lingering effects of economic stagnation from the 1970s, the static or dwindling fiscal resources arising from the Reagan strategy and accompanying attacks on the public fisc through tax-limiting reforms at state and local levels, along with growing public perceptions of governmental irrelevance and incompetence, spurred the effort.

This orientation introduced ideas, derived from the tumultuous restructuring of American business in the 1970s, for "reengineering" or "reinventing" the administration of public programs and the delivery of public services. The intellectual crafters of this orientation stressed what they regarded as a useless obsession with ideological disputes over the ends of government, a preoccupation that led incumbent officeholders and their challengers alike to ignore the real problems of citizens and to cripple *how* government goes about the work of addressing those problems. Contending that we "do not need another New Deal, nor another Reagan Revolution," and supported by the words of public officials calling for a new vision of government, the chief prophets of this movement stated the case forcefully. "Our fundamental problem today is not too much government or too little government. We have debated that issue endlessly . . . , and it has not solved our problems. . . . We do not need more government or less government, we need *better* government. To be more precise, we need better *governance*" (Osborne and Gaebler 1992, 23–24; emphasis in original; also see Gore 1993, 2, 8).

This "better government" orientation sought to distance itself decisively from past conceptions of government and public administration, offering a conception of "new governance" (e.g., D. John et al. 1994) that has outlived its service as political rhetoric and has gone on to reinforce and intensify the networked topography of governance, generating as one consequence, the appearance and perhaps the reality of a "hollow state" (e.g., Milward 1996).

At its inception, at least in the United States (for this was a worldwide phenomenon), the principal conceptual and metaphorical device employed was the distinction between "steering" and "rowing," borrowed from the longtime privatization advocate E. S. Savas (Behn 2012). This recalled the politics-administration dichotomy, and indeed, Osborne and Gaebler specifically discussed "separating" steering, which involves policy decisions, from rowing, which involves service delivery (1992, 34–37). They also argued that governments that steer "actively shape their communities, states, and nations" (32), however, and they discussed at length "community-owned government" and "empowerment," which involves government support for citizens in defining their goals as well as in finding the means to achieve them. Despite the attempt to create a conceptual separation that retained a distinctive role for government that might even hint at its formative nature, the overall aim of this neoliberal enterprise was to produce "more governance and less government" (Grell and Gappert 1992), or "governing without government" (Rhodes 1996), in ways that increased the spread and density of the interest networks surrounding the state. Through this expanded quasi-public sphere the enterprise purposely promulgated the values, principles, and even the rhetoric of the market and economizing rationality, pressuring if not directly forcing every social institution to be concerned about its "customers."

In the early 1960s, word first reached the public regarding a new kind of nuclear weapon, a "neutron bomb," or "enhanced radiation weapon" (see BBC News 1999), designed to wreak less destruction on buildings and infrastructure even as it destroyed more human lives by expanding the lethal dose of radiation through a far more powerful burst of neutrons. Attention to the potential of the neutron bomb peaked in the 1980s because of the Carter administration's decision to delay development, Ronald Reagan's decision to go forward with development, and China's announcement that it had developed the weapon. As the second Clinton term was ending, however, the neutron bomb had been relegated to a metaphor for destruction in which humans have disappeared and only artifacts remain. It is tempting to apply the neutron bomb metaphor to the intent and effects of the "new governance," especially with respect to the effects on career public servants. Despite the deregulation, devolution, and defunding efforts of both the Reagan agenda and the New Democrats, creating most notably stagnation in the size of federal civil service, the institutional structure of programmatic liberalism and the cadres of public servants populating that structure have nevertheless endured. Indeed, the new governance succeeded by reinventing the role of public sector bureaucrats, removing many more of them from direct service delivery and transforming them into the overseers of the networks of public, nonprofit, and private bureaucrats actually delivering services. Not surprisingly, especially for federal civil servants, this only increased the disharmony between the role they play and public expectations for the instrumental, service-oriented functions of administration that is the primary if not the only source of warm feelings citizens have for public servants. Despite the intentions of the designers of the new governance, this has only intensified the attacks on the programmatic liberal welfare state as spawning bureaucratic tyranny. For "movement conservatives," this has meant no diminution in "targets to mobilize against" (Skowronek 2011, 189).

A Conservative Postmodernism

The next success in that mobilization came with the election of George W. Bush, who gained the White House when Democratic candidate Al Gore, winner of the popular vote, lost the disputed electoral votes of the state of Florida through Supreme Court edict (*Bush v. Gore*, 531 U.S. 98 [2000]). The second Bush presidency proved a confusing disappointment to the faithful, however. President Bush started his presidency as the "first MBA president" (see Pfiffner 2007) and functioned initially in a way that produced policy results not much different than his predecessor and fully consistent with the neoliberal new governance orientation. The terrorist attacks of September 11, 2001, gave the neoconservatives in Bush's circle of advisors, especially Vice President Dick Cheney, policy control (Baker 2013), leading to expansion of the national security appendage of the administrative state, including a new "homeland security" dimension far exceeding what an American public suspicious of internal security structures had ever before tolerated, even during the Cold War (Dean 2004). Even as pronouncements about the constitutional importance of the unitary theory of the presidency (Yoo, Calabresi, and Colangelo 2005) and the return of the "imperial presidency" (Rudalevige 2006) came to prominence, the second Bush presidency foundered on the rocks of the neoconservative military gambits in Iraq and Afghanistan, leaving few permanent marks on the institutional structure of the programmatic liberal state. It would take the election of Sen. Barack Obama, a moderate Democrat, former community organizer, and first major-party African American presidential candidate, to ignite a far more furious assault by conservatives, fueled by enormous sums of money by corporate interests, especially in the fossil fuel and gun industries, and anchored, at least rhetorically, in the "categorical rejection of progressivism as a corruption of the original Constitution" accompanied by an "appeal back to a limited government that maximizes individual liberty" (Skowronek 2011, 189).

Despite the historical shallowness of some commentators (e.g., Cashill 2011) who found in President Obama the first postmodern president, that moniker most appropriately belongs to Ronald Reagan. Although there were strong hints of the reality-crafting art of postmodernism coming out of the Nixon White House, which included former advertising executive H. R. Haldeman, it was Ronald Reagan and his advisors who perfected the public spectacle (Miroff 2003) as a primary governing device. The spectacle is a prime feature of postmodernism and postmodernity (Debord 1977; Kreps 1998). It involves the attempt to create an alternative realty or "hyperreality," based on the postmodernist argument that what people accept as reality and truth are socially constructed (Berger and Luckmann 1966). The spectacle also relies on the evolution of social life in postindustrial democracies, indeed everywhere in the world given the effects of globalization, toward more and more time devoted to a virtual world of digital devices and social media. Although postmodernism originated in critiques of liberalism and modernist rationalism from the left, especially among those who argued that language itself was a field for the exercise of power and the maintenance of power differentials (e.g., Jacques Derrida), Ronald Reagan and especially his self-proclaimed heirs and torchbearers have proved to be the prime practitioners and adepts of a postmodern politics. Into this minefield walked Barack Obama, burdened by the imperative to respond to the worst economic crisis since the Great Depression, the polity-corroding effects of more than five years of war in Iraq and Afghanistan, and by his own agenda promoting change and hope.

By any reasonable historical reference, Obama appeared to be at best a moderately liberal Democrat, promoting a policy agenda very much in line with the neoliberal-tinged orientation of Clinton, Gore, and the New Democrats. His opposition painted him as far more radical, proposing dramatic growth in big government at the national level to rival anything the New Deal or Great Society had offered. And in one respect, Obama did propose to expand the programmatic liberal welfare state by taking another run at enacting a national health care plan that would cover most Americans not already covered by Medicare, Medicaid, the military retiree health care system, or employer-based private insurance. The program as envisioned would in many respects have closed the circle on the social welfare intentions of the New Deal. Although forced to accept compromises that included dropping the proposal's "public option," which would have provided health insurance directly from the public sector much like Medicare, Obama did succeed, with the passage of the Patient Protection and Affordable Care Act during the two years he enjoyed Democratic majority support in Congress. When the president signed the law in March 2010, he had narrowly accomplished what FDR, Harry Truman, Lyndon Johnson, and Bill Clinton had failed to achieve.

Opponents, primarily in the Republican Party and its wide field of ancillary and independent interest groups, painted the law as an existential threat to liberty, property, and the very foundations of the American republic. In a state of postmodern politics, in which hyperbole is the norm, the furious counterattack of Obama's conservative opponents nevertheless was stunning not just for its rhetorical excess, but also for its success in translating its hyperreal depiction of the destruction of the regime into actions that indeed seemed to threaten the institutional underpinnings of the programmatic liberal state. Winning back control of the U.S. House of Representatives in the 2010 election and twisting the Senate into knots through unprecedented use of the filibuster for even ordinary legislative action, Republicans forced substantial across-the-board cuts in federal spending in 2011 through "sequestration," or automatic spending cuts, triggered by exceeding targets for deficit spending. Even after Obama won re-election with solid electoral college and popular vote majorities, and Democrats reinforced party control in the Senate, the Republican House counterattacked furiously with threats of a government shutdown, which materialized, as well as the even more serious threat of preventing further increases in federal government borrowing authority, thus forcing the United States to fall short in fulfilling its fiscal obligations. Such a default would have seriously degraded the full faith and credit of the United States, threatening the global economy as well by weakening the world's major investment safe haven during troubled economic times. In late 2013, House Republicans capitulated and backed off on policy and spending demands, including changes to the new health care law, and allowed a vote on increasing the federal government's borrowing authority to go forward (Weisman and Parker 2013).

Whatever comes of the fury and chaos unleashed by the opposition to the Obama presidency, as well as by a host of social and economic issues that has sparked pitched battles at the state and local levels deep into the second decade of the twenty-first century, the conception and treatment of public administration in American politics and government has remained largely unchanged, not just in the last 30 years but all the way back to the New Deal. A recapitulation and reflection on the reasons for that state of affairs will help set the stage for a final contemplation of the status and meaning of public administration in the regime, its relationship and value to self-government, and the prospects for finally, fully realizing that value.

Postmodern American Politics and Public Administration

If one accepts the idea of an institutional thickening that has increased over time with each successive national reform effort, the New Deal nevertheless was a watershed. It not only transformed the regime fundamentally and solidified the progressive foundations of an administratively centered national politics but also diminished considerably the possibilities for further reform and reconstruction. A robust form of path dependency with more positive than negative feedback loops has increasingly locked institutions and political actors and their patterns of interaction into place. What the New Deal did not do was to make attempts at reform and reconstruction less likely. Instead, it further reinforced administration as the prime target for reform and reconstruction efforts. As a result, all three responses to the New Deal in the post–New Deal political order have rested fundamentally on the conception of politics, government, and public administration, bequeathed by progressive and New Deal reforms. Although its origins lie in the New Left critique of the New Deal state, the programmatic liberalism that emerged in the generation after the New Deal is mostly the New Deal's most direct and faithful descendant. Yet the neoliberal and neoconservative counterresponses have, in their own obvious and more subtle ways, reinforced New Deal and programmatic liberalism's instrumental conception of public administration.

The prophets of "new governance" praxis, Osborne and Gaebler (1992), did not shrink from stating exactly what they meant by governance. They saw it as "the process by which we collectively solve our problems and meet our society's needs. Government is the instrument we use" (24). Further, governance meant "'leading' society, convincing its various interest groups to embrace common goals and strategies" (34). The Osborne and Gaebler thinking, and the broader intellectual phenomena ("new public management" and "new governance") of which they were a part, encompass a complex blend of ideas. At the core of all this thinking, however, is what Osborne and Gaebler conveyed: that government, and by extension administration, is separate from the mysterious collective process of "governance." Further, although they suggest the community-shaping and goal-defining effects of steering, the separation of the constitutive and the instrumental is primary in their thinking: governance is the formative, constitutive process, while government is instrumental; it is what happens after we decide what we will do, and even what we will be.

Thus, the antipurposive reform strain, like its neoliberal anchor and the economizing rationality that undergirds both, has offered a resolutely instrumental conception of government and politics, in which the nation's problems, needs, goals, and norms of behavior are identified and defined through some mysterious process external to government, or those goals and norms have all been determined in the past and will never need any further consideration or refinement. Any further arguments on that score are simply tiresome distractions.

Politics and government, in this view, boil down to the art of persuasion: elected officials and other leaders convince groups to accept these predetermined problems, needs, goals, and norms. Public administrators are not involved even to this extent. They are responsible for "policy management," that is, finding the proper techniques and strategies to deliver products and services to citizen-customers (Barzelay 1992) in a manner that does not violate norms such as accessibility, responsiveness, and equity.

To be fair, the most thoughtful strains of the reinventing government movement manifested at least a vague recognition that democratic government and politics involve not just the satisfaction of the needs and wants of citizen-customers for a varied package of products and services but the never-ending project of a people to develop and refine its character. In appropriately associating many of the contemporary weaknesses in the responsiveness and effectiveness of American government to the institutional arrangements of the modern factionalism that emerged in the 1970s and 1980s, however, proponents of reinventing government completely dispensed with political theory as the basis for a theory of government. In place of political theory or ideology as the foundation for a philosophy of government, they sought to substitute a cascade of new principles of management, drawn largely from business, that together do not even amount to a coherent theory of management. This is hardly much different from the path many progressive reformers pursued in building the now-despised "bureaucratic paradigm" (Barzelay 1992), and predictably, this approach further reinforced an instrumental conception, not only of public administration but also of politics and government as a whole.

Of course, when it comes to economizing rationality, neoliberalism, and their manifestations in new public management and new governance thought about public administration, the constitutive is not actually absent. It is, instead, hidden in the rhetoric of the instrumental. To apply certain techniques, certain fiscal arrangements, and certain contractual relations is to give new shape and substance to public policy and thus, ultimately, to the character of the citizenry. In this particular case, that shape and substance is to create, or at least to facilitate and accelerate, the final emergence of a pure *homo economicus*, along with a polity based on market principles and economic rationality. This is bound to emerge even if it is not the ultimate aim of the reformers; it is the constitutive effect of their ideas and their approaches to carrying those ideas into effect. By hiding, or at least failing to fully recognize the constitutive effects of the government instruments to be employed, however, the newest reformers have sustained and even further exacerbated the serious tension and even conflict between the instrumental and the constitutive in the regime, to the detriment not only of harnessing the value of public administration in "governance" but also for modern self-government as a whole. The neoliberal orientation to government reform offers no permanent answers to the questions of liberal-democratic governance and certainly no answers to the question of how to integrate public administration into the American regime in a way that recognizes administration as both instrumental and constitutive, and in a way that, although privileging the instrumental, takes account of the constitutive in a manner that enables administration to contribute to, rather than undermine, self-government in an advanced, complex, "multiform" polity.

Although sharing neoliberalism's animosity toward programmatic liberalism, neoconservatism is an entirely different animal in its approach to government and public administration. First, neoconservatives acknowledge the importance of state power, in both its instrumental and constitutive effects. They seek to use administration not only as an instrument for the achievement of particular policy goals, especially in international affairs, protecting the security of the homeland, and policing immoral behavior and questionable social relations. They go further, however, in seeking, not unlike the Jacksonians and FDR, to structure and populate the administrative components of government in a way that will harness their formative power to shape the polity by altering social relations. Such alterations are meant to preserve, or if necessary recover, traditional values, traditional relations of authority and subservience, and traditional arenas of social, economic, and political power. The neoconservative animosity toward the liberal welfare state is thus not in the latter's conception of state and administration per se, but in the liberal state's standing as a force opposed to traditional values, traditional social relations, and traditional institutions of authority and power. Neoconservatives are the latest in a breed of intellectuals and activists horrified that the progressive–New Deal administrative state has had the effect of rearranging, or at least trying to rearrange, institutional structures, social relations, and thus authority and power in ways that express values different from, if not in opposition to, such traditional values as wealth and social standing, and the power that follows them.

In their assaults on programmatic liberalism, however, neoconservatives have sent their own mixed signals to add to public confusion about public administration's proper role. Their position on the importance of a muscular state to project power externally and protect traditional values and social relations internally implicitly acknowledges the constitutiveness of government and even public administration. Yet their furious efforts to destroy the welfare state and their unyielding rhetorical assaults on public bureaucracies and bureaucrats has signaled that administration in both its instrumental and its constitutive manifestations is to be despised and disparaged, especially when it is tied to a helping motivation that interferes with traditional forms of social assistance that maintain traditional values and social relations. Neoconservatives have been adept at differentiating the public order and safety preserving functions of police and the military as constitutionally legitimate core functions. This success as been muted by the sometime alliance of neoconservatism with neoliberalism's marketization of everything, which is itself a threat to some traditional nonmarket institutions and values. Still, neoconservatism, although it is less a coherent philosophy or ideology than a "persuasion" (Kristol 2003), at least acknowledges, if not always openly or positively, the constitutiveness of public administration.

Both neoliberalism and neoconservatism appear to recognize that Americans like the conception of the state as provider of services, the very essence of programmatic liberalism. In this sense, they have acknowledged the triumph of some version of FDR's vision. This triumph, that America has become, in the recent parlance, a nation of "takers" (Schweizer 2008) through the formative effects of programmatic liberalism tied to an administrative state, is precisely the focus of the combined neoliberal-neoconservative critique, suggesting that both orientations acknowledge more overtly than modern liberalism the constitutiveness of institutions. They abhor that quality when it is associated with the state, however, or, more precisely, when it is associated with a particular configuration and value orientation of the state. They are pleased, for the most part, with the constitutiveness of other institutions they embrace, such as the market or religion, although they remain confused in their insistence that such other institutions could function, let alone exist, without the purpose-serving and purpose-shaping functions and effects of government and its primary mechanism of action, public administration.

These representations of neoliberalism and neoconservatism are at best ideal types. Whatever their varied and messy incarnations, however, they have collided, mingled, and evolved in a bubbly and not always tasty brew that has lent a through-the-looking-glass quality to politics and government, which is the epitome of postmodern sensibilities. Having brought us to a new political version of William James's "blooming, buzzing confusion" (1890/1981, 462), the political movements of the post–New Deal political order have only sharpened and extended a subordinate, instrumental conception of administration. They have, further, sustained the New Deal's success in expunging from thoughtful public debate any coherent alternative conception of administration's role that might acknowledge its constitutiveness. Debates in legislative forums that might touch on broad questions about the role of administrative agencies and functions in governing rarely escape defaulting to the venerable and all too tiresome rhetorical practice of bureaucrat bashing.

There will be no thoughtful discussion and debate, of course, as long as opponents of programmatic liberalism and "big government" seek to gain control of the administrative state to use it as a battering ram against the egalitarian-welfare orientation of progressivism and New Deal liberalism. They do not seek to dismantle the whole battering ram itself, only what they see as the useless and undesirable parts of it, for they have, in ways they do not seem fully to comprehend, internalized the very programmatic orientation of the modern liberal state they claim to despise. The sharp polarization of elites, another prominent feature of current American politics (e.g., Hetherington 2009), reflects these battles over control of the administrative state as an instrument for competing programmatic ends. Sweeping incursions into the nation's politics and government, such as neoliberalism's marketization of the state, and the neoconservative culture wars, reflect those competing programmatic priorities. Such efforts to gain control of the state to serve priorities such as the wealth concentration and morals regulation around which neoliberals and neoconservatives can join hands, send the message that government can function best as a tool to serve particular interests and as a weapon to vanquish one's enemies. That such efforts will give new form and shape to the polity and the character of citizenry, in many and varied ways the initiators of such efforts do not entirely intend, is the great truth of the formative power of political institutions and processes hidden by an excessive focus on the instrumental.

Despite the greater array of controls on public administration imposed by both liberals and conservatives, and the ever more pronounced rhetoric and actions aimed at instrumentalizing administration in pursuit of that control, public agencies remain involved, in both large and small ways, in shaping public aims and the relations between citizens that define a political way of life. The rift between elite political rhetoric on the one hand, and public experience with the constitutive reality of government on the other, has simply grown even more acute. In confirmation of its transition to a postmodern condition, the public swings back and forth between revolt and anomie.

Chapter Seven

The Constitutive Dimension of Public Administration

Appreciating Consequences

S urvey research has shown repeatedly that majorities of Americans claim to want less government, and thus lower taxes and fewer government services, while also insisting that government be powerful and far-reaching enough to tackle long-smoldering problems and confront new threats as they arise. In the 2012 General Social Survey, for instance, "52.0% said their own federal income tax was too high, 45.5% about right, and 2.5% too low." Nevertheless, "more people have always favored increases in spending than cuts. In 2012, as in most years since the 1970s, people . . . backed more spending in about three-quarters of the areas and less spending in only the bottom quarter. Moreover, the number of areas with positive net spending scores not only outnumbered areas with nega- tive scores, but are also larger" (T. W. Smith 2013, 6). Such increases in spending are likely to be accomplished through administrative agencies and their contrac- tors, of course, but Americans think these entities waste considerable propor- tions of the tax dollars directed to them (Jones 2011). Even more confounding, cutting back on those wasteful bureaucracies might actually increase wasteful spending (Gravois 2011). Americans thus seem to want what government pri- marily does—deliver programs that at least some of the time help people—but not how it operates, namely, through complex organizations housing bureaucrats who make independent decisions that serve citizen needs but also shape people's lives, property, and communities. In short, Americans find themselves in a "love- hate relationship with administrative power" (Milkis 1993, 211). The American public's ambivalence about public administration and its place in both their private and public lives is not simply a product of the rise of the administrative state, however. The ambivalence and animosity have their roots in the struggle of American political leaders, from the founding onward across successive episodes of regime development and transformation, to comprehend and respond to the distinctive institutional character of administration, a character marked by an especially acute tension between the instrumental and constitutive qualities that typify all political institutions.

At several points in American political development, the nation appeared poised on the threshold of incorporating a constitutive understanding of administration into the nation's prevailing philosophies and practices, but each time the nation's leaders stopped short, and the chances that they would lead their fellow citizens across that threshold diminished correspondingly. It is worth pausing briefly here to reflect further on the first of those episodes before moving on to consider the present consequences of the succeeding choices, as well as what has not yet been lost. This sets the stage for considering in the final chapter, how, if at all, the value of understanding public administration in constitutive terms might be more fully attained.

Jefferson, Hamilton, and the Path Not Taken

In seeking to construct a republic, the Constitution's framers faced perhaps the ultimate regime design dilemma: how to preserve self-government, which from history appeared only possible in small, homogeneous states where government remained within reasonable reach of the citizenry, while ensuring sufficient energy in government for national survival, growth, and prosperity. One cannot easily fault Thomas Jefferson for concluding that it was critical, under the Constitution's scheme for an extended republic, to keep the administration of the people's affairs close to the people, where they could more easily keep an eye on that most active and continuous part of government, and even be part of it. This would not be only a matter of keeping government in check, however, but also a matter of learning firsthand the trials and tribulations, and in the long run, formative value, of republican self-government. Observers and commentators from Tocqueville, to Woodrow Wilson, to the most thoughtful of current critics of the state of American constitutionalism (e.g., Elkin 2006, ch. 7; Fung 2004) have made the same case. One might further conclude that perhaps the loss of a sense of the constitutiveness of administration is the result of the inexorable removal of the people from the administration of their own affairs as a result of the growth of the national state. Jefferson thus might reasonably have argued that the Constitution's design failed to bridge responsibly the two horns of the dilemma, forcing him into a stark choice effectuated in his self-styled "revolution."

Spurred by both conviction and ambition, however, Jefferson posed to his fellow citizens of the very young nation a false choice, for there was little in Hamilton's vision of an administrative republic that would have fundamentally undermined local government and the citizen experience with public administration in daily life local government provides. The Federalists, particularly Hamilton, sought to develop the balance between the empowerment of national administration necessary to build a new nation while simultaneously governing it (and the formative effects of administrative theory, structure, and practice such empowerment implied), with the combination of the political accountability necessary to conform to the aspirations for self-government of a whole nation and the protection of individual rights embodied in the new Constitution. By mimicking the worst of Whiggish fears and denunciations of monarchism, Jefferson and his followers injected a much harsher ideological conflict into the politics of the nation. Thus, Jefferson's politics not only aggravated the underlying tensions between the instrumental and constitutive in administration but also set in motion the constant battle over national administration that has diminished the lessons in accommodation and balance the Federalists offered, reduced the effectiveness of national administration and even in some sense all governance in the United States, and sown confusion and division among the citizenry about the meaning of self-government in a continental-sized nation, a meaning that at its core must accept the truth that administration through bureaucracy *is* day-to-day governance on any scale beyond the small town.

The great loss in not following the Hamiltonian path, or at least accommodating it more substantially than Jefferson's false choice allowed, was the forfeiture of the chance for American citizens to gain at the beginning of the republic the experience of national self-government by becoming accustomed, indeed empowered, to scrutinize national administration and shape its constitutive effects through direct interaction with the representatives of national government in their midst, rather than through a variety of intermediaries who had their own aims and interests. The irony is that citizens had this opportunity anyway and exercised it, because from the very beginning of the nation all the way to its twenty-first-century form, the vast majority of federal administrators have been widely dispersed across the nation rather than concentrated in the seat of the national government. Such citizen-administrator encounters occurred in the

shadow of an ideology of distrust and resistance, however, rather than a philosophy of citizen responsibility for engagement and guidance. The effect of the former
simply reinforced the contradiction between ideological rhetoric and reality in citizen experience with government where public administration is concerned.

The "second state" period brought slightly bolder incremental steps to introduce more extensive national administration, sparking repeated battles in which
the keepers of the Jeffersonian ideology sought to bend the agents of the new
policies to local ways. This was by then, however, much more a matter of serving
local centers of political power than a matter of giving citizens in their localities
a say in how policies would be carried out and thus teaching and empowering
them to guide its formative effects. By the time direct national administration
became much more prominent in local affairs, the control by local powers had
greatly diminished the chance of citizens gaining a real sense of control over
national policy affecting their lives through direct contact with federal administrators, which would also have provided a sense of their being a part of the formative enterprise going on across the nation. Political leaders and citizens did
accept direct federal administration, indeed, expected it to be vigorously pursued, under special circumstances: on the "margins" of the nation and in response to threats to peace and security (Balogh 2009, ch. 5). The combination of
this special exception with the dominant practice of keeping the force of the national government distant or hidden produced the perverse effect of citizens
rarely scrutinizing and questioning government in its work affecting marginal
populations and on the boundaries of the nation, both geographic and virtual,
while zealously challenging direct administration and even repeatedly seeking
to undermine it when associated with the Constitution's core domestic aspirations of pursuing justice and promoting the general welfare of all citizens.

The Federalists are hardly blameless in the development of these consequences, as it was the Federalist strategy to inject a populist element into their
drive for ratification of the Constitution, unleashing forces they could not entirely control, and requiring them to use some indirect forms of administration
for the energetic government actions they pursued. The Hamiltonian solution
was in part a response to this dynamic, but its attempt at a balance between local
and national administration, and between the instrumental and the constitutive
in administration, proved to be internally unstable, and it was swept away in the
Federalists' political defeat. It is, therefore, the Jeffersonian ideology that has
most persistently promoted the notions of instrumentalism, minimalism, and
subordination of administration to the people's will, setting the nation on edge

with a grinding friction between the necessities of government and the fantasy of small, local, amateur government as all that is needed to preserve liberty while coping with the many complexities of modernity.

To be sure, the fixation on the instrumental dimension of administration, which, when contrasted with the constitutive reality that is at the heart of the public's ambivalence and even hostility, has assumed its sharpest, most expansive form as the size and reach of the federal government have grown. This fixation is hardly surprising, signaling as it does the convergence of the irrepressible democratic impulse, the hegemony of economic progress that has lengthened the reach of economizing thought, and political leaders' repeated attempts to harness the formative power of administration for ideological ends. With the elements first fully recognizable in the Jacksonian era, this convergence has culminated in the programmatic liberal expression of what E. E. Schattschneider (1960) called the "socialization of conflict," in which problems previously defined and treated privately are identified as public goals (or ends), and public solutions (or means) are sought to address them. The solutions have come in the form of benefits and protections packaged as government programs. Programs must be administered, however, and to lessen the chances that these programs might be administered arbitrarily, political leaders have pursued an acutely instrumental approach to public policy intended to produce a public administration devoid of any "independent judgment" (Morone 1990, 128, 141). This is clearly contrary to both the historical and the current realities of the function, behavior, and effects of public administration in the regime. The contradictions and confusions about the role of public administration in American government and politics, rooted deep in the Republic's past and sustained by current arrangements, thus have generated a peculiarly conflictual politics centered on the administrative instrumentality.

First, public administration is the principal object of contention between activists across the ideological spectrum because it is the principal vehicle for delivering what political leaders and the public most prize about the modern state: the benefits and protections (and punishments on the marginal and deviant) it bestows. Second, these combatants seek to wield public administration as a weapon in a war to secure control of the state, not just for the kinds of services it dispenses and the means for dispensing them but also for the polity-shaping effects such control might generate.

For all the money, energy, and toil invested in this war to ensure that public bureaucracy as servant is under "political" control and responsive to the public will, as is pronounced repeatedly by those claiming to speak for that public, American citizens are no more comfortable than they ever were with an extensive presence of public bureaucracy in their lives. Indeed, they are as anxious and antagonistic as ever toward bureaucrats who seem to threaten both individual freedom and collective self-determination. And perhaps they should be, for a closer look at the intensely instrumental regard for and treatment of public administration suggests that perpetuating the contradiction between the conception and reality of public administration in American politics has been constitutive of a frustrated, dependent, unimaginative citizenry who suffer from weakened political institutions that are unlikely to satisfy strong aspirations to self-government.

Instrumental Administration and Its Consequences

The faceless bureaucrat, the rigidly rule-bound and unresponsive public servant, the mysterious labyrinth of corridors, the long customer service wait times—these are all part of the imagery of public bureaucracy deeply imbedded in American culture, some updated in the digital age by accounts of complicated or unresponsive websites and confusing call center menu options. All are in some way connected to real traits in the bureaucratic organizational form that may become pathological, but they have been magnified beyond all proportion as the instrumental conception of public administration has flourished. This disproportionate reaction to public bureaucracy is most pronounced in the applications of technology to administration and the use of nongovernmental "partners" in service delivery, and it illuminates one of the principal repercussions of a myopic understanding of administration.

Problem Displacement and the Vicious Circle of Control

In searching for collective solutions to societal problems that overwhelm both individuals and local communities, Americans have repeatedly supported either of two types of solutions that would keep the threat of bureaucratic tyranny at bay. One type encompasses automatic mechanisms and technological solutions as devoid as possible of human involvement, or at least of citizen contact with a bureaucrat. These mechanisms and technologies have, nevertheless, required "experts" and "managers" of one kind or another to make them work. Moreover, when human involvement becomes necessary because the automatic mechanism or the technology fails to function as expected, or the individual case is outside established system parameters, citizen contact with a bureaucrat may be all the more jarring for both parties, in part because the mysteries of the opaque system force the inexpert citizen to be even more compliant. The combination of high specialization, automatic processing, and complex technology in public administration has thus ironically reinforced among citizens the sense of loss of control, even of subservience, to machines and to bureaucrats. In a very real manifestation of the formative effect of tools on tool users, Americans have allowed their character as a people and their interactions with one another to be dictated by the formulas and technologies they have devised to address their problems in a way that might avoid the dreaded presence of bureaucratic administration in their midst.

This profound sense of loss of control of who we are, how we act, and how we govern ourselves is not due to the tyranny of the machine or the bureaucrat, however. It is grounded in the mechanistic, instrumental orientation itself. As William Leiss has stated it, "we are not tyrannized by the complex technical knowledge incorporated in our society's administrative structures; we simply expect too much of it" (1990, 22). The instrumental conception of politics, but especially of administration, embraced by American political leaders with increased intensity across the generations, has served as the repository for expectations for resolving the dilemmas of liberal democratic governance. These dilemmas became increasingly challenging and perplexing with the growing complications of industrial and postindustrial society. If the task of governance was, however, simply to craft the proper tools, in the form of public agencies and the public servants in them, and maintain proper control of those tools so that the fundamental goals of the regime could be attained, then the increasingly polycentric problems that emerged simply required more sophisticated tools, and more sophisticated controls on the use of those tools. At the national level, Congress's construction of a legislative-centered public administration is the epitome of this response, with new and more extensive formal and informal controls required to keep new or expanded administrative structures in check (see Rosenbloom 2000, ch. 3).

Embracing this definition of liberal democratic governance has shunted aside the central dilemmas posed by the combination of aspirations to strong protections for individual liberty and collective self-government, replacing them with the problem of imposing political controls on administration. Each successive wave of administrative reform has generated increased anxiety about control, responsiveness, and accountability, however. The result has been an upward spiral in collective worry about the control and accountability of the administrative establishment and about the manipulation of that establishment for partisan political purposes. An increasingly vicious circle has emerged in which anxiety about control and accountability of public administration has led to more extensive, more complex controls, which in turn have increased the social and operational distance between administrators and the public they are expected to serve. This distance then raises new worries about control and accountability and brings about the introduction of another layer of controls (see, for example, Schoenbrod 1983, 824). An expanding share of valuable political and governing resources is consumed in creating and tending this complex matrix of controls, with no noticeable improvement, in the aggregate, in the relationship between the public and public administrators, or in individual or systemic capacity for self-government. Indeed, precisely the opposite would appear to be the case.

The other prominent type of solution to large collective problems intended to avoid direct, centralized bureaucratic engagement is the strategy of keeping government "out of sight" (and presumably out of mind) through the use a wide spectrum of private intermediaries (Balogh 2009). This preserves the implicit bargain in which citizens can hold on to the myth of the sovereign individual as long as they don't know or at least aren't reminded of the extent to which their lives are administered. A strategy of energetic government action kept largely hidden, at least from the inattentive citizen, offered what Thomas Jefferson touted as the virtue of shaping loyalty to the republic through "economic independence and friendly intercourse" (71) rather than through the effective, forthright, and equitable administration of the law as envisioned by Alexander Hamilton. The Jeffersonian approach, reinvigorated as the "new governance," has the obvious limitation that when visible, vigorous exercise of governmental authority, which must always occur through administration, is necessary, citizen anger and resistance are all the more bitter because citizens have become so accustomed to the notion that government has not been all that powerful in shaping society. Even when indirect service provision is tried, through a combination of private and public entities, the effort of the state to reorganize, coordinate, and improve private functions still sparks anger and resistance, which in turn is easy to mobilize and manipulate for other more selfish ends. The attacks are all the more furious, in ways that can only be corrosive of the peace and integrity of the polity, when the results of direct and visible administrative action are formative or transformative, as in efforts such as fighting racial discrimination, creating and maintaining a stable financial system, or expanding educational opportunities and improving educational outcomes. In sum, by design the strategy of hiding the government in plain sight contributes nothing to helping citizens think about and appreciate the value of administration's constitutiveness.

Early manifestations of the effects of addressing the liberal democratic governance problem through an instrumental conception of administration appeared in dramatic fashion during the Jeffersonian embargo. In that instance, blunt and forceful, direct national administration that had such a profound effect on people's lives and livelihoods stood so much in contrast to Jefferson's philosophy of "a few plain duties performed by a few servants" that it nearly drove Federalist-dominated New England to secession. The effects surfaced again even more clearly in the Jacksonian reform effort. The practice of rotation in office and the nascent bureaucratic mechanisms that the Jacksonians put in place seemed to increase the aggregate accessibility and comprehensibility of administration, and they clearly had beneficial effects for the regime. The organizational norms, operating routines, and controls on behavior introduced by Amos Kendall and others, for instance, allowed for the retention of some administrative capacity and efficiency in the face of the greater turnover induced by rotation. Rotation and the spoils system in turn helped the growing public bureaucracy maintain public salience, and with it an important measure of legitimacy with a population that was expanding rapidly in its size, diversity, and embrace of a market-centered society (Larson 2010; Sellers 1991).

The spoils system was not, on the other hand, an easy system to navigate, raising questions about how much more accessible public employment had really become for any given individual, beyond the effects of the sheer increase in number of positions available. Nor did the spoils necessarily produce a more open, mutually supportive relationship in the face-to-face encounter between administrator and citizen. In some respects, the system diminished administrator ties to the citizenry by making the former answerable to party leaders, who may or may not have been sensitive to citizen needs. And it is not at all clear that administrative subordination to party, through the president or Congress, produced policy formulation or implementation that was much more consistent with the popular will than the system that preceded it.

In addition, the incipient bureaucratization, aimed as much at limiting corruption as increasing efficiency, combined with rotation to produce substantial administrative incapacity and inefficiency; the performance of the Union Army during the Civil War is perhaps the premiere example of this effect, with its parallels to the Jeffersonian "legacy of military incompetence in the Army and administrative ineptitude in the War Department" (Caldwell 1988, 179; but see Van Riper 1958, 43–44). A more serious consequence was that, because of rotation and routinization, fewer and fewer administrators had the sense of responsibility and the experience to understand and effectively deploy the practical judgment that lies at the core of administration as a political enterprise and the contributions it makes to the regime. Moreover, the eventually corrupt outcome of the spoils seemingly contradicted the Jacksonian pledges of moral restoration and subjugation of administration to the public will and interest. Hence, a new reform effort appeared, imposing new control arrangements and creating new and more complex challenges for accessibility, comprehensibility, and effectiveness.

The consequences for the vitality and fortitude of American aspirations to self-government are, however, most pronounced under the present system of controls and political relationships. Despite the greater openness to public influence, healthy skepticism, and "bottom-up reorientation of political forces" it exhibits (Heclo 1989, 298, 302), American politics and government are—to paraphrase Theodore Lowi's long-standing critique—open, accessible, intelligible, and beneficial for the organized but an impenetrable, frustrating, coercive enigma for the unorganized (see Lowi 1993a, 154–55). The complex matrix of political relationships and administrative controls built up around programmatic rights requires high-velocity, campaign-style political activism pursued from a platform of sophisticated organization. Attacks on the programmatic administrative state and its benefits, and beneficiaries, takes on the same form, but all the opponents have to offer in exchange is either more draconian impositions on certain civil liberties or the market's manic striving for advantage and the harsher consequences that follow. And self-proclaimed opponents of big government do not really want to get rid of the programmatic administrative state anyway. They just want to rid it of the programs that do not serve their purposes (see, for example, Farenthold 2013).

Organization provides to political interests, as it always has to pressure groups (see Ornstein and Elder 1978, 69–79, for example), the financial, leadership, and motivational resources to marshal the forces, including print, digital, and social media access, that are necessary to define and install new programmatic rights or to maintain and defend programmatic rights already won. This characteristic of the policy process does not appear to be very much of a reform of the self-interested basis of post–New Deal politics sought by the activists of the 1960s and 1970s. From the perspective of the individual citizen, moreover, the benefits of this system are concentrated on and enjoyed by relatively narrowly defined groups, while the burdens are diffuse, growing, and borne by an increasingly precarious middle class (see Elkin 2006, 264–65; Phillips 1993; Pressman 2007).

Furthermore, the procedures and requirements for administrative rule making that constitute a central feature of the current system, although important for opening up administrative decision making to a wider range of public viewpoints and bringing bureaucratic expertise into direct contact with the public's views, are nevertheless now so complicated and drawn out that influence rarely comes from anything but well-organized, directly affected constituencies who have the resources and stamina to maneuver through the process successfully. This situation is a mockery of the "reformation" of administrative law (Stewart 1975) that was central to the push by the reformers of the 1960s and 1970s to expand and protect newly defined rights and enhance popular participation, suggesting instead the "derangement of procedure" (Lowi 1993a, 158–59).

Over the course of the past generation, then, the cycle of worrying about accountability and control of administration, imposing new controls on administration in response, and spawning new and more elaborate concerns about accountability and control, has created an arrangement of nearly incomprehensible and inaccessible administrative controls and political relationships. Moreover, citizens see it as preventing them from enjoying the full benefits of the administrative state to which they believe they are entitled. This generates all sorts of feelings of bad faith between public administrators and their fellow citizens (Walsh 2012), and it presents serious barriers to meaningfully broad-based citizen engagement in politics and public life (Harris and Milkis 1989, 297–309; Mettler and Soss 2004; Milkis 1993, 250–55; Soss 2005; Wichowsky and Moynihan 2008).

In addition, the administrative controls that by now have reached their most elaborated patterns, and the political interactions that have reached their most convoluted, high-velocity forms, have revealed themselves to be serious obstacles to the effectiveness with which administrative agencies fulfill their "missions" (Moe 1989; but see Goodsell 2011). The fundamental structure of American governments, particularly the separation of powers, has from the beginning produced local, state, and national administrations fragmented in their structure and operational capacity. This has led to the search for the "philosopher's stone" of coordination (Seidman and Gilmour 1986, ch. 10). Further complication and aggravation of this fundamental condition, ironically, thwarts fulfillment of the instrumental conception of administration on which the rules and procedures and arrangements are predicated, a point not missed by advocates of neoliberal reforms. Far more serious, however, is that the complex, unwieldy matrix of controls and political relationships has weakened administrative effectiveness in the critical constitutive contribution that administration can make better than any other political institution: drawing on the day-to-day observations and experience its gains from occupying the space where state and society, public and private, meet, to rethink and suggest refinements to the polity's goals and the citizen relations that give them meaning, in light of both current exigencies and collective choices already made and legitimated (see Cook 2010; Rourke 1991, 1992).

Constitutional Space, Democratized Administration, and Policy Design

An exclusively instrumental conception of administration, especially of administration as a pillar in the foundation of the peculiarly American version of the modern welfare state, has served to cut off that institution from the liberal democratic constitutionalism of which it is a part. This has forced political leaders, public administrators, and scholars into a long and arduous search for legitimating arguments to reconcile and thus artificially reattach administration to a regime predicated on popular sovereignty and individual rights. As the bureaucratic form came more and more to embody what Americans understood by the term "administration," the legitimating arguments advanced and the structural reforms proposed became more elaborate.

Irrespective of the rate or extent of bureaucratization, however, the dominant view in American politics has always been that administration is foreign—an alien in a democratic land. This seems to be especially so with respect to good administration, that which is effective both in meeting goals and in helping to shape those goals and the citizen interactions that embody them. At the time of the founding, those with Whig sensibilities who embraced republican government most ardently denounced strong administration as monarchical. By the turn of the twentieth century, political leaders concluded that administration was more dangerous still, because it was by then clearly bureaucratized. They perceived that its potential for despotism was then much greater, and so it had to be domesticated, harnessed, and controlled or it would undermine the democratic way of life.

The best of the scholarly attempts to reconcile bureaucracy with American liberal democracy have been impressively creative, but all of them in one way or another ring hollow and artificial, for they accept the premises that administration is wholly instrumental in function and effect and that it must be forced to conform to a peculiarly American brand of democratic values. More important, the entire reconciliation project has been unsuccessful in finding an arrangement that the American people are comfortable with, largely because it is based on an erroneous, or at least an incomplete, conception of liberal democratic politics. Constituting a liberal democratic regime and engaging in liberal democratic politics consist not only in getting to some predetermined goal but also in deciding how best to get there. These are critical dimensions, no doubt, and public administration is particularly vital to the latter. But making and keeping a liberal democratic regime also entails considering and reconsidering what goals to strive for, and thus shaping and reshaping the character of a people. Public administration has a role here, too, and that role, in fact, is unavoidable.

Because American public administration, even in its most bureaucratized, centralized form, has a lineage that runs as deep as the Republic's, and because the nature of public administration as an institution is also consistent with the idea of the constitutiveness of political institutions inherent in democratic constitutionalism recognized by American political leaders across the generations, from the founders forward, American public bureaucracy does not inherently threaten to control what people think or how they interact with one another, or to otherwise enslave the populace. Instead, it is the repeated insistence by those same political leaders that administration is merely instrumental that poses such a threat. This is especially so for the most recent incarnation of the instrumental conception, in which citizens are recast as clients or customers. Emanating as it does from a neoliberal notion of individual autonomy that relies on untenable assumptions about the equality of parties in market exchange, this newest version fails to acknowledge and preserve a separate sphere of political autonomy and the freedom and power that come with it (W. Brown 2006, 703–4), much like what the Jeffersonians sought to preserve.

American public administration does not need to be artificially reconciled with or grafted onto the regime of the Constitution or suspended in an increasingly complex matrix of controls. Such controls have been devised, for the most part, to enhance the political power of their creators, rather than to enhance the freedom and sovereign power of the citizenry. Instead, because American political development generally, and the construction of the administrative state in particular, have not been guided by an understanding of administration that includes a robust constitutive perspective, administration has become separated from the regime. Just as serious, the instrumental perspective has led to legitimating arguments, which reconcile administration with liberal democracy principally on the basis of the former's neutrality and expertise. This does not mean that neutrality and expertise are unimportant aspects of public administration. On the contrary, they are crucial considerations. But heavy reliance on them has led to the seriously mistaken notion that expertise *is* authority (see Cook 1992, 426; MacIntyre 1981, chs. 7, 8; Mitchell and Scott 1987). This has allowed the social and psychic distance between citizen and formal administration to expand in unhealthful ways. Because of the nearly exclusive focus on deploying means to supposedly agreed-upon ends, the limits on public *and private* power at the heart of the design of the American constitutional system have increasingly become overwhelmed by institutions that are less accessible and responsive to citizens and less supportive of the everyday practice of self-government than the more representative institutions of the regime. These less accessible and responsive institutions are the courts (Calvin, Collins, and Eshbaugh-Soha 2011), and the much celebrated cross-boundary networks of the new governance (see, for example, Bevir 2010; Esmark 2007; Hendriks 2008).

Ensuring the creation and maintenance of a space between state and citizen is constitutionally wise, to give citizens a sense of assurance that the state in its various guises is not hovering directly overhead, and to give citizens room to grow and to develop abiding attachments to the regime without the coercion of the state. This space also provides the fertile ground in which citizens in a liberal democracy can cultivate institutions of their own making, which allow them to shape and control the state but which also serve as a nonthreatening platform for contact between citizens and the state. If the hidden state thesis is correct, the Jeffersonians and their successors recognized the wisdom of creating this kind of space and incorporated it into their preferred mode of governance for the national government, and proceeded to populate that critical social space directly or indirectly with private intermediaries that have sustained the sense of independence from the state that gives citizens confidence that self-government is being maintained. These intermediaries have included, most prominently, the political party, but also various private entities contracted to deliver services as well as the civic associations and similar organizations that loosely comprise what is called civil society. As the nation grew and public problems became increasingly national in scope and import, demands for national solutions increased. Political leaders responded with careful, limited encroachments by direct state administration into the social space between state and citizen, relying as much as possible on localized structures that appeared less oppressive, even though they may have been just as forceful an exercise of central authority. It was only in matters of domestic peace and security, protection against external threats, and the geographic "margins of the nation" (Balogh 2009, 385)—primarily the undeveloped western lands—that a direct, visible, and vigorous state, via administrative entities, was prominent.

During the early forays of the state into direct administrative action, political leaders engaged in much debate about the wisdom and appropriateness of such action, and some even offered ways of thinking about the incursions of the state in ways that suggested how to think about administration as contributing to the shape and health of the polity and thus of self-government. Such thinking was limited, however, and easily overwhelmed by the fear of central administration and the insistence that it be kept strictly instrumental, subordinate, and limited. As the stresses and strains of modernity grew in scope and intensity, however, and especially when the growth of the economy reflecting the success of the market revolution threatened to overwhelm the civic space with a leviathan other than the state—the corporation, trust, or conglomerate—policy makers turned increasingly to direct government action via large national bureaucracies. The greatly expanded role of administrative agencies, especially in a system of programmatic liberalism functioning on a narrow instrumental understanding rather than a more comprehensive understanding recognizing the formative nature of all political and governmental activity, has filled the constitutional space with more mechanistic and authoritarian manifestations of the state that give citizens little breathing room for thinking about the meaning and practice of *national* self-government. These forms of state presence can also narrow the pathways for reinforcing civic attachments to the regime (e.g., Geoghegan 2013).

Returning to the founding once more, it is possible to see Alexander Hamilton's conflict with Jefferson as at its heart a clash over the question of the proper relationship of the people with their government, and the effect of that relationship, particularly with respect to which institutions would best support formation of citizen attachments and embody a stable, vital, *republican* regime in the long run (see Milkis and Tichenor 1993, 14). Jefferson favored local government, civic associations, legislatures, and parties, for he insisted on individuals remaining completely independent of any government, creating a government as needed, and changing it as necessary, even on a whim. In Jefferson's view, the character of a people precedes government, and remains external to it, and their welfare is ultimately up to them, not government. Government, especially administration, is at best a necessary evil.

It was Hamilton's view that a close interconnection between citizens and government was inevitable, and even that the creation of a people by government, largely through administration, was not only likely, but necessary. Hamilton thus contended that administration, particularly a national administration essential for knitting together a fragmented political economy, must also be an important institutional pathway to citizen attachment and civic engagement, and that the design of administration must be sensitive to this. It is clear that Hamilton did not regard administration as the only institution that could cultivate attachments to the regime, but the success of good administration in promoting a commercial republic that would bring prosperity to the people and cement their allegiance to the regime was what he prophesied, and most passionately preferred. Hamilton sought unified national policy under executive control that would constitute the people and serve their welfare. This was clearly anathema to Jefferson's ideology, and being fully conversant with the formative power of political institutions, Jefferson set about creating, with Madison's assistance, a polity reflecting his ideology and institutional preferences, and they succeeded triumphantly.

When the progressives found the Jeffersonian polity frayed by the forces of modernity, they sought to bring a measure of Hamiltonian design to bear on the problem. It was Franklin Roosevelt who engaged in the greatest struggle to reconcile the two when he sought to make the unmet economic security needs glaringly illuminated by the Great Depression into basic rights best protected and provided by programs overseen by administrative agencies. The result, especially following reforms instituted in the 1960s and 1970s, was to expand the direct and visible presence of administration in the constitutional space between state and citizen. This expansion at first addressed critical problems, but as the problems and solutions continued to grow in complexity, the expansion created serious friction with the long-standing institutions of the Jeffersonian polity that had for so long been the principal cultivators of citizen attachments to the regime. A recognizable confusion about the nature of citizenship and the practice of self-government ensued, energizing most recently a volatile mix of fierce ideological battles and postmodern murkiness that only exacerbates the confusion.

The increasing presence of mechanistic, instrumental manifestations of the state in the constitutional space between state and citizen has, furthermore, forced attempts to democratize public administration to soften its impact and legitimate its direct presence in people's lives. It may indeed be a very good thing to enhance the voice of employees inside public organizations and the voice of citizens outside in their interactions with public agencies (e.g., Cooper, Bryer, and Meek 2006). It is also critical, as Woodrow Wilson argued, to make sure administration is connected to popular thought, sensitive to it, and adept at reading it. Attempting to transform administration into just another form of democratic politics, or even *the* form, is something else entirely, and, at least in the United States, would require a reformation of the regime far more radical than anything yet seriously contemplated.

Whatever definition of the proper scope of government is in force, public administration is expected to get some things accomplished, not just for customers or clientele but for the whole polity. Engagement in this effort is in fact the source of a great deal of the knowledge, valuable experience, and even expertise of public administrators. Organizational structures and operational modes that lean too far in the direction of citizen participation, democratic process, and deliberation hamper the ability of agencies to accomplish what is demanded of them. A conception of public administration that is principally concerned with how democratic it is, that seeks to democratize administration to make it more effective in its instrumental tasks, or that seeks to make administration the principal site of further democratizing the polity or fending off antidemocratic forces, serves neither public administration nor the regime well. Other institutions are better suited to embody fully—to constitute—the *democratic* spirit (Milkis 1993, 260).

An increasingly direct presence of an instrumental and mechanistic public administration in the space between state and citizen, the efforts to democratize it, and the positive reception citizens only give to administration's service delivery function, reveal the effect that instrumental conceptions of administration and liberal democratic politics have had on policy makers' attention to administration when they are designing policy. When working from an instrumental conception, the attention of policy makers to administration, indeed even their conception of the policy-making endeavor itself, is narrowed to the choice or development of means—programmatic, organizational, or institutional—that will achieve already settled ends. The choice may be made by the elected chief executive or by the legislature alone, or by the two in combination, or it may be left up to expert administrators. None of these approaches, however, effectively takes into account the multidimensional demands of policy design that concern administration. These demands include providing for the design of organizational structures and the mobilization of resources, functions at the core of the instrumental requirements of policy design. They also include, however, taking account of the constitutive impacts of administrative choices, especially the effect on citizen preferences, the development of relationships among distinctive classes of citizens, and the enriching or debilitating effects on citizen attachments to the regime. Because they are rarely considered in policy design, *unintended consequences* is the commonly used term for the manifestation of these constitutive impacts. When unintended consequences accumulate to the extent that the public perceives them as usually accompanying public policy initiatives, it is a sign that insufficient attention to administration is plaguing policy design.

Overall, then, the modern administrative system in the United States that has been constructed under this predominantly instrumental conception of administration, operating within an instrumental conception of liberal democratic politics, lacks the capacity to apply administration's distinctive institutional qualities to the complex problems of a postindustrial political economy. American public administrators are pulled away from greater innovation, creativity, and responsiveness, in part by the character of the bureaucratic form of organization, but to a far greater extent by the need to be defensive in a political system in which public organizations are under constant suspicion and subject to a complex matrix of controls, their weaknesses loudly condemned or completely ignored, and their strengths rarely respected for the contributions to the care and maintenance of the polity they make.

In a very real sense then, at all levels of American government, insensitive, unresponsive, and incompetent public bureaucracies are the *products* of instrumental conceptions of administration and liberal democratic politics. For most of the nation's political development, reformers have approached administration with the working assumption that the only necessity was to get control of and subordinate it, by disassembling or dispersing it or hiding its presence through intermediary forms, and the nation would be sustained or restored to greatness. To consider administration constitutively, however, requires acknowledging that public bureaucracies are fully and legitimately part of the governing complex, that they help shape the regime as well as achieve its goals, but also that their roles must be restrained to suit their strengths, limitations, and complex effects. Placing reasonable constitutional limits on what public institutions can and should do places an added burden on citizens, who must come closer to fulfilling the responsibility that the role of sovereign requires of them. A constitutive view also acknowledges the complexity of governing in a postindustrial society, a complexity that might appear to make it impossible for average citizens to engage in self-rule. The easier path is to rely heavily on public administration, which, much like the courts, does not seem to demand very much citizen time and effort in governing. The result, however, is to push administration beyond both practical and constitutional limits. The political response, not surprisingly, is then to attack, control, denigrate, and fear it when it fails to function well.

Administrative agencies in the United States face a constant struggle to maintain some balance between the dominant belief that they are simply tools of the popular will and the reality that they help shape public purposes and the relations between citizens, and thus the very essence of that popular will. This is in many respects the way the system has responded to the tension between the instrumental and the constitutive that lies at the heart of the design of a liberal democratic regime, and it may be necessary not to make this tension too explicit. Indeed, this may be the genius of limiting the visibility of the direct exercise of coercive government authority. Forcing administrative agencies to deal with the tension may also be the price all American citizens, but especially American public administrators, have to pay to enjoy the benefits of a modern, postindustrial society built on an eighteenth-century framework. Yet the consequences of a pervasively instrumental conception of administration and politics also offer a fundamental reason for attempting to recover and nurture a more complete understanding of administration that captures its constitutive side. Any conception of administration, the history of American political development shows, will invariably have a formative effect on politics, government, and the character of the citizenry. We may become what we do not like. Hence, it behooves political leaders and the attentive public to think long and hard and carefully about the conception they will embrace. To do otherwise will incur serious unintended and unwanted consequences. Being cognizant of the constitutive qualities of political institutions, most especially public administration, means, in other words, being more attentive to their formative consequences.

The Meaning of Constitutive Administration

An instrumental understanding of administration, articulated before the founding, formalized under the Constitution by the Decision of 1789, and subsequently reinforced and magnified by several waves of democratic expansion and political reform, has left American political leaders mostly wringing their hands about the problems of democratic controls on administrative discretion and increasingly blind to the possibility that good administration, its design carefully considered in the making of public policy, is integral to the regime and the capacity of the people for self-government. It is possible, nevertheless, to reconsider the path American political development has taken in its conception of the role of administration in politics and government and to seek a new path toward reconceiving administration to include a strong constitutive perspective. Such a reconception must aim to illuminate the distinctive contributions public administration can make to the health of the regime and the sustenance of self-government. The first step in this reconsideration is to examine the political nature of administration in its most basic sense, to identify, that is, the fundamental elements of a constitutive role for public administration in the American regime.

Regime Attachments and Tempering the Democratic Impulse

What features of a political and governmental system would best cultivate among a free people a long-term attachment to the regime and allegiance to the government? How could such a system be built on popular sovereignty and still avoid the fatal excesses associated with democracy? The responses to these questions offered during the debates at the founding were many and varied, and the Constitution emerged as the remarkable if imperfect plan to answer them. From the point of view of several of the framers, administration had a pivotal role to play in ensuring the Constitution's success with respect to both problems.

For the proponents of the Constitution, two qualities of the plan stood out as likely to win the hearts and minds of the American people. The first was its "aptitude and tendency to produce a good administration" (*The Federalist* No. 68) and the second was its capacity to maintain stability while keeping a proper "dependence upon the people" (No. 37). In the first instance, as Alexander Hamilton argued, administration, or more precisely *good* administration, would, in and of itself, be a key influence on the formation of citizen attachments to the regime. Because of their closer proximity to the people, the state governments would gain most of the advantage over the federal government from this formative effect of administration, "unless the force of that principle be destroyed by a much better administration of the latter" (No. 17). Hamilton expected, and later strove for, that very outcome. He enumerated along the way "various reasons" that "induced" a "probability that the general government will be better administered than the particular governments" (No. 27).

In the second instance, proponents claimed that the Constitution would gain general adherence because it offered, in place of the "irregular and mutable legislation" that characterized the Articles of Confederation, stability in government. Madison saw this as "essential to national character and to the advantages annexed to it, as well as to that repose and confidence in the minds of the people, which are the chief blessings of civil society" (*The Federalist* No. 37). Regularity and stability in public affairs would result from the decreased likelihood that public councils would succumb to the passions, demagoguery, and temporary delusions to which popular government was susceptible. The Senate was to play a pivotal role in this regard, providing duration, expertise, stability, and a "due sense of national character" (see Rohr 1986, ch. 3; also see Swift 1993). If the modern Senate cannot fulfill this role, in many respects the career civil service can (Rohr 1986, 32–39). It is also evident that several of the framers saw from the very beginning administration would help to fulfill this role in the regime (see *The Federalist* Nos. 72, 76).

As these views anchored in the Constitution's design signal, public administration is constitutive of the regime in the educative or formative sense—it influences what ideas about the regime citizens hold and it shapes the relations that develop among citizens—because it interacts extensively with citizens on a daily basis and is the institutional setting for much interaction among citizens of various kinds. It thus can cultivate, and in some instances, unfortunately, undermine, citizen attachment to or identification with the regime. Good administration, administration that is well organized, supported with ample resources, and populated by knowledgeable, practical, and judicious men and women who operate with a steady but not inflexible hand, will encourage good citizen relations and a commitment to supporting the regime (see Kravchuk 1992; Meier 1997). Administration without these qualities will erode that commitment. Furthermore, administration is constitutive of the regime because, by virtue of its premiere qualities—stability, durability, the application of knowledge to urgent problems while acknowledging settled law and tradition—it encourages the democratic temperament to value stability, continuity, and practical reason, thus helping to steady the sometimes passionate whim and impulse of democratic decision making.

Public administration is not simply the means to collectively determined ends. In a very real sense, it is a collection of those ends, and by its practices, it keeps them alive. Administration is the institutional expression of and gives an organized existence to the aspirations of republican self-government for stability, continuity, and temperance of democratic excess. To the extent one can say that the American polity has achieved these goals (see, e.g., Page and Shapiro 1989), public administration may deserve some credit for the achievement. This is what stood at the heart of Tocqueville's appreciation for the political effects of administration, especially at the local level. "Municipal bodies and county administrations are like so many hidden reefs retarding or dividing the flood of the popular will. If the law were oppressive, liberty would still find some shelter in the way the law is carried into execution" (1988, 263).

It is now almost wholly out of favor, as it has been for quite some time, to suggest that democracy needs to be reined in, that the people's immediate wants may not always be in their long-run interest, or that popular participation in governing should not be maximized without limit. The current American polity, with its much larger cohort of well-educated citizens enjoying better access to information and displaying much greater sophistication, and cynicism, about public affairs, is light years distant from the polity of two centuries ago. These characteristics may themselves serve as a break against the most risky expression of popular will. The pursuit of ever more expansive democracy, of greater popular participation and control, remains, however. It is thus critical not to lose sight of some essential traits of democracy. It is prone to demagoguery, to the instability of majority cycling, and to a present-orientedness that favors quick, easy, short-term solutions to complex problems (but see Barber 2003). Although the barriers to popular influence exhibiting these weaknesses on administration have eroded over the past several decades, to acknowledge and appreciate how public administration is constitutive of a regime that is predicated on more than simply the force of popular will means in part accepting the possibility that those barriers require some reinforcement so that administration can assist in tempering popular passions.

REPRESENTATION OF OBJECTIVE INTERESTS

One of the most basic, if not *the* most basic, of components in any liberal democratic regime established under a constitution is its scheme for representation. Representation is constitutive because, through elections, it periodically reconstitutes the polity. Through representation, citizens make a choice about how they will be recognized politically, and in the process, they become "self-conscious about who they are collectively" (N. L. Schwartz 1988, 129). Free, competitive elections are the foundation of the representation schemes in most liberal democracies. Elections thus appear to be the core of what makes representation constitutive. "Consent of the governed, which is the basis of democratic political authority, is periodically reconstituted or reaffirmed through elections of representatives, where citizens actively renew their membership" (N. L. Schwartz 1988, 128). By extension, then, elected officials enjoy a special status in liberal democracies, because they personify the reconstitutive or reaffirmative act of representation.

This poses a significant challenge to the legitimacy of administrative power in the United States, where, with the exception of several state government offices, public administrators are not selected in competitive elections. John Rohr argued that the centrality of elections in establishing public authority is misunderstood. Following Edward Corwin, he stressed that only the Constitution derives its authority from the people. All public officials, elected and nonelected, derive their authority from the Constitution, and Rohr noted that popular election is only one of 22 ways of holding office under the Constitution (1986, 185, 260–61 n. 31). To deal with the special legitimacy that elections impart, at least three general ways of establishing the legitimacy of public administrators, and thus recognizing the authority of their decisions and actions, have developed.

The hierarchical, or "overhead democracy," argument is grounded in a Hobbesian conception of representation as authorization and delegation (see Cook 1992, 405–10, for elaboration). Administrators do not achieve the status of representatives in this scheme, but their decisions and actions can be regarded as authoritative because they are delegated from true representatives, namely, elected officials, who are in turn following the supreme dictates of the people. This is, of course, the understanding of the status of public administrators at the heart of the instrumental conception of administration that has been dominant in American political development (also see Lowi 1993b, 262). Administrative authority in this view is predicated on the usefulness of administrators' technical expertise in achieving designated goals. The challenge posed by the idea of overhead democracy concerns: (1) how closely administrative decisions and actions adhere to the dictates of elected officials, (2) the efficacy of either internal controls (Friedrich 1940; Meier 1993, ch. 7) or external controls (Finer 1941; Gruber 1987; Meier 1993, ch. 6), and (3) how adept public officials, particularly members of Congress, are in applying external controls (Aberbach 1990; Morone 1985, 293–94; T. Schwartz 1989).

The pluralist view, in contrast to the hierarchical, rejects the possibility that there is some objective public will or public interest that elected officials represent (see Cook 1992, 410–14; Lowi 1979, 31–41; Morone 1985, 294–96). Instead, only organized or unorganized group interests exist; it is only through the pulling and hauling of these interests in the political arena that an agreement on public policy emerges, an agreement that usually favors some group or coalition over others. One version of the pluralist view of administrative authority overlaps with the hierarchical view in asserting that administrative agencies are simply the vehicles for putting group agreements into effect. Another version, however, depicts administrative agencies as true representatives, in the sense of delegates and advocates, of particular organized interests, hence the idea of the clientele agency. In the most extreme pluralist view, agencies themselves behave like organized interests (see Rourke 1984; Yates 1982).

Finally, the "representative bureaucracy" view presents public administrators as in some sense better representatives than elected officials, in part precisely because they are not elected and thus are not distanced from the people by elections that require compromises or dependence on campaign contributors. Thus, they are in some ways more like average citizens (Morone 1985, 297). The representative bureaucracy view mostly turns on the contention that administrators more accurately represent the public demographically—that many of the diverse traits of the populace are more clearly evident in the ranks of public bureaucracy than in the ranks of elected officials (Krislov and Rosenbloom 1981; Long 1952, 812–14; Rohr 1986, 45–50; Rosenbloom 1992, 136–39). A body of representatives that looks like the population it represents in terms of gender, race, ethnicity, and socioeconomic traits, so the descriptive representation argument goes (Pitkin 1967, ch. 4; also see Lim 2006), will think and act on questions of public policy as the whole population would if it were engaged in decision making. There are, furthermore, arguments that turn on bureaucrats functioning as active rather than passive representatives (e.g., Sowa and Selden 2003).

Each of the three arguments attempting to link public administration to representation as a way to give warrant to administrative authority is open to significant attack on its own terms (see Cook 1992; Meier 1993, chs. 6, 7). All three are commonly flawed, however, in that they conceive of representation in instrumental terms. This is inconsistent with basic constitutional thinking and reinforces the kinds of consequences assessed above. The hierarchical and pluralist arguments are obviously problematic because they are based on the authorization and delegation models of representation, in which representatives merely follow the orders of either the whole body of the public or of organized interests within it. The representative bureaucracy argument, whether based on passive or active representation, still expresses the idea that representatives do the bidding of those represented. None of these ideas of representation capture a constitutive understanding of representation, which involves the ongoing effort of a polity to decide what it is and what it seeks to achieve. Moreover, the concept of representation that prevailed at the founding was at least in part constitutive in just this way, because representation was conceived of by the founders as performing a transformative function. It would "refine and enlarge the public views" (*The Federalist* No. 10) by bringing the major parts of society together so that through deliberation and debate representatives, and ultimately the people themselves, would determine their "true" or "enlarged and permanent" interests in a way that was not just a second-best alternative to direct democracy but an improvement on it that would result in more effective self-government (Pitkin 1967, 191, 194–95; also Elkin 1993, 132–35; 2006, 40–41).

Public administration functions as a representative institution in just this way. Public administrators engage in deliberation and debate with each other, with other public officials (legislators, chief executives, judges), and with substantial segments of the public at large, not only about what are the best means for achieving designated policy goals, but about what those goals and the larger ends of the polity ought to be. Public bureaucracy "is a medium for registering the diverse wills that make up the people's will and for transmuting them into responsible proposals for public policy" (Long 1952, 810). Calls for public administrators to engage the general public more substantially and effectively in deliberation and debate about not just means but ends as well seek to enhance further this aspect of the representative function of public administration (e.g., Kathi and Cooper 2005; Reich 1988).

An important consideration, therefore, in conceptualizing the representative function of administration concerns the nature of the interests that administrators and administrative agencies represent. It is certainly true that many public agencies represent and promote the interests of (mostly) well-organized groups. These are interests understood to be, as James Madison depicted them, formulated out of individual self-interest, opinion, and passion, grouped by common impulse into factions. They are to be controlled and regulated, *by* representation, in the Madisonian scheme, or encouraged and celebrated *as* representation in the modern pluralist scheme.

But Madison's acknowledgment of the existence of "enlarged and permanent" interests, seems akin to what Edmund Burke conceived of as "unattached interests" (Pitkin 1967, 192). In Burke's representation theory, these are broad, relatively fixed interests that are objective and rationally discoverable (Pitkin 1967, 176), particularly "broad appropriative interests, such as labor, service, agriculture, and commerce, and deep associative interests, such as cities, states, churches, and schools" (N. L. Schwartz 1988, 142). A representative "speaks and acts for these yet is independent of any of them. . . . Dynamically, representatives can articulate new values and enable political formations to develop and change."

It is possible to think of public agencies representing not organized agricultural or commercial interests, for example, but the nation's interest in agriculture, commerce and other broad, relatively fixed concerns that are objective and rationally discoverable. Hannah Pitkin cautions that this idea can be taken too far. If these broad interests can be determined simply by knowledge accumulation and do not require active decision making, then experts can attend to them and no substantive representation is sensibly in force. If they are matters of questioning and debate as well as of knowledge, then political representation comes into play. If public administrators engage in deliberation and debate among themselves and with other public officials and segments of the general citizenry, they bring their specialized technical knowledge, normative training, and governing experience to bear to help determine the objective interests of the community, study them, and judge how they fit together to constitute the interest of the whole—the public interest (Cox, Buck, and Morgan 1994, 259; Goodsell 1990). Administrative agencies, in other words, represent ideas or rational constructs. They give organized existence to "the environment" or "the economy," for example, and help define how citizens are to relate to one another in environmentally or economically rational ways. In their capacities as implementers, moreover, administrators and their agencies enable political relations to develop and change (see C. N. Stone 1985). This dimension of the representative function of administration, with its focus on broad, long-term interests, reinforces the contributions public administration makes to stability in the regime. Its emphasis on rationality reinforces public administration's even more important contributions to the constitution of the regime, through practical reason.

Tradition, Law, and Experience: Social Learning and Practical Reason

One of the most remarkable characteristics of the instrumental conception of politics and administration is how unsophisticated it really is about the nature of liberal democratic politics. The notion that administration is simply the search for and then employment of the appropriate means toward previously determined goals implies a level of harmony incongruent with the conflict and competition engendered by democratic rule. It suggests that the "popular will" is fixed and predetermined and need only be elicited from the minds of the people or their representatives. Modern pluralism essentially emerged as a critique of this simplistic view of democratic governance, but for all intents and purposes, it simply replaced "popular will" with "group agreement," leaving administrative agencies still to carry out that agreement and, by extension, to be actively involved as contending groups in its creation.

To be sure, pluralism does acknowledge the conflict and competition indicative of liberal democracy. In the end, however, it is mostly a variation on the basic instrumental theme. The goals or ends of the polity are still established "out there," separate from governing, by the conflict, competition, bargaining, and accommodation that take place among organized groups. In the pluralist view, governing *is* the competition, bargaining, and accommodation among organized interests (Lowi 1979, 36). It may take place in the legislative, executive, judicial, or administrative arena, and thus legislators and legislative committees, elected executives and their staffs, attorneys at the bar, and administrative agencies can all be understood best as representing organized interests or even behaving politically just like interest groups. In pluralism's ultimate form, the competition, conflict, bargaining, and accommodation that produce the "parceling out of relative advantage" (J. Q. Wilson 1975, 93) constitute the be-all and end-all of government; the allocation of advantage is what government exists to provide.

The "popular will" is not fixed, however, nor does it simply emerge from the conflict and competition among organized groups. Democratic politics and government does involve conflict, competition, bargaining, and accommodation among varied interests. Yet it also involves confusion, uncertainty, and therefore the search, by at least some public officials, group leaders, and concerned citizens, for common interests that are not just the lowest common denominator of group agreements. They consist, instead, of "justice and the general good" (*The Federalist* No. 51). This returns us to the once discredited but recently reenergized concept of the public interest. In the view of some, it consists at minimum of the democratic consensus, a basic conception of the good society, and the adjustments to these made necessary by experience (e.g., Goodsell [1990], 100–101, drawing on Downs [1962] and Pennock [1962], among others; also see Long [1990]; for an alternative conception, see Elkin [2006] and the discussion below). Founding agreements, established traditions, and the experience with their consequences, combined with the more immediate elements of interaction, conflict, and competition among interests and ideas, create the ends of the polity. When the life of the regime is understood in this way, administration has a substantial role to play because it is involved in more than delivering goods and services. It is involved deeply, as the day-to-day operational manifestation of collective decisions expressed as government action, in conservative, restorative, and transformative activity (Morgan 1996).

"Much governmental activity . . . represents an attempt to employ government as an intermediary to alter some set of conditions that has complex origins" (C. N. Stone 1985, 486). Much of this kind of activity takes place in the realm of policy implementation and thus involves public administration directly and substantially. Instead of a "business-firm" model emphasizing the efficient production and delivery of goods and services and based on instrumental rationality, it requires a model of "social learning" (C. N. Stone 1985; also see Long 1952, 815–16; A. Brown and Wildavsky 1984; Stivers 1990, 263–64). The rational foundation of such a model is Aristotle's "practical wisdom," or *phronesis*, "to conjoin knowledge of the principles of right with considerations of what is suitable" (Morgan 1990, 74; also see Stivers 1990, 250, 260–61; Mainzer 1994, 360,

385–86 n. 2). Such practical wisdom is relevant to any "enterprise" (Anderson 1990), but it has special import in the public realm.

Recall that Herbert Storing linked what he labeled "practical reason" to Whig views on public administration. In Storing's version, it involves the application of instrumental rationality—the matching of means and ends—combined with a concern for the nature of the ends themselves in light of both experience and an abiding responsibility and morality (1980, 110–12). Practical reason in the public sphere is, therefore, centrally concerned with efficiency, in the sense that Charles Anderson gives it—"fittedness to purpose" (1993, 105). Most fundamentally, it is concerned with "institution fitting," that is, how properly to arrange institutional parts with respect to both their instrumental and constitutive contributions to the regime whole (Elkin 1987, 193–95). For administration, such reasoning is most required when the exercise of discretion is called for. Hence, administration discretion and practical reason are closely intertwined. Administrative discretion must be well grounded in accountability, that is, in the requirement that decisions be based on explicit reasons linked to clear, substantive rules, which are in turn grounded in the values that define the public interest. In the American case, this is the public interest of a commercial republic (see Elkin 2006, 132–36). This accountability is a necessary condition for fostering practical reason in the public sphere and the social learning that stems from it (Stivers 1990, 263–64; see also Anderson 1990, esp. chs. 9, 10). A regime function centered on the exercise of practical reason in everyday governing with an eye constantly on the public interest of a commercial republic is the firmest foundation for public administration claims to a constitutionally legitimate constitutive role grounded on something more than technical expertise.

This way of thinking about the contribution of administration to the regime is linked to what may be called its "informing function." When Delaware Representative John Vining likened the proposed secretary of foreign affairs to the president's arm and eye in the Decision of 1789 debates, it was no mere flight of rhetorical fancy. Vining's synecdoche captured what was in his time an already historically well-rooted recognition that perhaps the most fundamental function of government, and especially of administration, concerned the monitoring of the external environment for threats, and the state of society for developments that deserve attention. Indeed, the ancient roots of the legitimacy of government's effort to learn about and adapt to its social environment are found in the very etymology of the word *statistics* (Rose 1989; also see *Oxford English Dictionary*, s.v. "statistic," etymology). The American Republic's founders took as given that a key administration function was monitoring and reporting. As the nation developed, almost every new foray into addressing widespread social problems that involved the expansion of administrative capacity started with a new or existing administrative entity being charged with reconnaissance on the problem and any initial responses to it. As Congress began considering proposals for the expansion of the national government in the second state era, for example, those proposing new administrative entities almost invariably first emphasized their information-gathering function because the case for the legitimacy of the new entity was most easily made in connection with such a function, as in the case of James A. Garfield's proposal for a federal department of education, the purpose of which was "was to collect and disseminate information on educational practices in the various states" (Hoffer 2007, 92–93).

Certainly governments have an obligation to monitor conditions that bear on the health and safety of citizens. This is clearly an administrative function, ergo public administrators have an obligation to maintain the capacity and devote the resources to sustain such monitoring. Yet the role of public administration in the gathering, processing, and conveying of information goes far beyond this simple aspect. This was the insight Woodrow Wilson offered when he argued that "through Administration the State makes test of its own powers and of the public needs, makes test also of law, its efficiency, suitability" (Link et al. 1966–1994, 7:138). In contrast to law, which Wilson characterized as the summing up of the past, administration must be understood as always in contact with the present. It is thus the state's "experiencing organ," and the suggestions or initiatives of administration, Wilson insisted, are one of the most useful means of further developing public law. This was so because of the nature of administrative power, which Wilson defined as the power of the "coordinations of organizations" and "the irresistible energy and efficiency of harmony and cooperation." Cooperation was, for Wilson, "the law of all action in the modern world" (Link et al. 1966–1994, 17:135–136).

All administrative entities possess a special capacity to organize and coordinate their experiences and gather and share information efficiently. For public organizations, this special power of coordination and cooperation is specifically oriented toward monitoring and learning from the application of public law. Public organizations also orient cooperation and coordination toward reading and learning from more general engagements with the environment, through the use of discretion in such administrative activities as patrol and enforcement, as well as from broad, general observation. Yet public organizations go further, by also assessing in formal ways the implications of their monitoring, and communicating the formalized findings with the aim of guiding policy making, whether as the reform of existing law or the formulation of new laws.

What public agencies learn from their day-to-day contact with citizens in carrying out laws, and in addressing situations in which no existing law clearly applies, they can also contribute to the *processes* of revising existing law or fashioning new laws. All of this is part of the living, growing, adaptive life of state and polity, including the transparency that is essential for public assessments of adaptations to ensure their success. Thus, the monitoring, information gathering, analyzing, and reporting and recommending functions of public organizations are all aimed toward informing and refining public, collective choice, serving the public interest, especially the perpetual bargaining over what properly belongs in the public and private spheres.

Granted, many administrative agencies may be engaged in these functions for primarily instrumental concerns, such as carrying out the purposes of the laws they are tasked with implementing. Because public administrators and their agencies are wholly and exclusively accountable to public authority, however, their experiencing function also serves this accountability and expresses it; that is, by monitoring the suitability of the law, learning about changes in society that affect their areas of responsibility, and otherwise gathering information that might guide the refinement of public law, public organizations are being accountable and responsible. Furthermore, the informing function interwoven into public organizations and the staffs who embody their collective values is about preservation as well as refinement and change. It is about public administrators determining in the face of sometimes rapid and disruptive change how to preserve core, and very public, values expressed in public law and embodied in their organizations. This "administrative conservatorship" (Terry 2003) encompasses the use of monitoring, learning, and information gathering and sharing to make judgments, or to formulate advice for lawmakers, not only about what to change but also what to sustain and preserve. Through the power of information coordination, public administration supports the other constitutive institutions of the regime, the "branches" or "departments" of the familiar separation-of-powers scheme. Helping to maintain those constitutive institutions of the regime is thus administration's most vital way of serving the public interest (Elkin 2006, ch. 5).

Seeing administration in Wilsonian terms as government in contact with the people leads to the recognition that administration constantly encounters questions about adjustment, not just of means to ends, but of government functions to historical conditions and, ultimately, to shifting conceptions of liberty (see Link et al. 1966–1994, 7:116). Administration, then, is the embodiment of the "working constitution" (Long 1952, 816), because it is concerned with what will work in public policy with respect to fitting means to ends, determining the limits of public acceptability, and ensuring fidelity to the Constitution and the public interest of a commercial republic (Morgan 1990, 73–74; 1996, 52–54).

Public administration is constitutive of the regime, finally, because, more than any other political institution, it encompasses and must grapple with the tensions between the instrumental and the constitutive that are so acute in a liberal democratic polity. Public administration stands at the crossroads of the ideal and the real and must, on a continuing basis, demonstrate affinity to both. It is expected to help ensure that planes arrive on time and that hazardous waste sites are cleaned up promptly and thoroughly, while also helping to determine why such actions are necessary and how, with experience, they might be improved. It is constitutive because it helps to develop among citizens an appreciation that popular demands for action must be balanced against prior agreements etched in statutes or anchored in tradition or constitutional principle. Yet it also offers numerous lessons about making practical adjustments to what stands, in light of pressing needs and the careful assessment of current and future conditions. It is constitutive of the regime because, as the prime point of contact between government and citizens, it is in a position to help citizens cultivate an appreciation for practical reason and to support them in practicing it, making administration the active institutional expression of *responsible discretion* in the public sphere. It provides that function now, despite the dominance of the instrumental view of public administration's place in the regime as only a means to get results the qualities of which have not been very thoroughly explored. That such exploration must be expanded, with respect both to the time and resources allotted to it and to the number of citizens involved, seems clear if the capacity for self-government in an administrative, or "neo-administrative," state (Durant 2000) is to be not only preserved but enhanced. Public administration released from an overbearing instrumentalism could play an even more effective role across all these facets. What remains to be considered are the necessary conditions for, the potential consequences of, and the chances for imbuing our politics with a constitutive understanding of public administration.

Chapter Eight

Bureaucracy and the Future
of American Self-Government

In the penultimate chapter of *Progressive Democracy*, Herbert Croly characterized the "democratic political organization" he advocated as "fundamentally
educational." He admitted that, although it was "designed to attain a certain administrative efficiency, its organization for efficiency is subordinated to the gathering of an educational popular political experience. Indeed, it is organized for
efficiency chiefly because in the absence of efficiency no genuinely *formative*
popular political experience can be expected to accrue" (Croly 1914, 378; emphasis added). Croly thus juxtaposed the instrumental and the constitutive and intimated that they necessarily coexist in liberal democracy, indeed, not just coexist
but mutually interconnect, with the instrumental as a necessary condition for
the more profound constitutive effect. Together they form a governing whole.
That governing whole requires, in other words, that administration work well in
its primary instrumental task so that collective action through government,
which is primarily administration, can have the positive formative influences
the defenders of republican self-government claim for it.

The dominant way of thinking today about what makes for good political
organization—good governance—centers on the ability to make effective tradeoffs, such as the loss of some efficiency in favor of greater equity. Indeed, it is
difficult to avoid seeing politics as a matter of choosing between relatively equally
attractive but competing values or ends, such as equality, fairness, and efficiency.
To choose one, and to fashion public programs and societal institutions to

achieve it, inevitably involves losses on the ledgers of other values we hold dear (classic articulations include Calabresi and Bobbitt 1982; R. R. Nelson 1977; Okun 1975; Thurow 1980). Recall that one of the principal arguments of congressional opponents of FDR's original executive reorganization plan was that it weakened the traditional foundations of American democracy in exchange for an increase in the efficiency of government. They thus were able to portray the plan as an unacceptable tradeoff of democracy for efficiency. Similarly, the high-profile debates of more recent times about the national debt, how major entitlement programs contribute to it, and thus how they must be reined in are framed in terms of tradeoffs, especially between current and future generations (e.g., Howe and Jackson 2004).

Politics as tradeoffs is, however, a manifestation of the instrumental conception of politics and administration. Tradeoffs imply the pursuit of conflicting ends already defined. It should now be clear, however, that from the perspective of a constitutive understanding of politics, societal ends do not actually come out of nowhere or exist from some primordial time. They are the expressions of the interactions of citizens in a wide spectrum of societal relations. The ordering of these expressions is the work of political institutions. So far, so good, but the mistake American citizens and their political leaders have made is to see this institutional ordering, particularly through elections and legislative work, as merely the aggregating of individual or group wants and preferences, and resolving conflicts among them in favor of the most passionate or powerful (Schattschneider 1960; also see Elkin 2006, 86–89). Other institutions, particularly public administration, are then put to the task of achieving the ends designated.

An alternative way of thinking is evident in Herbert Croly's articulation of the nature of political organization in progressive democratic politics, one that emphasizes arranging public life so that one value—or one kind of conduct or mode of interaction—supports another rather than competing with or marginalizing it. Good politics, as in Croly's rendition, is then the enterprise of shaping and expressing values and fitting them together into a greater whole. Some tradeoffs will still be necessary, but it is not the aim of politics simply to make tradeoffs. Politics is much more about the ongoing formative experience of citizens living together in a community. For the United States, it is ultimately a community—a polity—that spans a continent. With this alternative way of thinking about politics, it does not seem at all far-fetched to conceive of the work of public administration as itself a political institution engaged in this same process of interaction, social learning, and constant recreation of the regime, that is, the public life of the citizenry. Along with its responsibilities to be organized efficiently to grapple with the practical problems that arise every day in the governing order, and to identify and put into effect efficient means to popularly desired ends, public administration contributes to the "formative popular political experience" that sustains and advances the regime. It does so in the ways explored in the preceding chapter, and it is readily conceivable that improvements in administrative efficiency enhance its formative contributions, including fostering stronger citizen attachments to the regime. At its foundation, this is the manner of thinking about public administration in a liberal democracy that deserves further illumination and development.

How can such illumination and development be coaxed out of a political process and public philosophy that discounts and disparages it? It is not unheard of that the ideas of scholars may find their way into the thinking and actions of policy makers and governmental practitioners. Within the scholarly discipline of public administration that developed along with the administrative state, a number of normative orientations have emerged that in various ways have taken account of the formative effects of administrative action and have attempted to guide those effects with particular value sets. These orientations include the focus on administrative ethics anchored in Carl Friedrich's conception of administrative responsibility grounded in professionalism, the "new public administration" with its concern for social justice, which was later revitalized with a further push for attention to social equity in public management (see, e.g., H. Frederickson 1990), and finally the more recent effort toward a "constitutional school" in the study of public administration (see, e.g., Newbold 2010b). Scholars and practitioners can learn much about what the constitutiveness of public administration means and the values that should guide its formative effects from these varied yet related efforts. Save for the development of the attention to ethics, however, these orientations have gained virtually no purchase outside the academy and have had no discernible effect on the political process or on how public administration is regarded and treated. Worse, outside the academy the ethics orientation has been thoroughly instrumentalized and aimed merely at preventing bad behavior and improving instrumental performance rather than considering the values that should guide the formative influences of administrative action.

A direct scholarly assault on the problem is thus unlikely to yield much change. Indirect influence through the introduction of these orientations in the education of future public officials and engaged citizens may produce some benefit. Because political leaders actually do understand the constitutive nature of public administration—even though they attempt to bury the reality of it behind rhetoric about democracy, subordination of administration to citizen sovereigns and their elected representatives, and the need to keep bureaucratic tyranny at bay—the path to open recognition and eventual legitimation of administration's constitutiveness lies along existing avenues of political rhetoric and political practice that may be open to consciousness raising about the links connecting attention to the constitutiveness of administration, improving the design of public policy, and preserving energetic but limited government.

Public Policy Design: Attending to Consequences

In the parlance of the "new institutionalism," or institutional rational choice as it is also known, the Madisonian foundations of American constitutional design manifest themselves most clearly as a configuration of institutional incentives. In instrumental terms, these incentives aim at channeling the self-interested motives that would otherwise lead to factionalism and tyranny so that the pursuit of self-interest will steer political actors into a dependence on reason and deliberation, allowing them to envision and commit to the "cause of an enlarged and permanent interest" (*The Federalist* No. 42) and fostering policy based on "moderation, good sense, and compromise" (Cain and Jones 1989, 17; also see Elkin 2006, 163–76). In constitutive terms, American institutional arrangements help to form a polity that does not seek to deny or disable fundamental self-interested motives but instead prefers to temper self-interested striving in ways that ensure the predominance of reason, the commitment to giving concrete meaning to the public interest, and compromise and moderation in public action.

Madison's approach to institutional design was, however, inductive, experimental, tentative, and pragmatic rather than deductive and axiomatic (Cain and Jones 1989, 12–15). As is often noted, Madison acknowledged that protecting liberty through an expectation of exclusively self-interested behavior and thus an absolute reliance on harnessing it was impossible. Some public spiritedness, manifested particularly in the selection of representatives, was required of the citizenry (see A. S. Diamond 1980, 30), but Madison's design has proved flawed in this respect (Elkin 2006, 65–68, ch. 7). Madison also recognized the limits of knowledge about human behavior and about what institutional designs would be most sensitive to the mix of motivations leading individuals to participate in public affairs. Hence, he fully conceded the potential for error and misjudgment in institutional choice and the consequent necessity that the workings of political institutions be closely observed, with an eye toward improving them incrementally. Unfortunately, Madison's recognition of the pitfalls of institutional design has proved all too prescient with respect to public administration, for a combination of initial institutional arrangements, subsequent institutional tinkering, and changes in American society have resulted in an American political and governmental system with policy maker incentives that are "not conducive to good administration" (Derthick 1990, 4; also see Elkin 2006, ch. 3).

ASSESSING ADMINISTRATIVE CONSEQUENCES

Certainly the framers, primarily in the guise of Alexander Hamilton, attended to the need for good administration in considering the design of the institutions created by the new constitution and the incentives such designs would generate. The discussions of the structure of the presidency and of the Senate in the *Federalist* papers, for example, read like an attempt to create incentives for elected officials to attend to good administration, accomplishing this by creating a bias in favor of stability through longer terms of office and no limit on reeligibility. Also, the provision for senatorial participation in the selection of top administrative officials suggests an attempt to create an incentive for senators to be concerned about the quality and capacity of these officials, by virtue of both the senators' accountability to the American public through the states, and their interest as legislators in selecting officials with sufficient capabilities and independence to provide at least a modest check on the behavior of the president. The Decision of 1789 weakened this arrangement of incentives to some extent, however, while increasing the incentive for the president to take special care that the laws would be stably, effectively, and efficiently executed, the accountability for administration being more clearly fixed in the president by that decision.

A combination of design features and political development has, however, undermined incentives favoring stability in the formation and administration of law. Specifically, a constitutional design based on individual rights *and* popular sovereignty manifested largely through electoral accountability, combined with societal changes reflecting the advance of democratic and egalitarian sentiment, have weakened many of the institutional checks on the influence of general public opinion. In addition, what is regarded as public opinion is now largely amorphous public sentiment seized by, manipulated by, and reexpressed in the passionate opinions of activists (whom Madison might have called factionalist leaders; see Heclo 1989) or manufactured by major business interests (M. A. Smith 2000) who have little regard for the public interest (see Elkin 2006, 262, 292). Additional structural changes, such as the Seventeenth Amendment (providing for the direct election of senators), the embrace of the popular presidential primary, the New Deal "economic bill of rights," and postwar "democratizing" congressional reforms cumulatively have served to create incentives for excessive responsiveness to "popular" activist demands. This responsiveness has led to an "extreme pragmatism" in which legislators constantly pursue policy fixes (Derthick 1990, 216) by responding to "fire alarm" rather than "police patrol" oversight and information gathering (Balla and Deering 2013; McCubbins and Schwartz 1984). Such an approach to policy making serves to exacerbate the mutability of public policy that Madison warned against (*The Federalist* No. 62), forcing administration to worker ever harder to provide the stability of policy that is one of its core contributions to the regime (Derthick 1990, 225).

In addition, a design in which separate institutions share power produces institutional incentives that encourage members of one branch to counteract the ambitions of another branch and thus to engage in competition and struggle over public policy. These basic incentives simply overwhelm whatever incentives may have been built into the system to encourage policy designers to care about good administration. This effect became increasingly evident as the stakes for organized interests rose so dramatically with the expansion in the size, responsibilities, and control of the federal government. Indeed, administration proved to be a major instrument in that increasingly high-velocity struggle, with public officials and their interest-group allies seeking to use bureaucracy to overturn losses they had suffered elsewhere in the policy process or preserve victories they had gained but could not easily protect legislatively. In some instances, the result was to expand administrative discretion substantially, while in others it was to limit it severely. In either case, however, interinstitutional competition translated into only intermittent regard for administrative capacity or effectiveness in further shaping or carrying out the law (T. M. Moe 1989; Poggione and Reenock 2009; but also see MacDonald and Franko 2007). Furthermore, the growth of federal government powers and responsibilities, and the concomitant reliance on administrative power, created enormous incentives, for legislators especially, to create new programs and new entitlements with little regard for the consequences, administrative or otherwise. The bureaucracy could simply be blamed for what went wrong, and legislators could take the credit for fixing it (Fiorina 1989).

While situating responsibility for attending to administration more clearly in the presidency and thereby creating the incentive to fulfill that responsibility, the Decision of 1789 also defined better the terms on which the legislative and executive branches would contend for control of administration. By defining administration in strictly hierarchical terms and thus discounting its constitutiveness, the Decision of 1789 made it justifiable for the president and Congress to use administrative agencies as instruments in their policy struggles with one another. The result, widely recognized and often deplored, is a fragmented, sometimes contradictory administrative establishment, designed better to serve the interests of its political masters than to ensure administrative effectiveness or minimize deleterious effects on the constitution of the citizenry.

Because the unintended effects of public policies reflect in part a failure to pay attention to the formative effects of administration, one avenue to getting policy makers to acknowledge administration's constitutive dimension is to get them to see the consequences, on the things they care about, especially impacts on constituents, of attending or not attending to administrative structure and capacity in policy design. Pessimism must prevail in considering the possibilities of overcoming fundamental structural obstacles to encouraging policy makers to attend to good administration in policy design through attention to unintended consequences. Nevertheless, Martha Derthick advanced some "modest proposals" for addressing the problem. Her proposals centered on providing information on agency capacities that may make clearer the potentially damaging administrative impacts of policy proposals and their consequences for constituents. The burden for making the impacts and consequences recognizable lies, Derthick stressed, with analysts, who must "demonstrate that present policy-making practices have administrative costs of a kind that politicians would care about were those costs to be specified. These are costs not just of inconvenience, disruption, and damaged morale in administrative agencies, but also in wasted money in the federal government's budget and in hardships to citizens" (Derthick 1990, 223–24).

For the analysis of agency capacities to be produced, Derthick argued, elected officials must tolerate the relatively low costs of maintaining small staffs to perform the analyses. Unfortunately, before, during, and soon after Derthick advanced her modest proposals, events offered evidence that the deck is stacked against even this modest commitment to a regard for administration in the behavior of elected officials. The number of staff members in the Office of Management and Budget assigned to management rather than budget analysis declined from 224 to 47 between 1970 and 1989 (R. C. Moe 1994, 116). The agenda of the leadership that came to power when the Republicans captured both houses of Congress in 1994 included cutting appropriations and staff for the General Accounting Office (now the General Accountability Office), which evaluates agency management for Congress (Salant 1995). Subsequently, Office of Management and Budget reorganizations completely eliminated separate management-specific expertise, folding management analysis into the program-specific "resource management offices," where the primary positions are titled "program examiner" and "budget preparation specialist" (General Accounting Office 1996). Putting such meso-level actions aside, however, when the political center supports macro-level reductions in the size, and the scope of responsibilities, of government, the elimination of agencies is the primary if not exclusive administrative focus of elected officials. Their attention is not trained on preventing the incapacity of administrative agencies that remain or improving their functions (indeed incapacity is proof of the need for elimination), however strategically counterproductive that may turn out to be (see, for example, Durant 1992).

Finally, the thrust to reinvent government was predicated on the notion that the incapacity and ineffectiveness of administration rests with bureaucracy as a particular form of organization, and its old, tired, rigid, and elephantine ways. Organizational capacity and effectiveness would be restored by adoption of "entrepreneurial" administration and management to create "public value" (Moore 1995, 2013). Restoration was thus to be the sole responsibility of agencies and agency heads, providing presidents and members of Congress with effective cover. They can continue to blame the bureaucracy for deleterious consequences, even when they as policy makers fail to take administrative structure and capacity into account, either in the design of new or consolidated programs (e.g., Pear, LaFraniere, and Austen 2013), or in their plans for program reductions or elimination.

The point of analyzing the institutional incentives for attending to administration in policy design is not to find ways to eliminate entirely incentives for the fragmentation, diffusion of power, and political manipulation of administration. Such an objective is out of reach (Derthick 1990, 213–15; also T. M. Moe 1989). Administration will therefore continue to be the object of political contention, especially in a system in which it is subordinated to institutions that are, at least in the eyes of their leaders, purposely set against one another. The point instead is to determine whether something like a Madisonian "balance" (Cain and Jones 1989) in the constitutional division of labor (Tulis 1987, 41–45; Wills 1999, chs.

4–5) can be achieved. Is it possible, in other words, to reduce the incentives to neglect administration in policy design and increase incentives for policy makers to concern themselves with implementation and attend to good administration in the framing of public policy?

The obstacles are still enormous. Invariably, policy implementation must be incremental, experimental, and adaptive, requiring some measure of patience on the part of legislators. The volatility of current factionalism and ideological combat makes for shortsighted and short-tempered policy makers, however. Beyond Martha Derthick's modest proposals emphasizing information and analysis, what might alter policy makers' understanding of the consequences of neglecting administration in policy design, and in turn lead them to acknowledge the legitimacy of administration's formative influences? Most American political leaders publicly proclaim their unswerving commitment to the rule of law. Offering them a way to think seriously about the scope and substance of the rule of law will appeal to their concerns about administrative discretion and illuminate the value of that discretion, while harnessing its properly bounded power, for improving the impact of public policy on the citizenry.

The Rule of Law and Administrative Consequences

Perhaps the best-known and thus most widely debated effort to give real meaning to the rule of law is Theodore Lowi's "juridical democracy." Lowi's "modest proposal for radical reform" was predicated on a reduction in the discretion of administrative agencies (Lowi 1979, 298–313; 1993a). The corrosive effects of interest-group liberalism on the regime, which Lowi cataloged in *The End of Liberalism*, including the neglect of administration in policy design because of unguided delegations of power, could only be neutralized, he argued, by a return to a fundamental regard for forms and formalisms. The rule of law—the requirement that the state express clearly the rule on which it seeks to take action—requires the state to make plain the purposes and means for any action. As Lowi succinctly stated, "the institutions of government ought to say what they are going to do to us before they do it; and if they cannot say they cannot act" (1979, 299).

Lowi's operational precept would seem to require policy makers, especially legislators, to take administration into account in policy design. To meet the test of the rule of law, policy makers would have to say something about how the rule behind a proposed action would be put into effect, and how the purposes would be achieved. The effect of this, however, would seem to be to reduce administration to an exclusively instrumental role. Indeed, Lowi defines administration as "a process of self-conscious, formal adaptation of means to ends. Administered social relations are all those self-conscious and formal efforts to achieve a social end" (1979, 22). His conception of the American regime under the rule of law is clearly legislative centered, making "bureaucratic expertise . . . redundant" (Ginsberg and Sanders 1990, 565), and some have charged that it is legislatively absolutist and highly centralized and hierarchical (see Schaefer 1988, 381–84; but see also Lowi 1988, 402–7, for clarification).

Lowi sounds like a progressive par excellence and an unwavering friend of the politics-administration dichotomy when he argues that "broad delegations are a menace to formal organization and to the ideal of the neutral civil servant," and they make "a politician out of a bureaucrat." This contradicts the *"raison d'etre* of administrative independence—neutrality and expertise." Improving the administrative process through adherence to the rule of law would, moreover, make "administrative power more responsible as well as more efficient" (1979, 304).

More fundamentally, Lowi's juridical democracy and its vision of a regime based on legal integrity—laws that have real, substantive meaning for citizens and articulate, with at least some precision and clarity, rules of behavior— appears to thoughtful critics to be an inappropriate response to the problems posed by the institutional arrangements of the Constitution and the regime developments that have followed. In particular, James Q. Wilson (1990) argued that juridical democracy is deficient on three counts. First, clearly defining and restricting the powers of administrators is inconsistent with a continued commitment to an activist welfare state; such a commitment requires more administrative discretion, not less. Second, many of the policies modern liberal democracies pursue cannot be reduced to clear rules of purpose and means, because some goals cannot be coherently and compellingly articulated in advance, some goals are in conflict with other goals, and some problems are so complex and interdependent ("polycentric") that the outcome of specific actions cannot be adequately predicted in advance. Hence, public bureaucracy must be "deregulated," that is, granted greater autonomy and discretion (also see J. Q. Wilson 1994). Third, the incentives faced by all public officials ("risk-averse bureaucrats, demagogic legislators, activist judges") do not favor the articulation of clear rules, because clear rules force the identification of winners and losers, and "our political system thrives on maintaining the illusion that no one need ever be a loser" (J. Q. Wilson 1990, 571).

Lowi hardly reads like a champion, or even a passive supporter, of either the scope or the aims of the American welfare state as it is currently configured, however. He argued that "what the state cannot do well, it should forego, rather than hand an impossibly vague mandate to bureaus, subcommittees, and their clientele groups" (Ginsberg and Sanders 1990, 565; also see Lowi 1971, 210: "chaos is better than a bad program"). Nor did Lowi's steadfast commitment to formalism appear to be founded on a commitment to a "sharp dichotomy of a government of laws or a government of men" (Brand 1988, 299). Lowi acknowledged that American legislatures would find it difficult to articulate a clear rule for every policy action, especially in the organic statute for an agency (see Lowi 1988, 402–3). The rule of law, he admitted, "could never eliminate all the vagueness in legislative enactments and could never eliminate the need for delegation of power to administrative agencies" (1979, 302). James Q. Wilson essentially acknowledged Lowi's argument in this regard but faulted Lowi for failing to specify the *policy* circumstances under which clear rules might be effectively developed and applied, an endeavor Lowi undertook on an independent track with his development of his concept of "arenas of power" (e.g., Lowi 1964, 1972, 2009a), an effort in which Wilson also engaged (e.g., 1980; 1989, ch. 9; 1992, ch. 23).

Lowi contended that the likelihood of vague legislative enactments requires the application, as a criterion independent of process, of the rule of law within administrative agencies. This would take place through early formal rule making. The effect, he argued, would be to shift the emphasis from agency-clientele bargaining on individual cases—he used the term *logrolling*—to bargaining on the rule. Lowi argued that, although bargaining on the rule would inevitably lead to bargaining on the case (allowing hard differences between winners and losers to be softened somewhat), the latter would then be helpful in refining the general rule (1979, 107–13, 303–4). The end result would be to reduce the "patronizing" effects of the informality of discretion (1993a, 171). Substantial political judgment—the central meaning of politics for Lowi is "the making of choices between good and bad, choices of priorities among competing good things" (1979, 267)—must, however, remain in the hands of administrators.

Lowi's argument suggested that a greater reliance on formalism would bring laws and people into closer consort while leaving administration plenty of discretion to adapt to changing circumstances and to undertake the arduous task of understanding and responding to complex, multifaceted problems. Of course, if politics means making hard choices, then Wilson was surely right in arguing that greater adherence to the rule of law would mean making more explicit the winners and losers created by any particular choice. That seems precisely to have been Lowi's point. If institutional arrangements and the prevailing public philosophy create incentives for policy makers to distance themselves from the hard choices, then changes in both are required. Asking political leaders to say what they mean when they invoke "the rule of law" might coax them into returning decision making to political representatives and the people themselves, rather than leaving it with administrators whose authority and legitimacy is for the most part dependent and always suspect.

Wilson argued that what would be required to accomplish this would be to change "all other features of the system at the same time" (1990, 571) in a manner that would create a regime foreign to our history and traditions. Lowi aimed for precisely that with his call for serious political discourse from which a new public philosophy could emerge (1979, 298), guided by political theory (313). The specific steps he advocated, however, hardly seem foreign to the regime: restoration of the Schechter Rule in the Supreme Court's scrutiny of the constitutionality of statutes; restoration of the tradition of codification, in which Congress reviews, updates, and sometimes simplifies statutes on the basis of administrative experience; limited tenure for statutes, which has become widely known and used in the form of "sunset" provisions. Lowi also expected that the move toward embracing the rule of law would have to come through changes in curriculum and philosophy in law schools, the pressure of social chaos resulting from public nonadherence to the rule of law, and the clarity with which interest-group demands are already made. Substantial debate followed publication of *The End of Liberalism*, which is exactly what Lowi had hoped to engender.

On the question of the proper function and status of administration in the regime, however, Lowi accepted it as fundamentally political and appropriately so within the constraints imposed by the rule of law and the Constitution's basic commitment to limited government. Lowi described juridical democracy as "working toward a fusion of fact and value," which "merely amounts to a fusion of political behavior, public administration, and public law" (1979, 312). He envisioned Congress revising and codifying laws "in light of administrative experience." To acknowledge the collective institutional responsibility of state action under the rule of law and to take seriously the experience of agencies, including policy failure under a clear rule (299), would allow policy makers to "fuse administrative experience" in the refinement of the law (307). It would also, presumably, reduce their temptation to deflect blame and claim short-term credit for quick fixes. Administrative experience, Lowi even suggested, might be among the most effective restraint on the excesses of legislative majorities (see Lowi 1971, 183–84; 1988, 403; Schaefer 1988, 381). When Lowi acknowledged the importance of administration in this way, he articulated essentially the same notion as Woodrow Wilson's idea of public administration as the state's "experiencing organ" and the informing function explored in the previous chapter. The formative effects of administrative discretion and experience on law and policy, and on the whole polity as a result, stemming from this role for administration would be far more to Lowi's liking than the debilitating effects of a patronizing system that arises from administrative discretion without the rule of law.

Rule of Law, Policy Design, and Deliberation

Of the two avenues briefly considered here for encouraging political leaders to acknowledge and even understand the constitutiveness of public administration, asking them to consider the real meaning of the rule of law through consideration of Lowi's juridical democracy is the most forceful, for it would imperatively require acceptance of administration's formative influence. Having to say something substantive about ends and means would force policy makers to consider the consequences of what they seek to do. They could no longer hide behind broad delegations of power, which make for a government and politics empty of all but process and thus constitute the epitome of an instrumentally rational, or "mechanistic," conception of governance (Lowi 1979, 63). Instead, legislators would have to consider the implications of their ends for the character and conduct of the citizenry and its relationship to government. This in turn would require them to think about implementation, about what administrators would actually do, and about how much and what kind of independent judgment would be left up to administration. The answers to these queries would indicate to them what might be the independent formative impact of administering the policies they devised, that is, the potential consequences of their pursuits.

Getting political leaders to explain what they mean when they claim allegiance to the rule of law is also the harder avenue to travel, however. It requires that legislators in particular take time to deliberate on a proposed law's substance and impact on the public interest. Deliberation is the hallmark of true representative bodies, even those made up of average politicians who collectively possess a diversity of talents and limitations, including more than a modicum of demagoguery (see Bessette 1994; also Elkin 1993, 134–35; 2004, 48–54). Deliberation in American legislatures is, therefore, frequently narrow, rushed, shortchanged, manipulated, and flawed. Operating under the rule of law, however, elected executives and courts, to some extent, but most especially administrative agencies could provide necessary correctives to flawed deliberation through their experience and expertise. Under the rule of law, administrative experience might be for the first time truly cumulative, and when combined with administrators' own well-developed conceptions of what the law, and the Constitution, require, lawmakers would have a much richer foundation on which to engage in deliberation. Moreover, Martha Derthick's proposed analyses of administrative capabilities would, under the rule of law, help legislators avoid major unintended consequences, and policy makers would have the incentive to support such modest analytical efforts, because, in operating with fidelity to the rule of law, they would demand information and analysis on administrative capacity so that they could choose more carefully and articulate more clearly the ends they sought and the means to be employed. They could also better assess administrative experience with policy operations and policy outcomes.

With these cumulative effects from both avenues, policy makers would gain a broad appreciation of the formative influence of administration in action and have the incentive to design law to guide it, thus securely legitimating it. That change, were it to come about, would have its own formative effect, altering citizen conceptions of and relations with administration, diminishing the excessive fear of bureaucratic tyranny that comes with a strictly instrumental conception of administration, and encouraging a greater sense of control over a public life that is inevitably dominated by administration.

Constitutive Administration and the Reinvigoration of Self-Government

With this assessment of two complementary avenues for raising the consciousness of political leaders and citizens regarding the formative bearing of public administration in the American regime, the analysis of this book has come full circle, for the question American political leaders have faced since the beginning of the republic remains how to balance the constitutiveness of administration against its substantial instrumental character in a manner consistent with the liberal democratic structure and principles of the Constitution. Lowi's critique and his declaration of reform raised that question anew and answered it by contending that the source of authority and legitimacy for administration at the national level is clear and unequivocal: it is delegated by Congress in statutes (also see Bensel 1980; Lowi 1993b, 262). Such authority and legitimacy can only be secured, however, if statutes have real substance and sufficient clarity about the rules of behavior policy makers intend to apply, so that administration, understood as government by officials rather than by laws, is properly constrained. The failure of policy makers to ensure these basic features of law puts administration in an untenable position and destroys its authority and legitimacy. Such failure also undermines the very authority and legitimacy of the government generally. This is the situation that has obtained in what Lowi called the Second Republic of the United States (or the fifth; see Lowi 2009b). Within the boundaries of law with real substance and clarity of rule, however, administration can, indeed must, act in ways that not only serve the purposes of the law but help to shape those purposes and the character of the citizenry. This may happen in ways that not even the rule of law can fully legitimate, however, suggesting again the necessity of anchoring administration and the discretion it must inevitably exercise not only in statutes but in the Constitution.

It is therefore helpful to contrast Lowi's answer to the core question of administration's place in the regime with that of John Rohr as advanced in his "normative theory of Public Administration . . . grounded in the Constitution" (Rohr 1986, 181). Rohr argued that public administrators often face situations in which the legal commands and instructions from their political superiors—the president, Congress, and the courts—are in tension or outright conflict, are insufficiently clear, or are constitutionally dubious. Indeed, even in a system where most commands are "clear and legally correct," the most important situations facing administrators are those "wherein the law empowers rather than commands," that is, where discretion is required (259–60 n. 25). These circumstances are proof, Rohr insisted, that administrators need an independent source of authority and legitimacy and guidance for their discretion that is grounded in the Constitution and not in statutory delegation.

Rohr found plenty of textual and historical evidence that the framers and later developers of the American regime intended public administration to be a core institutional component of the constitutional system, even though it is referenced only indirectly in the Constitution and then only in a subordinate capacity. This constitutional status is in fact the foundation of Rohr's conception of the independent authority, legitimacy, and guidance public administrators should recognize—the normative theory that should direct and teach them. Rohr argued for a conception of public administration as an instrumentality that is subordinate, yet professionally nonpartisan, institutionally autonomous, and constitutionally independent enough to serve as a "balance wheel" among the competing branches in the separation-of-powers system. Public administration can do this by way of individual administrators or entire agencies, choosing "which of its constitutional masters it will favor at a given time on a given issue" (1986, 182). Public administrators can do this within the discretion they possess, and they may do it in a way that "favor[s] those policies that they think are most likely to promote the public interest," but this must be pursued "against the broad background of constitutional principle" (183).

The great strength of Rohr's conception is also its great weakness. Rohr sought to anchor administrative behavior in the Constitution and encourage the public, as well as public administrators, to understand and judge administrative discretion in light of basic constitutional principles. It is difficult to see how anyone could disagree that this is in close keeping with the heritage of the founding and development of the constitutional system. It is also what a people who had embraced liberal democratic constitutionalism would want. In his conception of a subordinate yet autonomous public administration choosing among constitutional superiors, however, Rohr risked promoting exactly what he professed to abhor, namely, public officials claiming stewardship of the nation and the citizenry. This, he insisted, is a "threat . . . to the rule of law" (1986, 185; on the stewardship model, see Kass 1990). Lowi did not approve (see 1993b, 264).

The central political "problem" public administration poses for a liberal democratic constitutional regime is that administration is the manifestation of the ability of the state to reach where the law cannot quite grasp and to shape the aims of the polity and the character of the citizenry beyond the expressed intent of the law. Lowi sought to pull back on the reach of the state and bring it into line with what the law can grasp. Even he admitted, however, that this calibration can never be exact and, moreover, that public administration is central to the refinement and further clarification of substantive and rule-oriented law. Rohr sought to legitimate the reach of the state as it stands but also to ensure that it is guided by the higher law and purpose of the Constitution. Anything more than this, such as what Lowi sought, meant reconstructing the regime, which Rohr found beyond the work of administrative reform (Rohr 1986, 186; also see Bryner 1987, 216–17).

Lowi presented his proposal for juridical democracy as the initiation of a discourse intended to craft a new public philosophy. Likewise, Rohr and his companion authors of *Refounding Public Administration* promoted it as the initiation of a dialogue about the political and constitutional status of public administration (see Wamsley et al. 1990; Wamsley and Wolf 1996). The work of both stimulated a substantial body of additional scholarship and, at least in the case of

Lowi, political action as well. Along one important dimension, however, the political discourse and practical dialogue did not get very far. Political theorists and social commentators concerned with the future of liberal democratic constitutionalism have paid public administration very little heed, except, perhaps, for the concern about bureaucratic tyranny. That is a serious oversight, for any theory of democratic constitutionalism that does not incorporate, to use John Rohr's label, a "constitutional theory of public administration" is fatally deficient. What follows is a brief sketch of possible foundations for such a theory, stressing the centrality of a constitutive understanding of administration.

Democratic Constitutionalism and Responsible Discretion

In a democracy, it is inevitable that the reach of the people, in the guise of the state, will exceed the grasp of the law. This places public administration at the front lines of the contact and interaction between the state and the citizenry, confronting administrators with numerous opportunities to exercise discretion. The values of constitutionalism—limited government and the rule of law—invariably focus the attention and concern of the people and their political representatives on controlling that discretion and ensuring that administration serves designated ends. A wholesale concern for potentially irresponsible administrative behavior leads to extraordinary efforts to exact control, however. These efforts are inconsistent with the reality of political life in a liberal democratic regime, and they impair effective governance. It is the value of a constitutive perspective on public administration that it shows administration, and the discretion it inevitably exercises, as not simply a necessary evil but a critical positive force in keeping the regime in good repair and guiding its further development. Recognizing the constitutiveness of administration draws political leaders and the public away from a single-minded concern for control and directs their attention toward the fostering of responsible discretion. Within a general theory of constitutionalism, then, a constitutional theory of public administration is a theory of responsible discretion.

A constitutional theory of responsible discretion must be grounded in two core tenets. First, administrative discretion, to be responsible, cannot be unlimited. If it is, it will ultimately undermine not only public administration but also the regime. This was Lowi's core insight. Greater adherence to the rule of law in statutory design *and* implementation is fundamental. Despite the complexities and uncertainties of a postindustrial political economy and the worldwide commitments and influences faced by a modern nation-state, the rule of law is not too rigid or unadaptable. Moreover, it not only constrains unreasonable demands and expectations that delegation of excessive discretion might place on administration, it also returns liberal democratic politics and the accompanying obligations of citizenship to the center of the American polity. Administrative politics has its own important function in the constitution of the regime, but it is democratic politics, particularly the debate and deliberation associated with legislative forums, that must stand at center stage.

Second, the discretion of administrators must not be too tightly constrained, and this can only be realized if public administration is granted a sphere of legitimate action that is independently anchored in the Constitution. This is Rohr's central insight. He connected it to the administrator's oath of office. As important as administration's ministerial functions are to the integrity of the law, in following the commands of political superiors and fulfilling the clear purposes of the law, the discretionary function is the source of the most vital contributions administration makes to the regime because it allows administrators to probe the strengths and weaknesses of law and compile information on how to make it better, especially in light of the increasing speed of economic, social, and political dynamics (Scheuerman 2001). Especially when the bureaucratic form of organization dominates, it is also the source of some risk to constitutionalism and the rule of law. As long as recognition of the constitutiveness of administration prevails among political leaders and the interested public, however, that risk will be given due consideration, but not obsessive concern, in the ongoing debate about the structure and purposes of the regime that keeps the polity vibrant.

Where the state can reach but the law cannot quite grasp, administrators need sufficient security, emanating from a constitutionally grounded legitimation of their independence and authority, to take action. Such independence, set in the context of statutes with clear, substantive rules as required by the rule of law, is itself valuable. It signals broad political respect for administrators and recognition of their worth, and it provides an incentive for them to behave responsibly. This is the real import of Woodrow Wilson's observation that "large powers and unhampered discretion seem to me the indispensable conditions of responsibility" (W. Wilson 1887, 213). The point, Wilson stressed, was to fix the task and the responsibility clearly and then permit the administrator the independence to act. To grant broad discretion without clarity, and thus to divide and diffuse it, leads to obscurity and "remissness" (214; also see Bryner 1987, 217). To limit administrative power and discretion excessively leads to weak and ineffective government.

The actions administrators choose to pursue may be actions to prevent a harm or right a wrong, that is, to fulfill the purposes of the law even if the law does not expressly command it. The actions may generate practical experience about the impact of the law, which will be helpful in refining both means and ends. The actions may include administrators' cautioning political representatives, or even the public at large, that what is being sought by a statute is ambiguous, contradictory, or constitutionally dubious and very likely will lead to serious unintended consequences until the basic questions the issue raises are asked and answered. Finally, the actions may be those that allow administrators to explore the prospects for juxtaposing seemingly incompatible values, and the institutions that embody them, in ways that are mutually supportive, and thus to meet the dual tests of efficiency and the progressive development of the regime as championed by Herbert Croly.

All of these actions may be understood as expressing the idea of practical reason. Accountability in the exercise of administrative discretion readily follows when discretionary decisions are based on the giving of reasons linked to clear, substantive rules and to the underlying values and the democratic consensus that constitutes the public interest. Fidelity to the rule of law and an independent constitutional legitimacy for public administration are the prerequisites for the consistent exercise of practical reason in the public sphere. Public administrators exercising practical reason thus enable public administration as an institution to fulfill its most critical constitutive function: modeling practical reason, and thereby fostering its appreciation and practice, especially among lawmakers but also among the citizenry at large. It can thus serve the public interest in the most appropriate sense, understood "as the securing of the constitutive institutions that make a collectivity a republic and that enable it to maintain itself in that form" (Elkin 2006, 112). Recovering the legitimacy of a constitutive conception of public administration in American politics and government is thus imperative, because without that understanding, administration is severely hindered in the function for which it is well suited: champion of practical reason within the regime that brings to realization the instrumental and the constitutive as *together* composing the politics of self-government. To allow the absence of such a champion to continue is surely to put the regime in peril.

It is important to underscore, in thinking about a constitutional theory of public administration for the American regime, that action is the key, because it lies at the heart of public administration. Administration is not a contemplative enterprise. The knowledge it generates and the manner in which it is constitutive of the regime are the results of administrative action, the fulfillment of its need and obligation to act. This is what brings *practical* reason to the very heart of the matter.

The development and refinement of a constitutional theory of public administration that has as its object the positive effect of promoting practical reason through constitutionally anchored responsible discretion, rather than the negativity of merely preventing an unanchored, irresponsible discretion, is critical to dispelling the sense of loss of control and endangerment to self-government that so vexes the public and political leaders in the United States. Both the public and its political representatives will be able to accept as fundamentally legitimate a status and function for public administration that includes a constitutionally grounded independence, because adherence to the rule of law will ensure the positive value of administration's formative effects. In turn, the debilitating contradiction between the reality of administration's formative role in the regime and a doctrine of absolute instrumental subordination to political command will disappear because the absolutist doctrine will have lost its power. The security provided by adherence to the rule of law and responsible discretion will stand in its stead.

Final Reflections

With all the flaws in the design and practice of American government and politics that have emerged over time as worthy of careful and sustained scrutiny, a lack of conceptual coherence in American politics and public philosophy regarding the status and role of public administration in theory and practice hardly seems worth mentioning. It does deserve mention, and contemplation and argument, nevertheless, because it signals a larger problem— the failure of American government and politics at every level, but especially nationally, to harness consistently the power of administration "for the good of ordinary people," the ultimate aspiration of self-government as expressed by Woodrow Wilson (Link et al. 1966–1994, 5:399). Instead, the conceptual incoherence has led political leaders and citizens more generally to allow administrative power to be used for partial and factional ends, and it has led to their failure to grasp the complex, interwoven nature of state and society and to see it as a whole rather than divided into spheres to be jealously guarded from encroachment (Ansell 2011).

To govern at all means not only to fulfill designated purposes but also to shape those purposes and thus reshape the polity—the complex of relations among citizens that constitutes a public life, a regime. Administration is always at the vanguard of this dual action, so it is always in the cross fire of battles over who is to control that shaping and reshaping of purposes as well as who is to fulfill them, and how. The history of American political development is at its core a story about the gulf between the idealist visions of those seeking to control the shaping and reshaping, and the practical necessities of governing, which often do not comport with the visions. Public administration finds itself in that breach, and has often been the worse for trying to respond to the hailings and tuggings from both sides. It is at least plausible to contend, however, that the expansion, professionalization, and heightened sense of responsibility of a distinctive administrative cadre at all levels of American government has kept the breach between the ideal and the real from rending the fabric of the regime, as it did only once, so far, in the life of the nation.

The twenty-first century has thus far featured a great new agitation and flux in American politics. The American people are, in essence, locked in a struggle with themselves over who they are and what they will become as a political community. That this struggle can continue without causing undue injury may depend on whether the cliché that Americans are a pragmatic people has some foundation. It appears to be so, for they have, after all, given rise to the pragmatist school in philosophy (Garry 1992; Lacey 2008), and their commitment to liberal and democratic principles have not yet been reduced to one best way of arranging political institutions and policy choices (Anderson 1993, 110). What a tragedy it would be, then, if in their current confusion they so denigrated public administration as to utterly impair its capacity to assist them in their struggle to move closer to realizing their aspirations to self-government. The evidence suggests that as currently constituted, neither American citizens nor their leaders are up to the task (Elkin 2006, esp. chs. 6–7). This can change, however, with the exercise of "regime leadership" (Cook 2014), and it might very well be best if public administrators themselves, from the local to the national levels, led the charge.

References

Aberbach, Joel D. 1990. *Keeping a Watchful Eye: The Politics of Congressional Oversight.* Washington, DC: Brookings Institution.

Aberbach, Joel D., and Bert A. Rockman. 1988. "Mandates or Mandarins? Control and Discretion in the Modern Administrative State." *Public Administration Review* 48 (Mar.–Apr.): 606–12.

Ackerman, Bruce A., and William T. Hassler. 1981. *Clean Coal / Dirty Air.* New Haven, CT: Yale University Press.

ACSI. 2013. "Commentary on U.S. Federal Government: Citizen Satisfaction Continues to Rise for Federal Government Services." *American Customer Satisfaction Index*, Feb. 6. http://www.theacsi.org/news-and-resources/customer-satisfaction-reports/customer -satisfaction-reports-2012/acsi-federal-government-report-2012.

ACSI. 2014. "The Science of Customer Satisfaction." *American Customer Satisfaction Index.* http://www.theacsi.org/about-acsi/the-science-of-customer-satisfaction.

Adams, Guy B., Priscilla V. Bowerman, Kenneth M. Dolbeare, and Camilla Stivers. 1990. "Joining Purpose to Practice: A Democratic Identity for the Public Service." In Henry D. Kass and Bayard L. Catron, eds. *Images and Identities in Public Administration.* Newbury Park, CA: Sage Publications.

ADL. 2009. *Rage Grows in America: Anti-government Conspiracies.* New York: Anti-Defamation League.

Altman, O. R. 1938. "American Government and Politics: Second and Third Sessions of the Seventy-fifth Congress, 1937–38." *American Political Science Review* 32 (Dec.): 1099–123.

Anderson, Charles W. 1990. *Pragmatic Liberalism.* Chicago: University of Chicago Press.

———. 1993. "Pragmatic Liberalism, the Rule of Law, and the Pluralist Regime." In Stephen L. Elkin and Karol Edward Soltan, eds. *A New Constitutionalism: Designing Political Institutions for a Good Society.* Chicago: University of Chicago Press.

ANES. 2008. "Guide to Public Opinion and Electoral Behavior: Index of Tables." *American National Election Study.* http://www.electionstudies.org/nesguide/gd-index.htm.

Annals of the Congress of the United States, The. 1834. 1st Cong., part 1. Washington, DC: Gales and Seaton.

Ansell, Christopher K. 2011. *Pragmatist Democracy: Evolutionary Learning as Public Philosophy.* New York: Oxford University Press.

Appleby, Paul. 1952. *Morality and Administration in Democratic Government.* Baton Rouge: Louisiana State University Press.

Arnold, Peri E. 1976. "The First Hoover Commission and the Managerial Presidency." *Journal of Politics* 38 (Feb.): 46–70.

———. 1986. *Making the Managerial Presidency: Comprehensive Planning, 1905–1980.* Princeton, NJ: Princeton University Press.

———. 1994. "Reform's Changing Role: The National Performance Review in Historical Context." Paper prepared for the Division of United States Studies, Woodrow Wilson International Center for Scholars, Smithsonian Institution, Washington, DC.

"Assails Food Bill as Dictatorial." 1917. *New York Times*, June 15, 1, 7.

Bailey, Jeremy D. 2008. "The New Unitary Executive and Democratic Theory: The Problem of Alexander Hamilton." *American Political Science Review* 102 (Nov.): 453–65.

Baker, Peter. 2013. *Days of Fire: Bush and Cheney in the White House.* New York: Doubleday.

Balla, Steven J., and Christopher J. Deering. 2013. "Police Patrols and Fire Alarms: An Empirical Examination of the Legislative Preference for Oversight." *Congress & the Presidency* 40 (Feb.): 27–40. doi:10.1080/07343469.2012.748853.

Balogh, Brian. 2009. *A Government out of Sight: The Mystery of National Authority in Nineteenth Century American.* New York: Cambridge University Press.

Barber, Benjamin R. 2003. *Strong Democracy: Participatory Politics for a New Age.* Berkeley: University of California Press.

Barkow, Rachel E. 2010. "Insulating Agencies: Avoiding Capture through Institutional Design." *Texas Law Review* 89: 15–79.

Barzelay, Michael. 1992. *Breaking through Bureaucracy: A New Vision for Managing in Government.* Berkeley: University of California Press.

Bassani, Luigi Marco. 2010. *Liberty, State, and Union: The Political Theory of Thomas Jefferson.* Macon, GA: Mercer University Press.

BBC News. 1999. "Sci/Tech: Neutron Bomb: Why 'Clean' Is Deadly." *BBC Online Network*, July 15. http://news.bbc.co.uk/2/hi/science/nature/395689.stm.

Beach, John C., Elaine D. Carter, Martha J. Dede, Charles T. Goodsell, Rose-May Guignard, William M. Haraway, Monisha Kumar, Betty N. Morgan, and Virginia K. Sweet. 1997. "State Administration and the Founding Fathers during the Critical Period." *Administration & Society* 28 (Feb.): 511–30.

Behn, Robert D. 2012. "Motivating and Steering with Comparative Data: How the Bar Chart and 'The List' Might Help to Steer Social Integration." *International Public Management Review* 13 (1): 13–37.

Bell, Jonathan. 2004. *The Liberal State on Trial: The Cold War and American Politics in the Truman Years.* New York: Columbia University Press.

Benda, Peter M., and Charles H. Levine. 1988. "Reagan and the Bureaucracy: The Bequest, the Promise, and the Legacy." In Charles O. Jones, ed. *The Reagan Legacy: Promise and Performance.* Chatham, NJ: Chatham House.

Bensel, Richard F. 1980. "Creating the Statutory State: The Implications of a Rule of Law Standard in American Politics." *American Political Science Review* 74 (Sept.): 734–44.

Bentley, Arthur F. 1908. *The Process of Government: A Study of Social Pressures.* Chicago: University of Chicago Press.

Berger, Peter L., and Thomas Luckmann. 1966. *The Social Construction of Reality: A Treatise in the Sociology of Knowledge.* Garden City, NY: Anchor Books.

Bernstein, J. M. 2010. "The Very Angry Tea Party." *NYTimes.com*, June 13. http://opinionator.blogs.nytimes.com/2010/06/13/the-very-angry-tea-party/?_r=0.

Bernstein, Marver H. 1955. *Regulating Business by Independent Commission.* Princeton, NJ: Princeton University Press.

Berry, Jeffrey. 1977. *Lobbying for the People: The Political Behavior of Public Interest Groups.* Princeton, NJ: Princeton University Press.

Bertelli, Anthony Michael. 2010. "Congressional Ideology and Administrative Oversight in the New Deal Era." *Historical Methods* 43 (July–Sept.): 125–37.

Bessette, Joseph M. 1994. *The Mild Voice of Reason: Deliberative Democracy and American National Government.* Chicago: University of Chicago Press.

Bevir, Mark. 2010. *Democratic Governance.* Princeton, NJ: Princeton University Press.

Blunt, Barrie E. 1990. "Executive Constraints in State Constitutions under the Articles of Confederation." *Public Administration Quarterly* 13 (Winter): 451–69.

The Book of the States. 2010. Lexington, KY: Council of State Governments.

Boyd, James. 1970. "Nixon's Southern Strategy 'It's All in the Charts.'" *New York Times Magazine* (May 17): 215.

Brand, Donald R. 1988. *Corporatism and the Rule of Law: A Study of the National Recovery Administration.* Ithaca, NY: Cornell University Press.

———. 1989. "Reformers of the 1960s and 1970s: Modern Anti-federalists?" In Richard A. Harris and Sidney M. Milkis, eds. *Remaking American Politics.* Boulder, CO: Westview Press.

Brass, Clinton T. 2013. "Shutdown of the Federal Government: Causes, Processes, and Effects." *Congressional Research Service,* Sept. 25.

Breines, Wini. 1980. "Community and Organization: The New Left and Michels' 'Iron Law.'" *Social Problems* 27 (Apr.): 419–29.

Brinkley, Alan. 1989. "The New Deal and the Idea of the State." In Steve Fraser and Gary Gerstle, eds. *The Rise and Pall of the New Deal Order, 1930–1980.* Princeton, NJ: Princeton University Press.

Brown, Angela, and Aaron Wildavsky. 1984. "Implementation as Exploration." In Jeffrey L. Pressman and Aaron Wildavsky, eds. *Implementation,* 3rd ed., expanded. Berkeley: University of California Press.

Brown, Wendy. 2006. "American Nightmare: Neoliberalism, Neoconservatism, and De-democratization." *Political Theory* 34 (Dec.): 690–714.

Bryner, Gary C. 1987. *Bureaucratic Discretion: Law and Policy in Federal Regulatory Agencies.* New York: Pergamon Press.

Bullock, Charles J. 1895. "The Finances of the United States from 1775 to 1789, with Special Reference to the Budget." *Bulletin of the University of Wisconsin Economics, Political Science, and History Series* 1: 117–273.

Bush, George H. W. 1991. "Address before a Joint Session of Congress on the End of the Gulf War," Mar. 6. http://millercenter.org/president/speeches/detail/3430.

Cain, Bruce E., and W. T. Jones. 1989. "Madison's Theory of Representation." In Bernard Grofman and Donald Wittman, eds. *The Federalist Papers and the New Institutionalism.* New York: Agathon Press.

Calabresi, Guido, and Philip Bobbitt. 1982. *Tragic Choices.* New York: W. W. Norton.

Caldwell, Linton K. 1988. *The Administrative Theories of Hamilton and Jefferson: Their Contributions to Thought on Public Administration,* 2nd ed. New York: Holmes & Meier.

Calvin, Bryan, Paul M. Collins, Jr., and Matthew Eshbaugh-Soha. 2011. "On the Relationship between Public Opinion and Decision Making in the U.S. Courts of Appeals." *Political Research Quarterly* 64 (Dec.): 736–48.

Carpenter, Daniel P. 2001. *The Forging of Bureaucratic Autonomy: Reputations, Networks, and Policy Innovation in Executive Agencies, 1862–1928*. Princeton, NJ: Princeton University Press.

Cashill, Jack. 2011. *Deconstructing Obama: The Life, Loves, and Letters of America's First Postmodern President*. New York: Threshold Editions.

Chambers, John Whiteclay, II. 1980. *The Tyranny of Change: America in the Progressive Era, 1900–1917*. New York: St. Martin's Press.

Colton, Calvin, ed. 1897. *Works of Henry Clay*. Vol. 6. New York: Henry Clay Publishing.

Congressional Record. 1882. 47th Cong., 2nd sess., parts 1–3. Washington, DC: Government Printing Office.

Congressional Record. 1886. 49th Cong., 1st sess. Washington, DC: Government Printing Office.

Congressional Record. 1938. 75th Cong., 3rd sess., parts 1–6. Washington, DC: Government Printing Office.

Cook, Brian J. 1992. "The Representative Function of Bureaucracy: Public Administration in Constitutive Perspective." *Administration & Society* 23 (Feb.): 403–29.

———. 2002. "Expertise, Discretion, and Definite Law: Public Administration in Woodrow Wilson's Presidential Campaign Speeches of 1912." *Administrative Theory & Praxis* 24 (3): 487–506.

———. 2007. *Democracy and Administration: Woodrow Wilson's Ideas and the Challenges of Public Management*. Baltimore: Johns Hopkins University Press.

———. 2010. "The Organ of Experience: A Defense of the Primacy of Public Administrators in the Design and Reform of Policy and Law." *Administration & Society* 42 (3): 263–86. doi:10.1177/0095399710365483.

———. 2014. "Regime Leadership for Public Servants." In Douglas Morgan and Brian J. Cook, eds. *The New Public Governance: A Regime-Centered Perspective*. Armonk, NY: M. E. Sharpe.

Cooper, Terry L., Thomas A. Bryer, and Jack W. Meek. 2006. "Citizen-Centered Collaborative Public Management." Special issue: Collaborative Public Management, *Public Administration Review* 66 (Dec.): 76–88.

Corwin, Edward S. 1984. *The President: Office and Powers, 1787–1984*, 5th ed. New York: New York University Press.

Cox, Raymond W., III, Susan J. Buck, and Betty N. Morgan. 1994. *Public Administration in Theory and Practice*. Englewood Cliffs, NJ: Prentice-Hall.

Crenson, Matthew A. 1975. *The Federal Machine: Beginnings of Bureaucracy in Jacksonian America*. Baltimore: Johns Hopkins University Press.

Croly, Herbert. 1914. *Progressive Democracy*. New York: Macmillan.

Dahl, Robert A. 1961. "The Behavioral Approach in Political Science: Epitaph for a Monument to a Successful Protest." *American Political Science Review* 55 (Dec.): 763–72. http://www.jstor.org/stable/1952525.

Dahl, Robert A. 1982. *Dilemmas of Pluralist Democracy: Autonomy vs. Control*. New Haven, CT: Yale University Press.

Dean, John W. 2004. *Worse Than Watergate: The Secret Presidency of George W. Bush.* New York: Little, Brown.

Debord, Guy. 1977. *Society of the Spectacle,* rev. ed. Detroit, MI: Black & Red.

Denhardt, Robert B. 1993. *The Pursuit of Significance: Strategies for Managerial Success in Public Organizations.* Belmont, CA: Wadsworth.

Derthick, Martha. 1990. *Agency under Stress: The Social Security Administration in American Government.* Washington, DC: Brookings Institution.

Dewey, John. 1936. "A Liberal Speaks Out." *New York Times Magazine* (Feb. 23): 3, 24.

Diamond, Ann Stuart. 1980. "Decent, Even Though Democratic." In Robert A. Goldwin and William A. Schambra, eds. *How Democratic Is the Constitution?* Washington, DC: American Enterprise Institute.

Diamond, Martin. 1975. "The Declaration and the Constitution: Liberty, Democracy, and the Founders." *Public Interest* 41 (Fall): 39–55.

Diesing, Paul. 1962. *Reason in Society: Five Types of Decisions and Their Social Conditions.* Westport, CT: Greenwood Press.

Dimock, Marshall E. 1936. "Criteria and Objectives of Public Administration." In John M. Gaus, Leonard D. White, and Marshall E. Dimock, eds. *Frontiers of Public Administration.* Chicago: University of Chicago Press.

Downs, Anthony. 1962. "The Public Interest: Its Meaning in a Democracy." *Social Research* 29 (Spring): 1–36.

Durant, Robert F. 1992. *The Administrative Presidency Revisited: Public Lands, the BLM, and the Reagan Revolution.* Albany: State University of New York Press.

———. 2000. "Whither the Neoadministrative State? Toward a Polity-Centered Theory of Administrative Reform." *Journal of Public Administration Research and Theory* 10 (1): 79–109.

Easton, David. 1971. *The Political System: An Inquiry into the State of Political Science,* 2nd ed. Chicago: University of Chicago Press.

Eden, Robert. 1989a. "Introduction: A Legacy of Questions." In Robert Eden, ed., *The New Deal and Its Legacy: Critique and Reappraisal.* Westport, CT: Greenwood Press.

———. 1989b. "Dealing Democratic Honor Out: Reform and the Decline of Consensus Politics." In Richard A. Harris and Sidney M. Milkis, eds. *Remaking American Politics.* Boulder, CO: Westview Press.

Eisner, Marc Allen. 1993. "Demobilization and Development: Models of the State and the Reformation of the U.S. Political Economy in the Interwar Period." Paper prepared for delivery at the New England Political Science Association annual meeting, Northampton, MA, Apr. 3–4, 1993.

Elkin, Stephen L. 1985. "Economic and Political Rationality." *Polity* 18: 253–71.

———. 1987. *City and Regime in the American Republic.* Chicago: University of Chicago Press.

———. 1993. "Constitutionalism's Successor." In Stephen L. Elkin and Karol Edward Soltan, eds. *A New Constitutionalism: Designing Political Institutions for a Good Society.* Chicago: University of Chicago Press.

———. 2004. "Thinking Constitutionally: The Problem of Deliberative Democracy." *Social Philosophy and Policy* 21 (Jan.): 39–75.

———. 2006. *Reconstructing the Commercial Republic: Constitutional Design after Madison.* Chicago: University of Chicago Press.

Elkins, Stanley, and Eric McKitrick. 1993. *The Age of Federalism: The Early American Republic, 1788–1800*. New York: Oxford University Press.

Esmark, Anders. 2007. "Democratic Accountability and Network Governance—Problems and Potentials." In Eva Sorensen and Jacob Torfling, eds. *Theories of Democratic Network Governance*. New York: Palgrave Macmillan.

Farenthold, David A. 2013. "Austerity Proves to Be Hard Nut to Crack." *Washington Post*, Dec. 28, A1, A6–A7.

Farrand, Max, ed. 1911. *The Records of the Federal Convention of 1787*, 3 vols. New Haven, CT: Yale University Press. http://memory.loc.gov/ammem/amlaw/lwfr.html.

Finer, Herman. 1941. "Administrative Responsibility in Democratic Government." *Public Administration Review* 1 (Summer): 3–35.

Fiorina, Morris P. 1986. "Legislator Uncertainty, Legislative Control, and the Delegation of Legislative Power." *Journal of Law, Economics, and Organization* 2: 33–51.

———. 1989. *Congress: Keystone of the Washington Establishment*, 2nd ed. New Haven, CT: Yale University Press.

Fisher, Louis. 1985. *Constitutional Conflicts between Congress and the President*. Princeton, NJ: Princeton University Press.

Flaumenhaft, Harvey. 1981. "Hamilton's Administrative Republic and the American Presidency." In Joseph M. Bessette and Jeffrey Tulis, eds. *The Presidency in the Constitutional Order: An Historical Examination*. Baton Rouge: Louisiana State University Press.

Flexner, James T. 1969. *George Washington and the New Nation (1783–93)*. Boston: Little, Brown.

Foresta, Ronald A. 1984. *America's National Parks and Their Keepers*. Washington, DC: Resources for the Future.

Fowler, Dorothy Garfield. 1943. *The Cabinet Politician: The Postmaster General, 1829–1909*. New York: Columbia University Press.

Frederickson, H. George. 1990. "Public Administration and Social Equity." *Public Administration Review* 50 (Mar.–Apr.): 228–37.

Frederickson, H. George, and David G. Frederickson. 1995. "Public Perceptions of Ethics in Government." *Annals of the American Academy of Political and Social Science* 536 (Jan.): 163–72.

Frederickson, Kari. 2001. *The Dixiecrat Revolt and the End of the Solid South, 1932–1968*. Chapel Hill: University of North Carolina Press.

Freidel, Frank. 1990. *Franklin D. Roosevelt: A Rendezvous with Destiny*. Boston: Little, Brown.

Friedrich, Carl J. 1937. "The Rise and Decline of the Spoils Tradition." *Annals of the American Academy of Political and Social Science* 189 (Jan.): 10–16.

———. 1940. "Public Policy and the Nature of Administrative Responsibility." In Carl J. Friedrich and Edward S. Mason, eds. *Public Policy*. Vol. 1. Cambridge, MA: Harvard University Press.

Fung, Archon. 2004. *Empowered Participation: Reinventing Urban Democracy*. Princeton, NJ: Princeton University Press.

Garrett, R. Sam, James A. Thurber, A. Lee Fritschler, and David H. Rosenbloom. 2006. "Assessing the Impact of Bureaucracy Bashing by Electoral Campaigns." *Public Administration Review* 66 (Mar.–Apr.): 228–40.

Garry, Patrick M. 1992. *Liberalism and American Identity.* Kent, OH: Kent State University Press.

Garvey, Gerald. 1993. *Facing the Bureaucracy: Living and Dying in a Public Agency.* San Francisco, CA: Jossey-Bass.

Gaus, John M. 1958. "Leonard Dupee White 1891–1958." *Public Administration Review* 18 (Summer): 231–36.

Gellhorn, Walter. 1986. "The Administrative Procedure Act: The Beginnings." *Virginia Law Review* 72 (Mar.): 219–33.

General Accounting Office. 1996. "OMB 2000: Changes Resulting From the Reorganization of the Office of Management and Budget." United States General Accounting Office. Testimony before the Subcommittee on Government Management, Information and Technology Committee on Government Reform and Oversight House of Representatives, Feb. 7.

Geoghegan, Tom. 2013. "Why Are Americans Giving Up Their Citizenship?" *BBC News Magazine,* Sept. 26. http://www.bbc.co.uk/news/magazine-24135021.

Ginsberg, Benjamin, and Elizabeth Sanders. 1990. "Theodore J. Lowi and Juridical Democracy." *PS: Political Science and Politics* 23 (Dec.): 563–66.

Glenn, Brian J. 2010–11. "Conservatives and American Political Development." *Political Science Quarterly* 125 (4): 611–38.

Goldsmith, William M. 1974. *The Growth of Presidential Power.* Vol. 1. New York: Chelsea House.

Goodsell, Charles T. 1990. "Public Administration and the Public Interest." In Gary L. Wamsley, Robert N. Bacher, Charles T. Goodsell, Philip S. Kronenberg, John A. Rohr, Camilla M. Stivers, Orion F. White, and James F. Wolf, eds. *Refounding Public Administration.* Newbury Park, CA: Sage Publications.

———. 2004. *The Case for Bureaucracy: A Public Administration Polemic,* 4th ed. Washington, DC: CQ Press.

———. 2011. *Mission Mystique: Belief Systems in Public Agencies.* Washington, DC: CQ Press.

Gore, Al. 1993. *From Red Tape to Results: Creating a Government that Works Better and Costs Less.* Report of the National Performance Review. Washington, DC: U.S. Government Printing Office.

Gosar, Paul. 2013. "The IRS and EPA: Bureaucrats Out of Control." gosar.house.gov/sites/gosar.house . . . /The%20IRS%20and%20EPA_0.pdf.

Gravois, John. 2011. "More Bureaucrats, Please." *Washington Monthly,* Mar.–Apr. http://www.washingtonmonthly.com/features/2011/1103.gravois.html.

Green, Richard T. 1990. "Alexander Hamilton and the Study of Public Administration." *Public Administration Quarterly* 13 (4): 494–510.

———. 2002. "Alexander Hamilton: Founder of the American Public Administration." *Administration & Society* 34 (Nov.): 541–62. doi:10.1177/009539902237275.

Green, Richard T., Lawrence F. Keller, and Gary L. Wamsley. 1993. "Reconstituting a Profession for American Public Administration." *Public Administration Review* 53 (Nov.–Dec.): 516–24.

Grell, Jan M., and Gary Gappert. 1992. "The Future of Governance in the United States: 1992–2002." *Annals of the American Academy of Political and Social Science* 522 (July): 67–78.

Grossman, Andrew D. 2002. "The Early Cold War and American Political Development: Reflections on Recent Research." *International Journal of Politics, Culture, and Society* 15 (Spring): 471–83.

Gruber, Judith E. 1987. *Controlling Bureaucracies: Dilemmas in Democratic Governance.* Berkeley: University of California Press.

Gulick, Luther, and Lyndall Urwick. 1937. *Papers on the Science of Administration.* New York: Institute of Public Administration.

Hale, Jon F. 1995. "The Making of the New Democrats." *Political Science Quarterly,* 110 (Summer): 207–32.

Hall, Chester Gordon, Jr. 1965. "The United States Civil Service Commission: Arm of the President or Congress?" Unpublished Ph.D. dissertation, American University.

Hall, Thad E. 2002. "Live Bureaucrats and Dead Public Servants: How People in Government Are Discussed on the Floor of the House." *Public Administration Review* 62 (Mar.–Apr.): 242–51.

Halper, Stefan A., and Jonathan Clarke. 2004. *America Alone: The Neo-conservatives and the Global Order.* New York: Cambridge University Press.

Hardin, Russell. 1989. "Why a Constitution?" In Bernard Grofman and Donald Whitman, eds. *The Federalist Papers and the New Institutionalism.* New York: Agathon Press.

Harris, Richard A., and Sidney M. Milkis. 1986. "Programmatic Liberalism, the Administrative State, and the Constitution." Paper presented at the annual meeting of the American Political Science Association, Washington, DC, Aug. 31–Sept. 3.

———. 1989. *The Politics of Regulatory Change: A Tale of Two Agencies.* New York: Oxford University Press.

Harrison, Robert. 2004. *Congress, Progressive Reform, and the New American State.* Cambridge: Cambridge University Press.

Hays, Samuel P. 1987. *Beauty, Truth, and Permanence: Environmental Politics in the United States, 1955–1985.* Cambridge: Cambridge University Press.

Heclo, Hugh. 1989. "The Emerging Regime." In Richard A. Harris and Sidney M. Milkis, eds. *Remaking American Politics.* Boulder, CO: Westview Press.

———. 2008. *On Thinking Institutionally.* Boulder, CO: Paradigm.

Hendriks, Carolyn M. 2008. "On Inclusion and Network Governance: The Democratic Disconnect of Dutch Energy Transitions." *Public Administration* 86 (4): 1009–31. doi:10.1111/j.1467-9299.2008.00738.x.

Herring, Pendleton. 1936. *Public Administration and the Public Interest.* New York: McGraw-Hill.

Herson, Lawrence J. R. 1984. *The Politics of Ideas: Political Theory and American Public Policy.* Homewood, IL: Dorsey Press.

Hetherington, Marc J. 2009. "Review Article: Putting Polarization in Perspective." *British Journal of Political Science* 39 (2): 413–48.

Hill, Larry B. 1992. "Taking Bureaucracy Seriously." In Larry B. Hill et al., eds. *The State of Public Bureaucracy.* Armonk, NY: M. E. Sharpe.

Hirsh, Michael. 2013. "Analysis: Incompetence, but No Cover-Up in Benghazi." *Government Executive,* May 8. http://www.govexec.com/defense/2013/05/analysis-incompe tence-no-cover-benghazi/63057/.

Hoffer, Williamjames Hull. 2007. *To Enlarge the Machinery of Government: Congressional Debates and the Growth of the American State, 1858–1891*. Baltimore: Johns Hopkins University Press.

Hoogenboom, Ari. 1961. *Outlawing the Spoils: A History of the Civil Service Reform Movement, 1865–1883*. Urbana: University of Illinois Press.

Howe, Neil, and Richard Jackson. 2004. "Social Security Reform—Facing Up to the Real Trade-Offs." *Concord Coalition*. http://www.concordcoalition.org/publications/facing-facts/2004/0413/social-security-reform-facing-real-trade-offs.

Hubbell, Larry. 1991. "Ronald Reagan as Symbol Maker: The Federal Bureaucrat as Loafer, Incompetent, Buffoon, Good Ole Boy, and Tyrant." *American Review of Public Administration* 21 (3): 239–53.

Huntington, Samuel P. 1952. "The Marasmus of the ICC." *Yale Law Journal* 61 (Apr.): 467–509.

Hyneman, Charles S., and George W. Carey, eds. 1967. *A Second Federalist: Congress Creates a Government*. New York: Appleton-Century-Crofts.

Jackson, Michael. 2009. "Responsibility versus Accountability in the Friedrich-Finer Debate." *Journal of Management History* 66 (1): 66–77. doi:10.1108/17511340910921790.

James, William. 1981/1890. *The Principles of Psychology*. Cambridge, MA: Harvard University Press.

Jefferson, Thomas. 1787. "To James Madison from Thomas Jefferson, 20 December 1787," Founders Online, National Archives. http://founders.archives.gov/documents/Madison/01-10-02-0210, ver. 2013-12-27. In Robert A. Rutland, Charles F. Hobson, William M. E. Rachal, and Frederika J. Teute, eds. *The Papers of James Madison*. Vol. 10, *27 May 1787–3 March 1788*. Chicago: University of Chicago Press, 1977, pp. 335–339.

———. 1795. "From Thomas Jefferson to Jean Nicolas Démeunier, 29 April 1795," Founders Online, National Archives. http://founders.archives.gov/documents/Jefferson/01-28-02-0259, ver. 2013-12-27. In John Catanzariti, ed. *The Papers of Thomas Jefferson*. Vol. 28, *1 January 1794–29 February 1796*. Princeton, NJ: Princeton University Press, 2000, pp. 340–342.

———. 1819. "From Thomas Jefferson to Spencer Roane, 6 September 1819," Founders Online, National Archives. http://founders.archives.gov/documents/Jefferson/98-01-02-0734, ver. 2013-12-27. (This is an early access document from The Papers of Thomas Jefferson: Retirement Series. It is not an authoritative final version.)

John, DeWitt, Donald F. Kettl, Barbara Dyer, and W. Robert Lovan. 1994. "What Will New Governance Mean for the Federal Government?" *Public Administration Review* 54 (Mar.–Apr.): 170–75.

John, Richard R., and Christopher J. Young. 2002. "Rites of Passage: Postal Petitioning as a Tool of Governance in the Age of Federalism." In Kenneth R. Bowling and Donald R. Kennon, eds. *The House and Senate in the 1790s*. Athens: Ohio University Press.

Jones, Jeffrey M. 2011. "Americans Say Federal Gov't Wastes over Half of Every Dollar; Believe State and Local Governments Waste Proportionately Less Money." *Gallup Poll News Service*. Sept. 19.

Kaplan, Abraham. 1964. *The Conduct of Inquiry: Methodology for Behavioral Science*. San Francisco, CA: Chandler Publishing.

Karl, Barry D. 1963. *Executive Reorganization and Reform in the New Deal: The Genesis of Administrative Management*. Cambridge, MA: Harvard University Press.

———. 1983. *The Uneasy State: The United States from 1915 to 1945*. Chicago: University of Chicago Press.

———. 1987. "The American Bureaucrat: A History of a Sheep in Wolves' Clothing." *Public Administration Review* 47 (Jan.–Feb.): 26–34.

———. 1988. "The Constitution and Central Planning: The Third New Deal Revisited." *The Supreme Court Review 1988* (1988): 163–201. http://www.jstor.org/stable/3109624.

Kass, Henry D. 1990. "Stewardship as a Fundamental Element in Images of Public Administration." In Henry D. Kass and Bayard L. Catron, eds. *Images and Identities in Public Administration*. Newbury Park, CA: Sage Publications.

Kathi, Pradeep Chandra, and Terry L. Cooper. 2005. "Democratizing the Administrative State: Connecting Neighborhood Councils and City Agencies." *Public Administration Review* 65 (Sept.-Oct.): 559–67.

Kaufman, Herbert. 1965. "The Growth of the Federal Personnel System." In Wallace S. Sayre, ed. *The Federal Government Service*. Englewood Cliffs, NJ: Prentice-Hall.

Kessler, Charles R. 1989. "The Public Philosophy of the New Freedom and the New Deal." In Robert Eden, ed. *The New Deal and Its Legacy: Critique and Reappraisal*. Westport, CT: Greenwood Press.

Kettl, Donald F. 1988. *Government by Proxy: (Mis?)Managing Federal Programs*. Washington, DC: Congressional Quarterly Books / CQ Press.

———. 1993. *Sharing Power: Public Governance and Private Markets*. Washington, DC: Brookings Institution.

Klein, Ezra. 2013. "How Republicans Stopped Worrying and Learned to Love Big Government." *Washington Post*, June 21. http://www.washingtonpost.com/blogs/wonkblog/wp /2013/06/21/how-republicans-stopped-worrying-and-learned-to-love-big-government/.

Knickerbocker, Brad. 2010. "Government Employees Feel the Danger of Anti-government Anger." *Christian Science Monitor*, Mar. 27. http://www.csmonitor.com/USA/Politics /2010/0327/Government-employees-feel-the-danger-of-anti-government-anger.

Kohl, Lawrence Frederick. 1989. *The Politics of Individualism: Parties and the American Character in the Jacksonian Era*. New York: Oxford University Press.

Kolko, Gabriel. 1965. *Railroads and Regulation, 1877–1916*. New York: W. W. Norton.

Kravchuk, Robert S. 1992. "Liberalism and the American Administrative State." *Public Administration Review* 52 (July–Aug.): 374–79.

Kreps, David. 1998. "The Society of the Spectacle." http://www.kreps.org/ma/soc.html.

Krislov, Samuel, and David H. Rosenbloom. 1981. *Representative Bureaucracy and the American Political System*. New York: Praeger.

Kristol, Irving. "The Neoconservative Persuasion." *Weekly Standard* 8 (Aug. 25). http:// www.weeklystandard.com/Content/Public/Articles/000/000/003/000tzmlw.asp.

Krugman, Paul. 2011. "An Insurance Company with an Army." *New York Times*, Oct. 22. http://krugman.blogs.nytimes.com/2011/10/22/an-insurance-company-with-an-army-2/.

Kuttner, Robert. 1996. *Everything for Sale: The Virtues and Limits of Markets*. Chicago: University of Chicago Press.

Lacey, Robert J. 2008. *American Pragmatism and Democratic Faith*. Dekalb: Northern Illinois University Press.

Landis, James M. 1938. *The Administrative Process.* New Haven, CT: Yale University Press.

Landy, Marc K., Marc J. Roberts, and Stephen L. Thomas. 1990. *The Environmental Protection Agency: Asking the Wrong Questions.* New York: Oxford University Press.

Lane, Robert E. 1981. "Markets and Politics: The Human Product." *British Journal of Political Science* 1 (Jan.): 1–16.

Larson, John Lauritz. 2010. *The Market Revolution in America: Liberty, Ambition, and the Eclipse of the Common Good.* New York: Cambridge University Press.

Lasswell, Harold D. 1936. *Politics: Who Gets What, When, and How.* New York: McGraw-Hill.

Leiss, William. 1990. *Under Technology's Thumb.* Toronto: McGill-Queen's University Press.

Leopold, A. Starker, Stanley A. Cain, Clarence M. Cottam, Ira N. Gabrielson, and Thomas L. Kimball. 1963. "Wildlife Management in the National Parks." Washington, DC: Wildlife Management Institute.

Lim, Hong-Hai. 2006. "Representative Bureaucracy: Rethinking Substantive Effects and Active Representation." *Public Administration Review* 66 (Mar.–Apr.): 193–204.

Lindblom, Charles E. 1980. *The Policy-Making Process,* 2nd ed. Englewood Cliffs, NJ: Prentice-Hall.

Link, Arthur S. 1959. "What Happened to the Progressive Movement in the 1920s?" *American Historical Review* 64 (4): 833–51.

Link, Arthur S., et al., eds. 1966–1994. *The Papers of Woodrow Wilson.* 69 vols. Princeton, NJ: Princeton University Press.

Lipsky, Michael. 1971. "Street-Level Bureaucracy and the Analysis of Urban Reform." *Urban Affairs Review* 6 (June): 391–409. doi:10.1177/107808747100600401.

Long, Norton E. 1952. "Bureaucracy and Constitutionalism." *American Political Science Review* 46 (Sept.): 808–18.

———. 1990. "Conceptual Notes on the Public Interest for Public Administration and Policy Analysis." *Administration & Society* 22 (Aug.): 170–81.

Lowery, David. 1993. "A Bureaucratic-Centered Image of Governance: The Founders' Thought in Modern Perspective." *Journal of Public Administration Research and Theory* 3 (Apr.): 182–208.

Lowi, Theodore J. 1964. "American Business, Public Policy, Case Studies, and Political Theory." *World Politics* 16 (July): 677–715.

———. 1971. "A Reply to Mansfield." *Public Policy* 19 (Winter): 207–11.

———. 1972. "Four Systems of Policy, Politics, and Choice." *Public Administration Review* 32 (July–Aug.): 298–310.

———. 1979. *The End of Liberalism,* 2nd ed. New York: W. W. Norton.

———. 1985. *The Personal President: Power Invested, Promise Unfulfilled.* Ithaca, NY: Cornell University Press.

———. 1988. "Response to Schaefer." *Administration & Society* 19 (Feb.): 399–412.

———. 1993a. "Two Roads to Serfdom: Liberalism, Conservatism, and Administrative Power." In Stephen L. Elkin and Karol Edward Soltan, eds. *A New Constitutionalism: Designing Political Institutions for a Good Society.* Chicago: University of Chicago Press.

———. 1993b. "Legitimizing Public Administration: A Disturbed Dissent." *Public Administration Review* 53 (May–June): 261–64.

———. 2009a. *Arenas of Power.* Boulder, CO: Paradigm Publishers.

———. 2009b. "Bend Sinister: How the Constitution Saved the Republic and Lost Itself." *PS: Political Science and Politics* 42 (Jan.): 3–9.

Lowi, Theodore J., and Benjamin Ginsberg. 1990. *American Government: Freedom and Power.* New York: W. W. Norton.

Maass, Arthur A., and Lawrence I. Radway. 1959. "Gauging Administrative Responsibility." In Dwight Waldo, ed. *Ideas and Issues in Public Administration.* New York: McGraw-Hill.

MacDonald, Jason A., and William W. Franko, Jr. 2007. "Bureaucratic Capacity and Bureaucratic Discretion: Does Congress Tie Policy Authority to Performance?" *American Politics Research* 35 (Nov.): 790–807. doi:10.1177/1532673X07301654.

MacIntyre, Alasdair. 1981. *After Virtue: A Study in Moral Theory.* South Bend, IN: University of Notre Dame Press.

Macmahon, Arthur W. 1958. "Woodrow Wilson: Political Leader and Administrator." In Earl Latham, ed. *The Philosophy and Policies of Woodrow Wilson.* Chicago: University of Chicago Press.

Madison, James. 1785. "From James Madison to James Monroe, 21 March 1785." Founders Online, National Archives. http://founders.archives.gov/documents/Madison/01-08-02-0137, ver. 2013-12-27. In Robert A. Rutland and William M. E. Rachal, eds. *The Papers of James Madison.* Vol. 8, *10 March 1784–28 March 1786.* Chicago: University of Chicago Press, 1973, pp. 255–57.

Mainzer, Lewis C. 1994. "Public Administration in Search of a Theory: The Interdisciplinary Delusion." *Administration and Society* 26 (Nov.): 359–94.

Malecki, Edward S. 1977. "A Marxian Interpretation of the New Left." *Western Political Quarterly* 30 (Mar.): 35–59.

Marini, Frank. 1971. *Toward a New Public Administration.* Scranton, PA: Chandler Publications.

Marshall, Lynn. 1967. "The Strange Stillbirth of the Whig Party." *American Historical Review* 72 (Jan.): 445–68.

Martin, Daniel W. 1988. "The Fading Legacy of Woodrow Wilson." *Public Administration Review* 48 (Mar.–Apr.): 631–36.

Marx, Fritz Morstein. 1957. *The Administrative State.* Chicago: University of Chicago Press.

Mashaw, Jerry L. 2006. "Recovering American Administrative Law: Federalist Foundations, 1787–1801." *Yale Law Journal* 115 (Apr.): 1256–344.

———. 2007. "Reluctant Nationalists: Federal Administration and Administrative Law in the Republican Era, 1801–1829." *Yale Law Journal* 116 (June): 1636–740.

———. 2008. "Administration and 'The Democracy': Administrative Law from Jackson to Lincoln, 1829–1861." *Yale Law Journal* 117 (June): 1568–693.

———. 2010. "Federal Administration and Administrative Law in the Gilded Age." *Yale Law Journal* 119 (May): 1362–472.

Maslow, Abraham H. 1966. *The Psychology of Science.* New York: Harper & Row.

Matthews, Richard K. 1984. *The Radical Politics of Thomas Jefferson: A Revisionist View.* Lawrence: University Press of Kansas.

Mayer, David M. 1994. *The Constitutional Thought of Thomas Jefferson.* Charlottesville: University of Virginia Press.

Maynard-Moody, Steven, and Michael Musheno. 2003. *Cops, Teachers, Counselors: Stories from the Front Lines of Public Service.* Ann Arbor: University of Michigan Press.

McCubbins, Mathew, and Thomas Schwartz. 1984. "Congressional Oversight Overlooked: Police Patrols versus Fire Alarms." *American Journal of Political Science* 28 (Feb.): 165–79.

McNollgast. 1999. "The Political Origins of the Administrative Procedure Act." *Journal of Law, Economics, & Organization* 15 (Apr.): 180–217.

McWilliams, Wilson Carey. 1995. *The Politics of Disappointment: American Elections, 1976–94.* Chatham, NJ: Chatham House.

Meier, Kenneth J. 1993. *Politics and the Bureaucracy: Policymaking in the Fourth Branch of Government,* 3rd ed. Pacific Grove, CA: Brooks/Cole Publishing.

———. 1997. "Bureaucracy and Democracy: The Case for More Bureaucracy and Less Democracy." *Public Administration Review* 57 (May–June): 193–99.

Melnick, R. Shep. 1989. "The Courts, Congress, and Programmatic Rights." In Richard A. Harris and Sidney M. Milkis, eds. *Remaking American Politics.* Boulder, CO: Westview Press.

Mettler, Suzanne, and Joe Soss. 2004. "The Consequences of Public Policy for Democratic Citizenship: Bridging Policy Studies and Mass Politics." *Perspectives on Politics* 2 (Mar.): 55–73.

Milkis, Sidney M. 1993. *The President and the Parties: The Transformation of the American Party System since the New Deal.* New York: Oxford University Press.

———. 2007. "The Rhetorical and Administrative Presidencies." *Critical Review: A Journal of Politics and Society* 19 (2–3): 379–401. doi:10.1080/08913810701766272.

———. 2009. *Theodore Roosevelt, the Progressive Party, and the Transformation of American Democracy.* Lawrence: University Press of Kansas.

Milkis, Sidney M., and Daniel J. Tichenor. 1993. "The Progressive Party and Social Reformers: The 'Critical' Election of 1912." Paper prepared for delivery at the 1993 annual meeting of the American Political Science Association, Washington, DC, Sept. 2–5.

Milkis, Sidney M., and Michael Nelson. 2003. *The American Presidency: Origins and Development, 1776–2002,* 4th ed. Washington, DC: CQ Press.

Miller, Gary. 2000. "Above Politics: Credible Commitment and Efficiency in the Design of Public Agencies." *Journal of Public Administration Research and Theory* 10 (Apr.): 289–327.

Miller, James. 1987. *Democracy Is in the Streets: From Port Huron to the Siege of Chicago.* New York: Simon and Schuster.

Milward, H. Brinton. 1996. "Symposium on the Hollow State: Capacity, Control, and Performance in Interorganizational Settings." *Journal of Public Administration Research and Theory* 6 (Apr.): 193–95.

Miroff, Bruce. 2003. "The Presidential Spectacle." In Michael Neslon, ed. *The Presidency and the Political System,* 7th ed. Washington, DC: CQ Press.

Mitchell, Terence R., and William G. Scott. 1987. "Leadership Failures, the Distrusting Public, and Prospects of the Administrative State." *Public Administration Review* 47 (Nov.–Dec.): 445–52.

Moe, Ronald C. 1994. "The 'Reinventing Government' Exercise: Misinterpreting the Problem, Misjudging the Consequences." *Public Administration Review* 54 (Mar.–Apr.): 111–22.

Moe, Terry M. 1989. "The Politics of Bureaucratic Structure." In John E. Chubb and Paul E. Peterson, eds. *Can the Government Govern?* Washington, DC: Brookings Institution.

Montesquieu, Charles de Secondat. 1734. *Considerations on the Causes of the Greatness of the Romans and their Decline.* Translated by David Lowenthal. New York: Free Press. http://www.constitution.org/cm/ccgrd_l.htm.

Moore, Mark H. 1995. *Creating Public Value: Strategic Management in Government.* Cambridge, MA: Harvard University Press.

———. 2013. *Recognizing Public Value.* Cambridge, MA: Harvard University Press.

Morgan, Douglas F. 1990. "Administrative Phronesis: Discretion and the Problem of Administrative Legitimacy in Our Constitutional System." In Henry D. Kass and Bayard L. Catron, eds. *Images and Identities in Public Administration.* Newbury Park, CA: Sage Publications.

———. 1996. "Institutional Survival in the Postmodern Age: Administrative Practice and the American Constitutional Legacy." *Administrative Theory & Praxis* 18 (2): 42–56.

Morone, James A. 1985. "Representation without Elections: The American Bureaucracy and Its Publics." In Bruce Jennings and Daniel Callahan, eds. *Representation and Responsibility: Exploring Legislative Ethics.* New York: Plenum Press.

———. 1990. *The Democratic Wish: Popular Participation and the Limits of American Government.* New York: Basic Books.

Mosher, Frederick C. 1968. *Democracy and the Public Service.* New York: Oxford University Press.

Munro, William Bennett. 1930. *The Makers of the Unwritten Constitution.* New York: Macmillan.

Nardulli, Peter F. 1992. "The Constitution and American Politics: A Developmental Perspective." In Peter F. Nardulli, ed. *The Constitution and American Political Development: An Institutional Perspective.* Urbana: University of Illinois Press.

Nathan, Richard. 1975. *The Plot That Failed: Nixon and the Administrative Presidency.* New York: Wiley.

———. 1983. *The Administrative Presidency.* New York: Wiley.

NBCWashington.com. 2013. "Rally at World War II Memorial Ends at White House." *NBC4 Washington*, Oct. 14. http://www.nbcwashington.com/news/local/Vets-Plan -Rally-at-World-War-II-Memorial-227574101.html.

Nelson, Michael. 1982. "A Short, Ironic History of American National Bureaucracy." *Journal of Politics* 44 (2): 747–78.

Nelson, Richard R. 1977. *The Moon and the Ghetto: An Essay on Public Policy Analysis.* New York: W. W. Norton.

Nelson, William E. 2006. *The Roots of American Bureaucracy, 1830–1900.* Reprinted with a new preface. Washington, DC: Beard Books. First published 1982 by Harvard University Press.

Newbold, Stephanie P. 2010a. *All but Forgotten: Thomas Jefferson and the Development of American Public Administration.* Albany: State University of New York Press.

———. 2010b. "Toward a Constitutional School for American Public Administration." *Public Administration Review* 70 (July–Aug.): 538–46.

Newbold, Stephanie P., and David H. Rosenbloom. 2007. "Critical Reflections on Hamiltonian Perspectives on Rule-Making and Legislative Proposal Initiatives by the Chief Executive." *Public Administration Review* 67 (Nov.–Dec.): 1049–56.

Newbold, Stephanie P., and Larry D. Terry. 2006. "The President's Committee on Administrative Management: The Untold Story." *Administration & Society* 38 (Nov.): 522–55.

Norton, Anne. 2004. *Leo Strauss and the Politics of American Empire*. New Haven, CT: Yale University Press.

Novak, William J. 2008. "The Myth of the 'Weak' American State." *American Historical Review* 113 (June): 752–72.

Okun, Arthur M. 1975. *Equality and Efficiency: The Big Tradeoff*. Washington, DC: Brookings Institution.

Ornstein, Norman J., and Shirley Elder. 1978. *Interest Groups, Lobbying and Policymaking*. Washington, DC: Congressional Quarterly Press.

Osborne, David, and Ted Gaebler. 1992. *Reinventing Government: How the Entrepreneurial Spirit Is Transforming the Public Sector*. Reading, MA: Addison-Wesley.

Ostrom, Vincent. 1987. *The Political Theory of a Compound Republic: Designing the American Experiment*, 2nd ed. Lincoln: University of Nebraska Press.

Overeem, Patrick. 2010. *The Politics-Administration Dichotomy: Toward a Constitutional Perspective*, 2nd ed. New York: CRC Press.

Page, Benjamin I., and Robert Y. Shapiro. 1989. "Restraining the Whims and Passions of the Public." In Bernard Grofman and Donald Wittman, eds. *The Federalist Papers and the New Institutionalism*. New York: Agathon Press.

"Panaceas Offered by the New Party." 1912. *The New York Times*, August 8: 1, 3.

Parker, Ashley. 2013. "Border Deal by 2 in G.O.P. Lifts Chances of Immigration Bill." *New York Times*, June 22, A14.

Parmelee, Lisa Ferraro. 2000. "The Year Was . . . 1946." *Public Perspective* (Mar.–Apr.): 48–49.

Patterson, James T. 1967. *Congressional Conservatism and the New Deal*. Lexington: University of Kentucky Press.

Pear, Robert, Sharon LaFraniere, and Ian Austen. 2013. "From the Start, Signs of Trouble at Health Portal." *New York Times*, Oct. 12, A1.

Pemberton, William E. 1986. "Struggle for the New Deal: Truman and the Hoover Commission." *Presidential Studies Quarterly* 16 (Summer): 511–27.

Pennock, J. Roland. 1962. "The One and the Many: A Note on the Concept." In Carl J. Friedrich, ed. *The Public Interest, Nomos V*. New York: Atherton.

Peskin, Allan. 1999. *Garfield*. Kent, OH: Kent State University Press.

Pessen, Edward. 1978. *Jacksonian American: Society, Personality, and Politics*. Homewood, IL: Dorsey Press.

Pew Research Center. 2010. "Distrust, Discontent, Anger and Partisan Rancor: The People and Their Government." Pew Research Center for the People and the Press, Apr. 18. http://www.people-press.org/2010/04/18/distrust-discontent-anger-and-partisan -rancor.

————. 2013a. "Majority Says the Federal Government Threatens Their Personal Rights." Pew Research Center for the People and the Press, Jan. 31. http://www.people-press .org/2013/01/31/majority-says-the-federal-government-threatens-their-personal-rights.

————. 2013b. "State Governments Viewed Favorably as Federal Rating Hits New Low." Pew Research Center for the People and the Press, Apr. 15. http://www.people-press .org/2013/04/15/state-govermnents-viewed-favorably-as-federal-rating-hits-new-low.

Pfiffner, James P. "The First MBA President: George W. Bush as Public Administrator." *Public Administration Review* 67 (Jan.–Feb.): 6–20.

Phillips, Kevin. 1993. *Boiling Point: Republicans, Democrats, and the Decline of Middle-Class Prosperity.* New York: Random House.

Pitkin, Hanna Fenichel. 1967. *The Concept of Representation.* Berkeley: University of California Press.

Poggione, Sarah J., and Christopher Reenock. 2009. "Political Insulation and Legislative Interventions: The Impact of Rule Review." *State Politics & Policy Quarterly* 9 (Winter): 456–85.

Polenberg, Richard. 1966. *Reorganizing Roosevelt's Government: The Controversy over Executive Reorganization, 1936–1939.* Cambridge, MA: Harvard University Press.

Posner, Richard A. 1974. "Theories of Economic Regulation." *Bell Journal of Economics and Management Science* 5 (Fall): 335–58.

President's Committee. 1937. "Report of the Committee: With Studies of Administrative Management in the Federal Government/Submitted to the President and to the Congress in accordance with Public Law No. 739, 74th Congress, 2d session." Washington, DC: Government Printing Office. http://hdl.handle.net/2027/mdp.39015019768939.

Pressman, Steven. 2007. "The Decline of the Middle Class: An International Perspective." *Journal of Economic Issues* 41 (Mar.): 181–200.

Proceedings of the National Civil-Service Reform League Annual Meeting. 1884. New York: National Civil-Service Reform League, August 6.

Purcell, Edward, Jr. 1967. "Ideas and Interests: Business and the Interstate Commerce Act." *Journal of American History* 54: 561–78.

Register of Debates in Congress. 1848a. 23rd Cong., 2nd sess., part 1. Washington, DC: Gales and Seaton.

Register of Debates in Congress. 1848b. 23rd Cong., 2nd sess., part 2. Washington, DC: Gales and Seaton.

Reich, Robert B. 1988. "Policy Making in a Democracy." In Robert B. Reich, ed. *The Power of Public Ideas.* Cambridge, MA: Ballinger.

Rhodes, R. A. W. 1996. "The New Governance: Governing without Government." *Political Studies* 44 (Sept.): 652–67.

Richardson, James D. 1898. *A Compilation of the Messages and Papers of the Presidents.* Vol. 8. Washington, DC: Published by authority of Congress.

————. 1911. *A Compilation of the Messages and Papers of the Presidents.* 11 vols. Washington, DC: Bureau of National Literature.

Roberts, Alisdair. 1996. "Why the Brownlow Committee Failed: Neutrality and Partisanship in the Early Years of Public Administration." *Administration & Society* 28 (May): 3–38.

Roberts, Robert North, and Marion T. Doss. 1997. *From Watergate to Whitewater: The Public Integrity War.* Westport, CT: Greenwood Press.

Rogers, Lindsay. 1938. "Reorganization: Post Mortem Notes." *Political Science Quarterly* 53 (June): 161–72.

Rohr, John A. 1986. *To Run a Constitution: The Legitimacy of the Administrative State.* Lawrence: University Press of Kansas.

———. 1989a. "Public Administration, Executive Power, and Constitutional Confusion." *Public Administration Review* 49 (Mar.–Apr.): 108–14.

———. 1989b. *The President and the Public Administration.* Washington, DC: American Historical Association.

———. 1989c. *Ethics for Bureaucrats: An Essay on Law and Values*, 2nd ed. New York: Marcel Dekker.

Roosevelt, Franklin D. 1938. *The Public Papers and Addresses of Franklin D. Roosevelt.* Vol. 5. New York: Random House.

Roosevelt, Theodore. 1912. "Confession of Faith." http://www.theodore-roosevelt.com /images/research/speeches/trarmageddon.pdf.

Rose, Richard. 1989. "Signals for Steering Government: A Symposium of the Wissenschaftszentrum, Berlin." *Journal of Public Policy* 9 (July–Sept.): 233–40.

Rosenbloom, David H. 1971. *Federal Service and the Constitution: The Development of the Public Employment Relationship.* Ithaca, NY: Cornell University Press.

———. 1992. "Democratic Constitutionalism and the Evolution of Bureaucratic Government: Freedom and Accountability in the Administrative State." In Peter F. Nardulli, ed. *The Constitution and American Political Development: An Institutional Perspective.* Urbana: University of Illinois Press.

———. 2000. *Building a Legislative-Centered Public Administration: Congress and the Administrative State, 1946–1999.* Tuscaloosa: University of Alabama Press.

Rosenthal, Alan. 1990. *Governors and Legislatures: Contending Powers.* Washington, DC: CQ Press.

Rossiter, Clinton. 1962. *Conservatism in America: The Thankless Persuasion*, 2nd ed., rev. ed. New York: Knopf.

Rourke, Francis E. 1984. *Bureaucracy, Politics, and Public Policy*, 3rd ed. Boston: Little, Brown.

———. 1991. "American Bureaucracy in a Changing Political Setting." *Journal of Public Administration Research and Theory*, 1 (2): 111–29.

———. 1992. "American Exceptionalism: Government without Bureaucracy." In Larry B. Hill et al., eds. *The State of Public Bureaucracy.* Armonk, NY: M. E. Sharpe.

Rudalevige, Andrew. 2006. *The New Imperial Presidency: Renewing Presidential Power after Watergate.* Ann Arbor: University of Michigan Press.

Ruderman, Richard S. 1997. "Aristotle and the Recovery of Political Judgment." *American Political Science Review* 91 (June): 409–20.

Sabato, Larry. 1978. *Goodbye to Good-time Charlie: The American Governorship Transformed.* Lexington, MA: Lexington Books.

Salamon, Lester M., ed. 1989. *Beyond Privatization: The Tools of Government Action.* Washington, DC: Urban Institute Press.

———. 2000. "The New Governance and the Tools of Public Action: An Introduction." *Fordham Urban Law Journal* 28 (5): 1611–74.

Salant, Jonathan D. 1995. "Senate Passes Spending Bill for Legislative Branch." *Congressional Quarterly Weekly Report* 53 (July 22): 2142–44.

Sandalow, Marc. 2004. "New Analysis: Record Shows Bush Shifting on Iraq War / President's Rationale for the Invasion Continues to Evolve." *SFGate.com*, Sept. 29. http://www.sfgate.com/politics/article/NEWS-ANALYSIS-Record-shows-Bush-shifting-on-2690938.php.

Sandel, Michael J. 2012. "What Isn't for Sale?" *The Atlantic*, April. http://www.theatlantic.com/magazine/archive/2012/04/what-isnt-for-sale/308902/.

Sanders, Jennings B. 1935. *Evolution of Executive Departments of the Continental Congress 1774–1789*. Chapel Hill: University of North Carolina Press.

Savage, Charlie, and Edward Wyatt. 2013. "U.S. Secretly Collecting Logs of Business Calls. *New York Times*, June 76, A16.

Savage, Charlie, Edward Wyatt, and Peter Baker. 2013. "U.S. Confirms That It Gathers Online Data Overseas." *New York Times*, June 7, A1.

Savas, E. S. 1987. *Privatization: The Key to Better Government*. Chatham, NJ: Chatham House.

Schaefer, David Lewis. 1988. "Theodore Lowi and the Administrative State." *Administration & Society* 19 (Feb.): 371–98.

Schattschneider, E. E. 1960. *The Semi-sovereign People: A Realist's View of Democracy in America*. New York: Holt, Rinehart and Winston.

Scheuerman, William E. 2001. "Liberal Democracy and the Empire of Speed." *Polity* 34 (Fall): 41–67.

Schoenbrod, David. 1983. "Goals Statutes or Rules Statutes: The Case of the Clean Air Act." *UCLA Law Review* 30 (Apr.): 740–828.

Schroeder, John Fredrick. 1855. *Maxims of Washington; Political, Social, Moral, and Religious*. New York: D. Appleton & Co.

Schultze, Charles L. 1977. *The Public Use of Private Interest*. Washington, DC: Brookings Institution.

Schwartz, Nancy L. 1988. *The Blue Guitar: Political Representation and Community*. Chicago: University of Chicago Press.

Schwartz, Thomas. 1989. "Checks, Balances, and Bureaucratic Usurpation of Congressional Power." In Bernard Grofman and Donald Wittman, eds. *The Federalist Papers and the New Institutionalism*. New York: Agathon Press.

Schwarz, Jordan A. 1970. *The Interregnum of Despair: Hoover, Congress, and the Depression*. Urbana: University of Illinois Press.

Schweizer, Peter. 2008. *Makers and Takers*. New York: Doubleday.

Scigliano, Robert. 1989. "The President's 'Prerogative Power.'" In Thomas Cronin, ed. *Inventing the Presidency*. Lawrence: University Press of Kansas.

Seidenfeld, Mark. 1992. "A Civic Republican Justification for the Bureaucratic State." *Harvard Law Review* 105: 1512–76.

Seidman, Harold, and Robert Gilmour. 1986. *Politics, Position, and Power: From the Positive to the Regulatory State*, 4th ed. New York: Oxford University Press.

Sellers, Charles. 1991. *The Market Revolution: Jacksonian America, 1815–1846*. New York: Oxford University Press.

Shapiro, Martin. 1986. "APA: Past, Present, and Future." *Virginia Law Review* 72: 460–520.

Shaw, Albert. 1887. "The American State and the American Man." *Contemporary Review* 51 (May): 695–711.

Short, Lloyd Milton. 1923. *The Development of National Administrative Organization in the United States.* Baltimore: Johns Hopkins Press.

Skowronek, Stephen. 1982. *Building a New American State: The Expansion of Administrative Capacities, 1877–1920.* New York: Cambridge University Press.

———. 1997. *The Politics Presidents Make: Leadership from John Adams to Bill Clinton.* Cambridge, MA: Belknap Press of Harvard University Press.

———. 2011. *Presidential Leadership in Political Time: Reprise and Reappraisal,* 2nd ed. Lawrence: University Press of Kansas.

Smith, Louis. 1942. "Alexis de Tocqueville and Public Administration." *Public Administration Review* 2 (Summer): 221–39.

Smith, Mark A. 2000. *American Business and Political Power: Public Opinion, Elections, and Democracy.* Chicago: University of Chicago Press.

Smith, Tom W. 2013. "Trends in National Spending Priorities 1973–2012." *General Social Survey Trend Report,* Mar. 8. Chicago: NORC.

Somit, Albert. 1948. "Andrew Jackson as Administrator." *Public Administration Review* 8 (Summer): 188–96.

Soss, Joe. 2005. "Making Clients and Citizens: Welfare Policy as a Source of Status, Belief, and Action." In Anne L. Schneider and Helen M. Ingram, eds. *Deserving and Entitled: Social Constructions and Public Policy.* Albany: State University of New York Press.

Sowa, Jessica E., and Sally Coleman Selden. 2003. "Administrative Discretion and Active Representation: An Expansion of the Theory of Representative Bureaucracy." *Public Administration Review* 63 (Nov.–Dec.): 700–710.

Spicer, Michael W. 2010. *In Defense of Politics in Public Administration: A Value Pluralist Perspective.* Tuscaloosa: University of Alabama Press.

Stewart, Richard B. 1975. "The Reformation of Administrative Law." *Harvard Law Review* 88: 1669–813.

Stillman, Richard J. 1991. *Preface to Public Administration: A Search for Themes and Direction.* New York: St. Martin's Press.

Stivers, Camilla M. 1990. "Active Citizenship and Public Administration." In Gary L. Wamsley, Robert N. Bacher, Charles T. Goodsell, Philip S. Kronenberg, John A. Rohr, Camilla M. Stivers, Orion F. White, and James F. Wolf, eds., *Refounding Public Administration.* Newbury Park, CA: Sage Publications.

Stone, Clarence N. 1985. "Efficiency versus Social Learning: A Reconsideration of the Implementation Process." *Policy Studies Review* 4 (Feb.): 484–90.

Stone, Deborah A. 1988. *Policy Paradox and Political Reason.* Boston: Scott, Foresman / Little, Brown.

Storing, Herbert J. 1980. "American Statesmanship: Old and New." In Robert A. Goldwin, ed. *Bureaucrats, Policy Analysts, Statesmen: Who Leads?* Washington, DC: American Enterprise Institute.

———. 1981. *What the Anti-federalists Were For.* Chicago: University of Chicago Press.

Storrs, Landon R. Y. 2013. *The Second Red Scare and the Unmaking of the New Deal Left.* Princeton, NJ: Princeton University Press.

Swift, Elaine K. 1993. "The Making of an American House of Lords: The U.S. Senate in the Constitutional Convention of 1787." *Studies in American Political Development* 7 (Fall): 177–224.

Terkel, Studs. 1984. *"The Good War": An Oral History of World War Two.* New York: Pantheon Books.

Terry, Larry D. 1990. "Leadership in the Administrative State: The Concept of Administrative Conservatorship." *Administration & Society* 21 (Feb.): 395–412.

———. 2003. *Leadership of Public Bureaucracies: The Administrator as Conservator,* 2nd ed. Armonk, NY: M. E. Sharpe.

Thach, Charles, C., Jr. 1922. *The Creation of the Presidency, 1775–1789.* Baltimore: Johns Hopkins Press.

Thurow, Lester C. 1980. *The Zero-Sum Society: Distribution and the Possibilities for Economic Change.* New York: Basic Books.

Tichenor, Daniel J., and Richard A. Harris. 2002–2003. "Organized Interests and American Political Development." *Political Science Quarterly* 117 (4): 587–612.

Tocqueville, Alexis de. (1835) 1945. *Democracy in America.* Translated by Henry Reeve. Edited by Phillips Bradley. Reprint, New York: Vintage Books.

———. 1988. *Democracy in America.* Translated by George Lawrence. Edited by J. P. Mayer. New York: Perennial Library.

Tribe, Laurence. 1973. "Technology Assessment and the Fourth Discontinuity." *Southern California Law Review* 46 (June): 617–60.

Truman, David B. 1971. *The Governmental Process: Political Interests and Public Opinion,* 2nd ed. New York: Knopf.

Tulis, Jeffrey K. 1987. *The Rhetorical Presidency.* Princeton, NJ: Princeton University Press.

U.S. Civil Service Commission. 1871. "Report of the Commission." U.S Congress, Senate. 42d Congress, 2d Session, Ex. Doc No. 10. https://archive.org/details/presidemessageofoounitrich.

U.S. Department of Interior. 2013. "National Park Service: NPS Stats." https://irma.nps.gov/Stats/.

U.S. Department of State. 2013. "Report of the Accountability Review Board." www.state.gov/documents/organization/202446.pdf.

U.S. Department of Treasury. 2013. "Inappropriate Criteria Were Used to Identify Tax-Exempt Applications for Review." Treasury Inspector General for Tax Administration, May 14. Ref. No. 2013–10–053.

Van Riper, Paul P. 1958. *History of the United States Civil Service.* Evanston, IL: Row, Peterson.

———. 1983. "The American Administrative State: Wilson and the Founders—an Unorthodox View." *Public Administration Review* 43 (Nov.–Dec.): 477–90.

van Wagtendonk, Jan W. 1991. "The Evolution of National Park Service Fire Policy." *Fire Management Notes* 52 (4): 10–15.

Wagner, Joseph. 1990. "Groups, Individuals & Constitutive Rules: The Conceptual Dilemma in Justifying Affirmative Action." *Polity* 23 (Fall): 77–103.

Walsh, Katherine Cramer. 2012. "Political Understanding of Economic Crises: The Shape of Resentment toward Public Employees." http://www.polisci.wisc.edu/Up loads/Documents/wisc/Walsh_Oxford_Econ%20Crisis.pdf.

Wamsley, Gary L., Robert N. Bacher, Charles T. Goodsell, Philip S. Kronenberg, John A. Rohr, Camilla M. Stivers, Orion F. White, and James F. Wolf, eds. 1990. *Refounding Public Administration*. Newbury Park, CA: Sage Publications.

Wamsley, Gary L., and James F. Wolf, eds. 1996. *Refounding Democratic Public Administration: Modern Paradoxes, Postmodern Challenges*. Thousand Oaks, CA: Sage Publications.

Wang, Jessica. 2005. "Imagining the Administrative State: Legal Pragmatism, Securities Regulation, and New Deal Liberalism." *Journal of Policy History* 17 (3): 257–93.

Weber, Gustavus A. 1919. *Organized Efforts for the Improvement of Methods of Administration in the United States*. New York: D. Appleton & Co.

Weisman, Jonathan. 2013. "Documents Show Liberals in I.R.S. Dragnet." *New York Times*, June 25, A14.

Weisman, Jonathan, and Ashley Parker. 2013. "Shutdown Is Over." *New York Times*, Oct. 17, A1.

Wharton, Francis. 1889. *The Revolutionary Diplomatic Correspondence of the United States*. Washington, DC: Government Printing Office.

White, Jay D. 1990. "Images of Administrative Reason and Rationality: The Recovery of Practical Wisdom. In Henry D. Kass and Bayard L. Catron, eds. *Images and Identities in Public Administration*. Newbury Park, Calif.: Sage.

White, Leonard D. 1926. *An Introduction to the Study of Public Administration*. New York: Macmillan.

———. 1948. *The Federalists: A Study in Administrative History*. New York: Macmillan.

———. 1951. *The Jeffersonians: A Study in Administrative History*. New York: Macmillan.

———. 1954. *The Jacksonians: A Study in Administrative History*. New York: Macmillan.

———. 1958. *The Republican Era, 1869–1901: A Study in Administrative History*. New York: Macmillan.

Wichowsky, Amber, and Donald P. Moynihan. 2008. "Measuring How Administration Shapes Citizenship: A Policy Feedback Perspective on Performance Management." *Public Administration Review* 68 (Sept.–Oct.): 908–20.

Wiebe, Robert H. 1967. *The Search for Order: 1877–1920*. New York: Hill and Wang.

Will, George F. 1991. "If Saddam Survives, He Wins." *Washington Post*. Jan. 27, C7.

Williams, Robert F. 1988. "Evolving State Legislative and Executive Power in the Founding Decade." *Annals of the American Academy of Political and Social Science* 496 (Mar.): 43–53.

Willoughby, William F. 1930. "Appendix III: A General Survey of Research in Public Administration." *American Political Science Review* 24 (Feb.): 39–51.

Wills, Garry. 1994. "What Makes a Good Leader?" *Atlantic Monthly* 273 (Apr.): 63–80.

———. 1999. *A Necessary Evil: A History of American Distrust of Government*. New York: Simon & Schuster.

Wilson, James Q. 1975. "The Rise of the Bureaucratic State." *The Public Interest* 41 (Fall): 77–103.

———. 1980. "The Politics of Regulation." In James Q. Wilson, ed. *The Politics of Regulation*. New York: Basic Books.

———. 1989. *Bureaucracy: What Government Agencies Do and Why They Do It*. New York: Basic Books.

———. 1990. "Juridical Democracy versus American Democracy." *PS: Political Science and Politics* 23 (Dec.): 570–72.

———. 1992. *American Government: Institutions and Policies*, 5th ed. Lexington, MA: D. C. Heath.

———. 1994. "Can the Bureaucracy Be Deregulated?" In John J. Dilulio, ed. *Deregulating the Public Service: Can Government Be Improved?* Washington, DC: Brookings Institution.

Wilson, Woodrow. 1887. "The Study of Administration." *Political Science Quarterly* 2 (June): 197–222.

———. 1908. *Constitutional Government in the United States*. New York: Columbia University Press.

———. (1885) 1981. *Congressional Government: A Study in American Politics*. Reprint, Baltimore: Johns Hopkins University Press.

Wiltse, Charles M., and David G. Allen, eds. 1977. *The Papers of Daniel Webster: Correspondence*. Vol. 3. Hanover, NH: University Press of New England.

Wiltse, Charles M., and Alan R. Berolzheimer, eds. 1988. *The Papers of Daniel Webster: Speeches and Formal Writings*. Vol. 2. Hanover, NH: University Press of New England.

Wood, B. Dan. 1988. "Principals, Bureaucrats, and Responsiveness in Clean Air Enforcements." *American Political Science Review* 82 (Mar.): 213–34.

Wood, Gordon S. 1980. "Democracy and the Constitution." In Robert A. Goldwin and William A. Schambra, eds. *How Democratic Is the Constitution?* Washington, DC: American Enterprise Institute.

Yates, Douglas. 1982. *Bureaucratic Democracy: The Search for Democracy and Efficiency in American Government*. Cambridge, MA: Harvard University Press.

Yoder, Eric. 2013. "Threats and Attacks against Public Lands Employees Rise." *Washington Post*, June 17. http://www.washingtonpost.com/blogs/federal-eye/wp/2013/06/17/threats-and-attacks-against-public-lands-employees-rise/?tid=up_next.

Yoo, Christopher S., Steven G. Calabresi, and Anthony J. Colangelo. 2005. "The Unitary Executive in the Modern Era, 1945–2004." *Iowa Law Review* 90 (2): 601–755.

Zavodnyik. Peter. 2007. *The Age of Strict Construction: A History of the Growth of Federal Power, 1789–1861*. Washington, DC: Catholic University of America Press.

Index